CLASS AND STRATIFICATION

AN INTRODUCTION TO CURRENT DEBATES

Second Edition

ROSEMARY CROMPTON

Polity Press

First edition published 1993; reprinted 1995, 1996, 1998.
This edition published in 1998 by Polity Press in association with Blackwell Publishers Ltd.

Editorial office:
Polity Press
65 Bridge Street
Cambridge CB2 1UR, UK

Marketing and production:
Blackwell Publishers Ltd
108 Cowley Road
Oxford OX4 1JF, UK

Published in the USA by
Blackwell Publishers Inc.
Commerce Place
350 Main Street
Malden, MA 02148, USA

ISBN 0–7456–1792–1
ISBN 0–7456–1793–X (pbk)
A catalogue record for this book is available from the British Library.

Library of Congress Cataloging-in-Publication Data
Crompton, Rosemary.
    Class and stratification : an introduction to current debates /
Rosemary Crompton. — 2nd ed.
        p.   cm.
    Includes bibliographical references and index.
    ISBN 0–7456–1792–1 (alk. paper). — ISBN 0–7456–1793–X (pbk. :
alk. paper)
    1. Social classes.   2. Social structure.   I. Title.
HT609.C77   1998
305.5—dc21
                                                                    98–23965
                                                                    CIP
Typeset in 10.5 on 12 pt Times
by Wearset, Boldon, Tyne and Wear
Printed in Great Britain by MPG Books, Bodmin, Cornwall

This book is printed on acid-free paper.

Class and Stratification

To Jenny and Anne

CONTENTS

Introduction to the First Edition   viii

Introduction to the Second Edition   xii

1 Explaining Inequality   **1**
Introduction   1
Social order and theories of social differentiation   6
Stratification and the debate on social class   9
The growing critique of 'class analysis'   16
Concluding summary   22

2 Class Analysis: The Classic Inheritance and its Development   **24**
Introduction   24
Marx   26
Weber   32
Class and sociology after the Second World War   36
The development of theoretical accounts of the 'class structure'   37
Culture, class and history   40
Once again, the indivisibility of structure and action   44
Social class, urban sociology and the turn to 'realism'   47
Conclusions   50

3 Measuring the 'Class Structure': Goldthorpe and Wright   **54**
Introduction   54

Occupations   56
'Commonsense' occupational hierarchies and the
analysis of 'social classes'   58
Scales of occupational prestige or 'status'   61
Theoretical ('relational') class schemes: I Goldthorpe   64
Theoretical ('relational') class schemes: II Wright   69
Conclusions   76

4 Problems of Class Analysis   **79**
Introduction   79
Changes in the structure of work and employment   81
The expansion of women's employment   84
Class, politics and action   86
The failure of class action   89
Gender and class   92
Gender and the 'employment aggregate' approach   94
Are social classes dying?   98
Converging approaches   100
The absence of theory   101
The continuing relevance of employment aggregates   104
Conclusion   106

5 Farewell to Social Class?   **112**
Introduction   112
Bringing status back in   116
Recent social theory   123
Farewell to class societies?   127
Discussion and conclusions   134

6 Lifestyle, Consumption Categories and Consciousness Communities   **140**
Introduction   140
Consumption-sector cleavages   142
Culture, class and occupation   146
Social class and the work of Pierre Bourdieu   148
The 'new middle classes'   150
The middle classes and the gender question   158
From 'abstract labour' to 'customer care'   160
Summary and conclusions   164

7 Citizenship, Entitlements and the 'Underclass'   **169**
Introduction   169
T. H. Marshall and the development of the concept of
citizenship   171

Women and citizenship 180
Race and citizenship 186
Social citizenship and the 'underclass' 190
Conclusion 199

8 Retrospect and Prospect **203**
Introduction 203
Social mobility 208
Social polarization 218
Conclusions 225

References **231**

Index **251**

Introduction to the First Edition

Introductions to books are usually the last thing to be written, and this one is no exception. I would like to take this opportunity, however, to describe some of the factors which led me to write this textbook, not least because many of the themes developed within it are rather different from positions taken up in my previous work – particularly *Economy and Class Structure* (Crompton and Gubbay 1977).

During the 1960s and 1970s, sociology underwent a period of rapid expansion as an academic subject. Within the social sciences, sociology had always been a critical discipline. During this period, therefore, one major focus of sociological criticisms was the ideas and hypotheses relating to the 'end of ideology' thesis. This thesis included arguments to the effect that industrial societies were characterized by a broad consensus on values and attitudes, and that conflicts relating to 'class' were rapidly becoming outdated in such societies. In contrast, sociological sceptics argued that, even in welfare capitalism, class conflicts persisted, and that class inequality and conflicts could not be eradicated or even 'managed' in capitalism. During the 1960s and 1970s, therefore, 'class theory' came to assume an increasingly important place within sociology. This was accompanied by a revival of interest in the classical theorists, especially the work of Marx. In particular, Braverman's *Labor and Monopoly Capital* (1974) provided a number of insights as to how the divisions revealed by the Marxist analysis of the labour process might be mapped on to the structure of jobs and occupations. *Economy and Class Structure*, written during the 1970s, reflected these developments. It sought to provide a Marxist altern 'ive to the pre-dominantly Weberian mapping of social classes w,thin sociology which had prevailed hitherto.

Theoretical ideas relating to social class in sociology had been grafted on to an existing approach to social stratification in which 'classes' were taken to be occupational aggregates. Other existing conventions were also carried forward into these new developments in 'class analysis' – most notably, the assumption that as the class of the household corresponded to that of the main breadwinner, and that as the 'head of household' would usually be a man, then the 'class structure' could be reliably assumed to correspond to the structure of male employment. Without exception, therefore, in Britain all of the major surveys in the area of class and stratification had, until the 1970s, drawn upon men-only samples.

This practice came under increasing attack from the feminist cri-tique within sociology which developed from the early 1970s. These criticisms, however, were not only directed at the exclusion of women from empirical investigations, but also at the underlying assumptions upon which the identification of a class structure within the structure of employment was predicated. That is, it was argued that the class (employment) structure was itself 'gendered'. Logic-ally, therefore, the effects of 'class' and 'gender' could not be disen-tangled within the structure of employment. These feminist arguments were paralleled by developments in social theory, which, particularly in Giddens's account of 'structuration', argued that action could not be separated from structure in sociological invest-igations – including investigations into 'social classes'.

As a consequence of these and other developments, 'class analy-sis' in sociology moved in a number of different directions. How-ever, during the 1980s, debates within sociology itself were somewhat overshadowed by the crisis which sociology faced as an academic discipline in Britain, as departments were 'rationalized' and subject to increasing economic pressures, and sociologists them-selves underwent the (often painful) process of adapting to 'new times'. Perhaps because of these developments, a number of key sociological concepts – in particular, class – came under increasing, and critical, scrutiny. The end – or at least, the irrelevance – of class analysis in sociology was ever more frequently argued.

By the end of the 1980s, therefore, the empirical work of those pursuing a theoretical interest in class within sociology had fragmented into (at least) three areas: first, the macro-level analysis of large data sets, gathered by those who had developed theoretical, relational, approaches to 'social class' (Goldthorpe and Wright); second, socio-historical accounts of class formation (Lash and Urry 1987; McNall et al. 1991); and third, a growing interest in the *cultural* construction and reproduction of class associated with a developing 'sociology of consumption' and fuelled by the emphasis on consumerism which seemed, increasingly, to characterize contemporary societies (Bourdieu 1986). Those sociologists not directly concerned with these debates carried on doing what they had always done – that is, using the convenient sociological shorthand whereby 'occupation' was taken to be a measure of 'class' without worrying too much about the finer details – even though, as we shall see, this assumption is highly problematic. It is one of the major arguments of this book that the largely unacknowledged fragmentation of approach within 'class analysis' in sociology is one of the reasons why its practitioners were not well placed to respond to the growing tide of criticisms of both the class concept and class analysis in general, which had emerged by the end of the 1980s.

This book, therefore, was written with the aim of providing an overview of the field which would facilitate the moving forward of debate in an area which had, in my view, got somewhat bogged down in arguments between and within different schools of 'class analysis'. The unfortunate result was that many outsiders – even within the sociological community – had lost any real sense of what was going on. Despite claims to have provided an 'overview', however, there are a number of gaps in this text which I would freely acknowledge. As reflects my own interests, the question of gender is discussed reasonably thoroughly, but the important topic of race and ethnicity is discussed only in relation to the question of citizenship. Other crucial stratification issues – such as, for example, age – are not discussed at all. Nationalism, which following the break-up of the Eastern bloc is emerging as a central topic for the 1990s, is not considered. I can only apologize in advance for these and other deficiencies.

It would have been pleasant to record the fellowships, scholarships, and sabbatical leaves which had contributed to the writing of this book, but unfortunately there were none. Roger Burrows organized a debate on class at the 1990 British Sociological Association Conference, to which I contributed along with Ray Pahl and Gordon Marshall, and which was important in getting me started. Gordon Marshall was the first to suggest that I was writing a book, not an article, and has read the first draft of chapter 5. Communications with Mike Savage over the last few years have done much to clarify my thinking, as did conversations with Bob Holton in 1990. I would also like to thank David Held and Tony Giddens at Polity Press for their advice and comments, as well as an anonymous Polity reader for detailed comments on the first draft. Gerald Crompton has had to listen to far more monologues on class and stratification than an economic historian has any reasonable right to expect. Justine Clements has made the final alterations to my word-processed text, for which many thanks. Many others have contributed, directly and indirectly, to the writing of this book and I hope that a general acknowledgement will suffice – the good bits (if any) are theirs, and the faults are all mine.

Rosemary Crompton
University of Kent

Introduction to the Second Edition

The first edition of this book was written in order to provide an overview of an area of sociology which had become somewhat fragmented – with, I argued, somewhat negative consequences. This fragmentation continues to be reflected in the many books, commentaries and articles on the subject of class and stratification which have appeared since 1993, although a measure of clarification has been achieved as well. In Britain, an extended debate was stimulated by Goldthorpe and Marshall's (1992) defence of 'class analysis' as they saw it (Lee and Turner 1996). Further afield, Clark and Lipset's critical contribution was seen as having a particular significance given Lipset's historic role in establishing the centrality of 'class' within sociology (Bendix and Lipset 1967a). Two major cross-nationally comparative class projects have delivered their final reports (Erikson and Goldthorpe 1993; Wright 1997). If judged only by the number of publications with 'class' in the title, therefore, then within sociology class and stratification might still appear, relatively speaking, to be very much alive.

Nevertheless, the 'end of class' continues to be asserted with some regularity, and the postmodern and culturalist 'turn' in British sociology shows no sign of abating. A second edition of this book, therefore, seemed justified not only in relation to the volume of new and relevant work which had appeared on the scene, but also in order to restate the continuing significance of the topic within sociology (and indeed, the social sciences more generally).

In this second edition I have tended to concentrate on developments in the theoretical debates relating to class and stratification analysis, rather than providing a detailed empirical account of the various dimensions of class structures. This is in large part because there are a number of recent books which do an excellent job of summarizing the empirical evidence (Devine 1997; Breen and Rottman 1995; Reid 1998). This does, not mean, however, that I do not attach considerable importance to the need to justify statements with reference to empirical evidence, and this evidence is provided where necessary.

My own views have not radically changed, although there have been some shifts in emphasis which are reflected in the second edition. I am more convinced than ever that the way ahead in class and stratification analysis is to recognize the *de facto* plurality of conceptual frameworks and methodologies in the field. Thus I do not think it is particularly useful to argue about which class scheme is the 'best', for example – which is one reason why I have dropped 'Testing and refining measures of employment class' (1993: chapter 5) from this edition. In 1997, I would be even more cautious of laying an excessive emphasis on the unity of 'structure' and 'action' than I was in 1993. In sociological terms, structure and action are indeed interdependent, but as far as empirical research is concerned – and this is no more true than in the case of class analysis – an analytical separation has to be assumed (Layder 1990; Archer 1996).

The first edition of this book has been extensively revised and updated, but some chapters have been reworked more than others, and others have virtually disappeared. Chapters 1, 2 and 3 have probably changed least. Chapters 4 and 5 have been virtually rewritten. In chapter 4, I have taken out much of the emphasis on 'where to put people' (in line with my argument that there can be no single 'best' class scheme, then it is likely that different schemes will vary in their allocations of particular jobs, despite their broad similarities of purpose). Recent debates on 'class' have been incorporated, and the emerging convergence of Goldthorpe and Wright's recent work is emphasized. In chapter 5 I have systematically considered the implications of recent social theories (in particular, poststructuralism and postmodernism) for class and stratification analysis. I suggest that these debates remain a prime source of confusion and 'pseudo-debate' – that is, sociologists talking past, rather than to, each other. In particular, I stress the need to distinguish between theoretical arguments relating to the possibility of a fundamental shift in the very nature of society itself (as is suggested in some versions of 'postmodernism' or 'reflexive modernity'), and the 'employment-aggregate' approach of Goldthorpe and Wright, which is largely concerned with the persisting consequences of job-related inequalities. These are two very different kinds of arguments, and should be seen as such.

The order of chapters 6 and 7 has been reversed from the first edition, although they still deal with the same broad topics. Chapter 6, on culture and consumption, has been extended to include a discussion of recent developments in employment and their likely implications for class consciousness and identity, as well as a section on gender and the middle classes. Chapter 7 is largely unchanged in outline, but the discussion of the 'underclass' debate has been extended and developed in order to provide a 'worked example' of the necessity of a multidimensional empirical approach. Chapter 8 has been completely rewritten. Rather than providing a descriptive outline of the 'class structure', as in the first edition, I have chosen to examine in some depth the related topics of social mobility, educational opportunity, and social polarization. This is in part because it may be argued that the culturalist and postmodernist turn in sociology is in some danger of removing altogether any requirement that we systematically examine those structures and processes in society which repeatedly ensure that some are less equal than others – in other words – social class.

I conclude that although contemporary capitalist societies continue to be fundamentally stratified by systematic inequalities associated with access to property, jobs, and 'life chances' in general, the fragmentation of being and experiences brought about by developments such as the flexibilization of employment, privatism and 'home-centredness', and the growth of insecurity – of jobs, of 'falling off the ladder' in an increasingly competitive and 'marketized' environment – make the development of a cohesive, collective, occupationally-based 'class consciousness' of a 'Fordist', 'trade-union', variety not very likely. Thus in this sense recent criticisms have some validity. Nevertheless, at the end of the millennium, the actual capacity of dominant economic interests to be realized shows little sign of being undermined. Class processes still count, even if the class interests of particular groups remain poorly articulated. It might be argued, therefore, that rather than sociologists continuing to argue for the 'end of class', together with a refocusing of interests away from the 'material' to the 'cultural', we should, rather, be going in the *opposite* direction.

Finally, I would like to thank the Research School of Social Sciences, the Australian National University, for inviting me to take up a visiting scholarship, and the University of Leicester for giving me leave of absence to take it. I would never have achieved this rewrite without this assistance, which is gratefully acknowledged. Fiona Devine and Mike Savage read first drafts of the manuscript, and Lisa Adkins the first draft of chapter 5. Many other people have helped in lots of different ways – from a willingness to tolerate a certain level of abstractedness (and lack of sweetness of temper) to answering specific academic enquiries. I really am very grateful to you all.

Rosemary Crompton
University of Leicester
December 1997

1 Explaining Inequality

Introduction

All complex societies are characterized, to varying extents, by the unequal distribution of material and symbolic rewards. It is also the case that no persisting structure of economic and social inequality has existed in the absence of some kind of meaning system(s) which seek both to explain and to justify the unequal distribution of societal resources.

'Social stratification' is a general term which describes these systematic structures of inequality. In pre-industrial or traditional societies, inequalities and thus social stratification were widely held to be natural, and/or to reflect an aspect of a cosmology which provided an account of the society itself. Thus, for example, in ancient Greece Aristotle asserted that: 'It is thus clear that there are *by nature* free men and slaves, and that servitude is just and agreeable for the latter ... Equally, the relation of the male to the female is *by nature* such that one is superior and the other inferior, one dominates and the other is dominated' (cited in Dahrendorf 1969: 18). A pre-established harmony is being asserted between things natural and things social. This is a view which effectively rules out any sociological treatment of the issue – if inequalities are 'natural', then there is no need to investigate them further.

Besides this assumption of 'naturalness', inequalities have been viewed as deriving from the divinely ordained structuring of society, as in the Hindu caste system in classical India. In this system, social rank corresponded to religious (ritual) purity. Lower castes polluted the higher and, as a consequence, a series of restrictions were imposed on low-caste individuals and their families. Thus the caste system corresponded (although not precisely) to the overall structure of social inequality.[1] Two religious concepts, *karma* and *dharma*, sustained the system. Karma teaches a Hindu that he or she is born into a particular caste or sub-caste because he or she deserves to be there as a consequence of actions in a previous life. Dharma, which means 'existing according to that which is moral', teaches that living one's present life according to the rules (dharma) will result in rebirth into a higher caste and thus ultimate progression through the caste system. Both existing inequalities of caste, therefore, as well as any possibility of change in the future, are related to universal religious truths and are thus beyond the reaches of systematic sociological examination.

The justification of material inequality as stemming from some 'natural' or divine ordinance, therefore, is a common feature of traditional or pre-industrial societies. Such accounts not only explain inequality, they also assert that it is part of the natural order of things that the 'best' should get the majority share of the rewards that society has to offer. In feudal Europe as in classical India, stratification was accompanied by religious and moral justifications. From the ninth century onwards, Western Europe was an essentially rural society, in which an individual's condition was determined by access to the land. This was largely controlled by a minority of lay and ecclesiastical proprietors. It was a hierarchical society, in which the enserfed peasantry were subject to the domination of secular and ecclesiastical lords. The Church possessed both economic and moral ascendancy. As Pirenne (1936) has argued, the Church's conception of the feudal world 'was admirably adapted to the economic conditions of an age in which land was the sole foundation of the social order'. Land had been given by God to men in order to enable them to live on earth with a view to their eternal salvation. The object of labour was not to grow wealthy, and the monk's renunciation was the ideal 'on which the whole of society should fix its gaze'. To seek riches was to fall into the sin of avarice, and poverty was of divine origin (Pirenne 1936: 423).

In traditional societies, therefore, relative economic stagnation was also associated with social rigidity in respect of stratification systems. These societies, however, did not endure, and throughout the seventeenth, eighteenth and nineteenth centuries Western Europe, and much of the rest of the world, was transformed by the development of capitalist industrialism – the most significant element of the process which has been described as the coming of 'modernity'. The profound economic and social changes which took place throughout these centuries were accompanied by a developing critique of the traditional systems of belief which for over two millennia had served to explain material inequalities and render them legitimate.

In direct opposition to the idea that human beings are naturally or divinely unequal at birth, therefore, there developed from the seventeenth century onwards the argument that, by virtue of their humanity, all human beings were born *equal*, rather than unequal.[2] From this assumption derives the beginnings of a sociological approach to the explanation of inequality. If equality, rather than inequality, is assumed to be the 'natural' condition of human beings, then how are persisting inequalities to be explained and justified? If each individual is endowed with natural rights, why do some individuals dominate others? These questions remain as the central problems of social and political theory. In the sphere of political thought, some of the first answers to these questions were supplied by the social contract theorists. Hobbes (1588–1679) argued that in a state of nature life was 'nasty, brutish and short', characterized by the war of 'every man against every man'. The solution to this 'problem of order' was submission to the state, in the absence of which there would be chaos. Locke (1632–1704) also argued that the 'natural rights' to life, liberty and property are best protected by the authority of the state. In a famous statement which has resounded through history, Rousseau (1712–78), asserted that 'man was born free, and he is everywhere in chains'. He did not consider that complete equality could ever be achieved but argued that direct democracy, expressed through the 'general will', would afford the greatest protection for the individual. Thus the foundations of the argument that all 'citizens' were entitled to political rights, as expressed in universal suffrage and democratic institutions, were laid in the eighteenth century.

The passing of traditional society and the growth of capitalist industrialism was accompanied by an emphasis on the rationality of the modern social order. Not customary rules, but rational calculation, were held to be the principles which should govern economic conduct in the developing capitalist societies. The expansion of markets and transformation of the processes of production which accompanied the Industrial Revolution would have been difficult to achieve without the erosion of customary rights in trade and manufacture – which affected all its aspects and included cartels, wage and price fixing, restrictions on the mobility of labour, and so on.

Thus the political changes which created the formally free individual also created the landless labourer. This individual was, however, entitled to sell what only she or he possessed – labour, or the capacity to work. People themselves had become commodities.

The English and French revolutions were first amongst the political changes which accompanied the transition to capitalist industrialism. However, the 'bourgeois freedoms' which they achieved came under critical scrutiny from that foremost social theorist of the nineteenth century, Karl Marx. As described in the *Communist Manifesto*, Marx saw the unfolding of human history as an outcome of economic, rather than merely political, conflicts: 'The history of all hitherto existing society is the history of class struggles' (Marx and Engels 1962: 34). Inequality was, and always had been, a reflection of differential access to the means of production and what was produced. For Marx, state power was inseparable from economic power, and the 'sovereign individual' of capitalism was but a necessary condition of the development of the capitalist mode of production. Political equality could coexist with material inequalities and indeed, by defining the inequalities associated with the dominant system of production, distribution and exchange as 'non-political', bourgeois ideology served to make them legitimate. The landless labourers created as a consequence of political and economic change constituted a new class which was emerging as a consequence of the development of industrial capitalism – a class which would eventually transform capitalist society – the proletariat.

The development of capitalist industrialism has been identified as a major element in the transition to 'modernity'. The idea of modernity describes not just the development of industrialism *per se*, but also of the corresponding modes of surveillance and regulation of the population of nation states – nation states have been identified as one of the characteristic social forms accompanying the transition to modernity. Modernity is accompanied by the extensive development of *organizations*, that is, reflexively monitored systems which have the capacity to act upon the social world. The transition to modernity ushered in a world which is peculiarly dynamic, a world which is in the process of constant change and transformation.

In this book, 'class' will be discussed as a peculiarly modern phenomenon. As we shall see, the concept of class has a number of different meanings. To describe class as 'modern', however, is to suggest that it is primarily a characteristic of modern stratification systems, of 'industrial' societies, in contrast to the 'traditional' structures of inequality associated with ascribed or supposedly natural characteristics such as those of feudal estates or religiously defined hierarchies, as well as gender and race. In the modern world, class-based organizations – that is, organizations claiming to represent classes and class interests – have been the dynamic source of many of the changes and transformations which have characterized the modern era. This does not mean that 'classes' did not exist prior to modernity, but rather that the discourse of 'class' has become one of the key concepts through which we can begin to understand it.[3]

'Class', therefore, is a major organizing concept in the exploration of contemporary stratification systems. However, although inequalities associated with the structures of production, distribution and exchange assume greater significance with the transition to industrialism, this does not mean that established forms of social distinction and differentiation simply disappear overnight. Customary inequalities, particularly those associated with ascribed statuses associated with age, gender and race, have persisted into the modern era.

Not only customary inequalities, but many of the ideas which underpinned them, persisted into the modern age. Hirsch (1977) has argued that the 'moral legacy' of pre-capitalist institutions supplied the social foundations for the developing capitalist order. The ideologies associated with religion and custom in traditional societies, besides identifying the levels of material reward which were properly associated with the different ranks in society, and giving hope for the future beyond this life, supplied a powerful moral justification for the unequal distribution of resources. They also included rules relating to individual behaviour such as truth, trust, customary social obligations and the restraint of appetites. Hirsch argued (1977: 117) that by the late twentieth century capitalism was facing a 'depleting moral legacy': 'The social morality that has served as an understructure for economic individualism has been a legacy of the procapitalist and preindustrial past. This legacy has diminished with time and the corrosive contact of the active capitalist values.' In a related argument, Goldthorpe (1978) extended the logic of Hirsch's analysis to argue that the period of rapid inflation in Britain during the 1970s was in part a consequence of the decay of the *status order*, that is, it reflected an erosion of customary assumptions which had provided a normative underpinning for the differential distribution of rewards in a market society. If customary assumptions relating to inequality have and are being eroded, then how do unequal societies cohere, particularly given the presumption of a fundamental equality amongst human beings?

Social order and theories of social differentiation

Inequality is a feature of all complex societies. One response, therefore, to the question posed above might be to argue that material inequalities are not, in themselves, necessarily a bad thing. Indeed, this has been a consistent theme in neo-liberal arguments concerning inequality. Such arguments distinguish between legal or formal equalities – for example, equality before the law; equality of opportunity – and equality of outcome. However, the pursuit of equality of outcome – for example, through programmes of affirmative action – contradicts, the neo-liberals argue, the principle of legal or formal equality. This is because positive or affirmative treatment for supposedly disadvantaged groups would treat the supposedly advantaged as less than equal. Thus in recent years we have witnessed, for example, the phenomenon of white male applicants to college courses in the United States utilizing equal-opportunity legislation in order to challenge the allocation of a quota of places on prestige courses to ethnic-minority applicants. Another important strand in neo-liberal arguments has been that, in any case, material inequalities are positively beneficial in modern societies. Economists such as Hayek have argued that in a capitalist society, the pursuit of self-interest encourages innovation and technological advance. Inventors and entrepreneurs may succeed or fail, but society as a whole will nevertheless benefit from the advances which these dynamic individuals have achieved – mass transport and communication, consumer goods such as cars, washing machines, and so on.[4] Capitalism is dynamic *because* it is unequal, and attempts at equalization will ultimately result in the stifling of initiative. Thus neo-liberals such as Berger have argued that: 'If one wants to intervene politically to bring about greater material equality, one may eventually disrupt the economic engine of plenty and endanger the material living standards of the society' (1987: 48).

These neo-liberal arguments have their parallel in the functionalist theory of stratification in sociology (Davis and Moore 1945; reprinted 1964). 'Social inequality', they argued, 'is thus an unconsciously evolved device by which societies insure that the most important positions are conscientiously filled by the most qualified persons' (1964: 415). In the particular case of advanced industrial societies, individuals must be induced to train for positions requiring a high level of skills, and compensated for having to take risks. In brief, their theory suggested that in industrial societies, characterized by a complex division of labour, a new consensus concerning inequality was emerging as a replacement for the old. Whereas the old consensus was grounded in customary, religious (and therefore non-rational) perceptions of worth, the new consensus reflected the rationality of modern industrial societies. Differentiated groupings are not percieved as necessarily antagonistic; they are, therefore, often described from within the functionalist perspective as socio-economic 'strata', rather than 'classes'.

The immediate origins of functionalist theories of stratification may be found in the Parsonian structural-functionalism which dominated sociological theory in the United States after the Second World War. These ideas will be discussed at greater length in chapters 2 and 3. Functionalist theories of stratification also reflected elements of Durkheim's analysis of the ultimate social consequences of the division of labour in industrial society. Durkheim (1968) was acutely aware of the negative consequences of the division of labour (poverty, social unrest etc.) consequent upon the development of industrial capitalism, but he argued that, nevertheless, 'normal' forms of the division of labour would lead to the development of 'organic solidarity' – that is, solidarity through interdependence – in complex industrial societies.

Functional theories of stratification, therefore, suggested that inequality in complex societies was rendered legitimate via an emerging consensus of values relating to the societal importance of particular functions. It is important to recognize that such theories incorporate a moral justification of economic inequality which has been commonplace since the advent of economic liberalism – that is, in a competitive market society, it is the most talented and ambitious – in short, the *best* – that get to the top, and therefore take the greater part of societies' rewards. However, for many commentators, such arguments rest upon the presumption of equality of opportunity (as Durkheim expressed it, the 'equality of the partners to the contract' in the division of labour). Thus the conditions and possibility of equality of opportunities have loomed large in debates on stratification.

Equality of opportunity is a powerful justification for inequality. If all have an equal opportunity to be unequal, then the unequal outcome must be regarded as justified and fair, as a reflection of 'natural' inequalities of personal endowments, rather than of structured social processes. Although a true equality of opportunity has never, in fact, been achieved, the assumption that it was nevertheless a Good Thing dominated the liberal consensus which prevailed in

most Western societies after the Second World War, and which saw
the extension of state expenditure on education, health and welfare.
However, neo-liberals have always argued against such assumptions,
and in recent decades the political and policy influence of such views
has been increasing. Within the sociological field, Saunders (1990a;
1996) has argued for a return to the functionalist perspective in
stratification theory and research.

Two closely associated arguments, therefore, have been used by
functionalists to explain and justify material inequalities in a society
of political and legal equals. These are, first, that unequal rewards
provide a structure of incentives which ensure that talented individuals will work hard and innovate, thus contributing to the
improvement of material standards for the society as a whole; and,
second, that a broad consensus exists as to the legitimacy of their
superior rewards, as such innovators are functionally more important to society.

Others, however, have stressed the continuing tensions, instability
and tendencies to crisis which are associated with persisting structures of inequality. Marx predicted that the underlying structure of
class inequality, associated with differential access to the ownership
and control of productive resources, would lead, via the class
struggle between labour and capital, to the revolutionary overthrow
and eventual transformation of capitalist industrialism. Many theorists of stratification who are not Marxists, however, have also
stressed the inherent instability of capitalist market societies, rather
than any tendency toward an emergent consensus and stability. In
contrast to the functionalists, 'conflict theorists' of stratification such
as Dahrendorf (1959), Rex (1961) and Collins (1971) have emphasized the significance of power and coercion in any explanation of
inequality. However, although such writers stress the persistence of
conflict and are sceptical of the emergence of any genuine agreement concerning the existing structure of inequalities, they do not,
unlike Marx, envisage the imminent break-up of the social and stratification order.

This is in part because persisting conflict exists in an uneasy tension with tendencies to regulation in capitalist market societies. The
'depleting moral legacy' which Hirsch identified may be argued to
have been supplemented to some extent by institutions developed
within the framework of capitalism. Dahrendorf (1988), Lockwood
(1974) and Rex (1986), for example, have all drawn upon T. H. Marshall's account of 'citizenship' (1963), arguing that the development
of social citizenship (for example, universal provisions such as

education and welfare state benefits) in particular has contributed to the mitigation of class inequalities (chapter 7 below). During the twentieth century, there have been long historical periods (extending over many decades in countries such as Sweden) in which such a corporatist bargain has been struck between capital and labour (Therborn 1983).

A feature common to authors who may be characterized as working within the 'conflict' approach to social stratification is that they all identify social *classes* as the primary 'actors' within stratification systems in industrial societies. However, there is a marked lack of precision or agreement as to the definition and meaning of 'class'.

Stratification and the debate on social class

In recent years, a common theme within sociology (and, indeed, in commentaries on society and politics more generally) has been that 'class' is becoming increasingly irrelevant in the late twentieth century. Thus Pahl (1989: 710) has argued that 'class as a concept is ceasing to do any useful work for sociology', and Holton and Turner have asserted that 'class' is 'an increasingly redundant issue' (1989: 194). Pakulski and Waters (1996b) continue to argue that 'class is dead', and Clark and Lipset (1991) that social classes are 'dying'. The retreat from class, it may be suggested, is becoming the sociological equivalent of the new individualism. In this book it will be argued that although it is certainly the case that much confusion surrounds the use of the term, there are insufficient grounds for the wholesale rejection of class as an 'outmoded nineteenth-century concept'.

It is paradoxical that these recurring statements as to the redundancy of 'class' within sociological analysis should be emerging at a time when the level of non-sociological interest in the topic shows little sign of diminishing. For example, in the contest for the Conservative Party leadership (and Prime Ministership) in Britain during 1990, much was made of the 'classlessness' – or rather, upward mobility – of the eventual winner, John Major.[5] This was a powerful argument, and supporters of his opponents were driven to attempt to demonstrate their *lack* of 'class advantages' despite their patrician backgrounds and antecedents. This led Douglas Hurd (another contestant for the leadership) to describe his father as a farmer (classless?), who had managed to 'scrape together' the funds to send his son *on a scholarship* to Eton, and a supporter of Heseltine (a third competitor) to recount that his candidate had personally applied the wallpaper in the boarding-house which was the foundation of his (Heseltine's) property empire. In the same week as the leadership contest Lord Justice Harman ruled that the Conservative Westminster City Council could not sell property whose leasehold specified that the properties should be used as 'dwellings for the working class ... and for no other purpose'. Westminster had argued that the term 'working class' no longer had any meaning. However, the judge ruled that although parliament no longer used the term in housing legislation this did not mean that it no longer had any meaning in ordinary English speech (the protagonists were well aware that, once on the open market, the properties would rise in value to a level outside the reach of the 'working class'). In 1996, BBC2 ran a three-part documentary on class ('Parsons on Class'), but in the same year, no less a pundit than Prince Edward declared that 'the class system is dead' (*Daily Express*).

Sociologists might argue that the use of the term 'class' in academic discourse is in fact quite different from its use in ordinary speech, the everyday use of the word being much closer to the notion of social distinction or prestige. This would seem to be confirmed by the journalistic view: 'observation of class difference has, over the years, been reduced to a question of style' (*Observer*, 6 October 1991). The use of 'class' to indicate lifestyle, prestige or rank is probably the most commonly used sense of the term. Here 'class' is bound up with hierarchy, of being 'higher than' or 'lower than' some other person or group. Rank is often indicated by lifestyles, and particular patterns of consumption. For example, in an often-repeated television comedy sketch of the 1960s, the 'upper class' was represented by a bowler hat, the 'middle class' by a trilby, and the 'lower class' by a flat cap ('Frost over England'). Thirty years later, a conscious parody of the sketch ('Parsons on Class') had the 'upper class' wearing a deerstalker, the 'middle class' a peaked golfing cap, and the 'lower class' a football supporters' woolly hat. In the BBC2 programme, demonstrating that 'class' is a redundant term meant contrasting aristocrats who sent their children to state schools with low-paid workers who paid for private education, keen golf club members who lived in local authority housing, and self-made men who had bought their own private shooting rights. In these kinds of debates, the 'end of class' rests on the argument that particular kinds of consumption practices are no longer tied to particular status groups.

'Class', therefore, is a word with a number of meanings. Although

these will be extensively rehearsed throughout this book, it is nevertheless useful to attempt a summary at this early stage. With some
over-simplification, three different meanings of the class concept
may be identified:

- 'Class' as prestige, status, culture or 'lifestyles'.
- 'Class' as structured inequality (related to the possession of eco-
  nomic and power resources).
- 'Classes' as actual or potential social and political actors.

Sociologists, as well as journalists, have also paid considerable attention to class-differentiated lifestyles, as in Goldthorpe et al.'s (1969)
discussion of the 'privatized' lifestyle of the 'affluent worker'. Occupational classifications have been devised by market research com-
panies in order to give an indication of lifestyles and consumption
patterns. When occupations are ranked according to their perceived
levels of prestige or social standing, these are described as status
scales.

A second common use of the 'class' concept is as a general
description of structures of material inequality, reflected in differential access to economic and power resources (these could be the
ownership of capital or productive resources, skills and qualifications, networks of contacts, etc.). Unequally rewarded groups are
often described as 'classes'. These groupings are not characterized
by any formal, legal distinctions; rather, they summarize the outcome, in material terms, of the competition for resources in capitalist market societies. A very common basis for classification in
modern societies is occupation – for example, the Registrar-
General's 'social class' groupings, maintained by the Office of
National Statistics (ONS). These occupational groupings are
amongst the most useful indicators of patterns of material advantage
and disadvantage in modern societies, and are widely used in social-
policy, market and advertising research, and so on. Sociologists have
also devised their own 'class' schemes.

The term 'class', however, has not just been used to *describe* levels
of material inequalities, social prestige, or legal or traditional rankings. 'Classes' have also been identified as actual or potential social
forces, or social actors, which have the capacity to transform society.
Marx considered the struggle between classes to be the major
motive force in human history. His views were certainly not shared
by conservative commentators; nevertheless, from the French Revolution and before, 'classes' – particularly the lower classes – have been
regarded as a possible threat to the established order. Thus 'class' is

also a term with significant *political* overtones. The use of the single word 'class', therefore, may describe rankings of lifestyles or social prestige, patterns of material inequalities, as well as revolutionary or conservative social forces. It is a concept which is not the particular preserve of any individual branch of social science – unlike, for example, the concept of marginal utility in economics. Neither is it possible to identify a 'correct' sociological perspective, or an agreed use of the term.

The variety of meanings which have been attached to the concept of class, it will be argued in this book, has contributed to the lack of clarity which characterizes many contemporary debates in stratification. However, two further sets of factors have also added to the general muddying of waters which were never particularly clear: first, debates in social theory, and second, the very rapidity of the social and economic changes which these theories sought to explain.

Debates in social theory have had a profound impact on the manner in which sociologists and others have approached the study of the social world. What Giddens (1982a) and others have described as the 'orthodox consensus' that emerged in the social sciences during the 1950s and 1960s had decisively shaped class analysis in sociology in the immediate postwar period. This 'orthodox consensus' was influenced by the logical framework of positivism; thus social science investigations were closely modelled on those of the natural sciences, and social facts treated as 'things'. Sociologists sought to establish general (or law-like) statements about social behaviour through factual observations. The second element of the consensus, the predominance of a broadly functionalist approach, has already been briefly described. The third element of this consensus, according to Giddens, was the influence of a conception of 'industrial society', whereby the technology of industrialism and its attendant social characteristics (rationality of technique, extensive division of labour, and so on) was seen to be the main motive force transforming the contemporary world.

Although the orthodox consensus had its critics – for example, the 'conflict theorists' identified above – their critiques were developed and shaped within its framework. In particular, as we shall see in chapters 2 and 3, this approach structured research and theorizing in the area of class and stratification in a number of significant respects. First, the influence of positivism meant that classes were conceived as objective entities which could be empirically investigated – and to this end, the occupational structure was conventionally regarded as providing a framework within which the 'class structure' could be located. Second, much of the debate between 'functional' or 'consensus' approaches, on the one hand, and 'conflict' theories, on the other, took place on the terrain of stratification theory. Third, developments in systems of occupational stratification were a key feature of the industrial society thesis. It was argued that the stratification systems of advanced industrial societies would have a tendency to converge, and moreover that this would be in the direction of more open structures in which 'middle-class' occupations predominated (Mayer 1963). As the 'middle mass' expanded, so the conflict between classes would be reduced.

Mainstream class and stratification theory – as represented, for example, by writers such as Bendix and Lipset (1967b), had appropriated the Marxist distinction between a class 'in itself' and a class 'for itself' – that is, between a class which existed as a historical reality, on the one hand, and a class which had acquired a consciousness of its identity and a capacity to act, on the other. Bendix and Lipset, however, viewed the question of class action as contingent – a class might, or might not, manifest a particular consciousness. This approach fits unproblematically with broadly 'positivist' modes of social investigation: 'classes' may be identified, factual observation will reveal whether they are 'class conscious' or not. However, one aspect of the developing critique of positivism – as expressed, for example, in Giddens's theory of 'structuration' – argued that neither subject nor object, 'structure' nor 'action', should be regarded as having primacy. These arguments meshed with those already developed by some Marxist theoreticians – particularly historians such as E. P. Thompson – regarding the indivisibility of class from the notion of consciousness.

The theoretical challenge to normative functionalism developed by Lockwood (1956) and others was closely bound up with the development of sociological approaches to class. The persistence of conflict (in particular, *class* conflict), in contemporary societies was emphasized, rather than stability. The US tradition of social stratification came in for particular criticism. It was argued that it focused upon social status or prestige, rather than class. From the 1950s there was a renewed sociological interest in European class theoretical writings, particularly the work of Marx and Weber (these will be discussed in the next chapter). The developing interest in class theory was paralleled by developments in sociological methods. The increasing methodological sophistication of the social survey was complemented by a huge increase in scope and capacity for data processing facilitated by the development of computer technology.

As a consequence of these parallel developments, ambitious programmes of 'class analysis' were devised during the 1970s in which developments in class theory and survey analysis were combined (Wright 1997; Erikson and Goldthorpe 1993). One important feature of such programmes is that they sought to link two of the major aspects of class identified above: that is (a) class as a source of structured social inequality, and (b) class as a source of social and political identity, consciousness, and action. As we shall see, this approach has developed into a major specialty within the field of 'class analysis'.

However, the 'class' concept has been widely used to describe the broad contours of inequality in contemporary societies, and has not always been primarily concerned – or even concerned at all – with the issues of class consciousness and action. In nineteenth century investigations of the poor, for example, the unfortunates had to be identified – indeed the empirical definition of 'poverty' absorbed much of the energies of early investigators. As, increasingly, extensive national statistics were gathered, so classification schemes were devised to bring order to the data. In a society where increasing numbers were dependent on paid employment, one obvious indicator of social advantage or disadvantage was occupation. Thus from the beginning of the twentieth century it has become commonplace for statisticians to divide the population into occupational aggregates or classes, depending (more or less) on the material rewards accruing to particular occupational groupings. The term 'class' is universally employed to describe these occupational aggregates, although they are clearly not of the same order as the 'classes' discussed in the theoretical work of Marx and Weber. However, occupational indices developed in the context of applied or policy research have constantly overlapped with theoretical discussions and empirical research relating to social class, and class consciousness and action, and therein lies the source of much confusion.

Chapter 3, therefore, has a major focus on different strategies which have been developed to investigate the employment or class *structure*. All of these accounts focus mainly upon employment and the associated structure of occupations. However, although the structure of employment in industrial societies is the major empirical source of the generation of these 'classes', there is no agreed index of classification. It will be suggested that class schemes can be usefully divided into three broad categories.

These are, first, the 'commonsense' schemes which lack theoretical pretensions, and which arrange occupations into an approximate hierarchical order to which a number of (hopefully not too arbitrary) cut-off points are applied. In an industrial society, occupation is an excellent indicator of both levels of material reward and social standing, and over the years such indexes have been found to correlate with a range of factors, such as rates of infant mortality, access to education, voting behaviour, and so on. Second, there are indexes of occupational prestige or status, which attempt to measure the societal ranking or worth of particular types of occupations within the population at large. Occupational prestige scales were initially constructed with a view to the investigation of social mobility. The similarity of occupational prestige scales as between different nation states, and the relative 'openness' (or otherwise) of occupational structures, have been essential data in the development and investigation of the 'industrial-society' thesis, which, as we have seen, Giddens has described as a key element of the 'orthodox consensus' developed within postwar sociology. Both commonsense occupational indexes and occupational prestige scales are descriptive indexes. They are also hierarchical, and thus 'gradational' measures of a more or less particular quantity (income, prestige, social standing, and so on). However, the third category of class index identified in chapter 3, that is, 'relational' or theoretical class schemes, have been constructed with explicit reference to class theories – particularly those of Marx and Weber. Thus they claim to be a measure of the dynamics and actualities of class *relations*, rather than simply to describe structures of inequality or prestige. The two major examples of theoretically grounded, relational class schemes which will be investigated are the Marxist class scheme of Erik Wright, and the neo-Weberian class scheme of John Goldthorpe.[6] Both of these authors claim that their class schemes are not hierarchical or 'gradational', but 'relational'.

However, although these three different types of class scheme have been constructed for very different purposes, there are in practice considerable similarities between the location of occupations and employment statuses as between the different schemes. Thus the three types of scheme are often treated as equivalent. However, the fundamental differences in the bases and assumptions on which they have been constructed suggest that considerable care should attend upon their application, particularly in respect of theoretical arguments relating to social class. The very different nature and claims of the different 'class' indexes available have not been widely acknowleged within the sociological community, and this has been a further source of confusion in the area of 'class analysis'. This confusion, as we shall see, has been somewhat clarified in recent discussions, and in many respects the work of the major protagonists has tended to converge.

It has been argued, therefore, that there is great diversity in the conceptualization and measurement of 'social class'. It is important that the growing body of criticism of class analysis is evaluated in the light of this diversity. Since the nineteenth century, there is no time when class has not been a contentious issue, but the recent pace of social and economic change has served to increase the range and intensity of the debate.

The growing critique of 'class analysis'

As we shall see in chapter 2, a major point of contrast between the theoretical approaches of Marx and Weber concerns the question of class action. Although Marx's writings are famously ambiguous on the point, there can nevertheless be little doubt that he viewed class conflict as the major motor of historical change, and thus some kind of class action to be inevitable. Weber, on the other hand, regarded class conflict as contingent – that is, as highly likely to occur, but by no means inevitable. He certainly did not regard such conflict as the only, or even the major, force of societal transformation. In a similar vein, much recent debate has focused on 'the declining significance of class'.

Changes in the structure of work as employment, as well as in the kinds of persons engaged in it, have supplied much of the empirical basis for arguments concerning the declining significance of class in late twentieth-century industrial societies. In countries such as Britain, America, Canada, Australia and much of Western Europe, there has been a massive decline in the numbers employed in heavy manufacturing and traditional extractive industries such as mining, steelmaking, shipbuilding and heavy engineering. The reasons for this decline are complex. Technological innovation has played a major part, as has technical obsolescence – newly automated processes simply require fewer people, new forms of energy replace old – but there have also been shifts in the global division of labour – South East Asia, for example, is now the centre of the shipbuilding industry. The collapse of heavy industry in the West was enormously accelerated by the impact of the world recession which followed upon the oil crisis of the 1970s (cause and effect are virtually impossible to disentangle here). The economic restructuring which followed decline and massive unemployment did increase the number of jobs available, but mainly in the service economy of finance and retail services. These changes have all led to a decline in the numbers of what had long been considered to be the traditional 'working-class', that is, geographically concentrated, manual employees in heavy industry. There has been a corresponding growth in non-manual, 'white-collar' employees, who had conventionally been regarded as located in the 'middle' classes or strata.

Together with these changes in the occupational structure, it has also been argued that 'work' as employment has become of considerably less significance in the shaping of social attitudes. People in employment spend less of their time in paid work, and increasing numbers of people are less dependent on paid work for their livelihood than in a previous era. This is partly because technical change and continuing economic uncertainty mean that there is simply less work (as employment) available, but also because the expansion of state provisions (in education, health and welfare) has made people less dependent on the sale of their labour in order to obtain the services they need. The continuing 'roll-back' of welfare states might imply there is some need to modify these arguments, but nevertheless it is still argued that work as employment is of declining importance as a source of social identity in the second half of the twentieth century. To borrow Gorz's title (1982), it is argued that we should bid a 'Farewell to the Working Class'.

The real implications of these changes in work and employment have, however, been hotly contested. In particular, in 1974 Braverman's influential book, *Labor and Monopoly Capital*, argued that the capitalist mode of production embodied an inherent tendency towards the routinization and 'deskilling' of labour. These tendencies affected all workers, and thus the apparent 'upgrading' of the labour force consequent upon the growth of non-manual employment was more apparent than real. White-collar workers, and even management, would in their turn become deskilled employees. Braverman's intervention stimulated considerable controversy as to the real nature of the changes, in class terms, which were occurring in respect of the occupational structure; but a (perhaps unintended) consequence of the revitalized debate on the class structure was that the question of class action was increasingly treated as a separate issue – or even not considered at all.

The question of class action, however, still remained problematic. The definition and relative size of the 'working class' might be contested, and the evidence of occupational class schemes might continue to demonstrate that occupational class and voting behaviour were still closely related; nevertheless, it would be difficult to make a strong case to the effect that the working class (or any other class) in the West has been engaged in sustained revolutionary activity since the end of the Second World War. The collapse of 'state socialism' in the Eastern bloc seems to have been accompanied by a turning away from socialist ideals, rather than their revitalization. During the 1970s and 1980s, therefore, there have developed a number of important political debates which have challenged the significance of 'class' for contemporary politics.

These debates are also linked to the wider social and economic changes which took place during the 1970s, which have already been briefly discussed in respect of their effects on employment. It is increasingly being suggested, amongst theoreticians of the political left, that these changes are in fact epochal and signify a significant shift in the development of capitalist industrialism. Many different labels have been used to describe this transition – from Fordism to post-Fordism, from modernity to postmodernity, from organized to disorganized capitalism. They describe the continuing break-up of older, mass-production industries and the growth of new, computer-based production and 'flexible specialization'. Individuals are being forced to adapt rapidly to these 'new times', long-term employment in mass industries and mass bureaucracies, which provided a solid foundation for the articulation of industrial-class action, is rapidly becoming a thing of the past.

Thus a major theme which runs through these commentaries is that of *individualization*. As employment fragments, so individuals are forced to negotiate their own trajectories through an increasingly unstable labour market (Beck 1992). In politics as much as in employment, it is argued, individualistic values are on the increase, and the old solidarities which fostered class identity and struggle have disappeared. 'Old politics' stands accused of 'productivism'; the 'new socialism', it is argued, must recognize that there are no objective class interests as such, but that there are many different points of antagonism, and thus potential for oppositional organization between capitalism and the population of late twentieth-century industrial societies. These kinds of argument, therefore, not only attempt to take on board the apparent decline in political significance of the old-style working class, but also to identify new focuses of political concern.

In contrast to the distributional issues which were the focus of the 'old politics', it is argued that the growth of 'new social movements' has transformed the political scene. Such movements are concerned with the environment, and the rights of various groups which have been historically excluded from full economic and political participation – women and subordinate ethnic groups in particular (Offe 1985a). The notion of rights is being extended, beyond those of adults, to include those of animals and children. It is a feature of new social movements that their support cuts across class boundaries, thus further weakening the basis of the old class politics, and class-based political action.

The growth of 'second-wave' feminism, which accompanied the increasing participation of women in paid employment, has also been of considerable importance in debates relating to the declining significance of 'class'. Class politics, it might be argued (as well as the institution of citizenship itself) were decisively shaped by the interests of male employees, as well as male owners and controllers of the means of material production. Men might have subordinated other men, and struggled for power and control, within the 'public' sphere of employment, politics and warfare, but, as the feminist critique demonstrated, women were subordinate not only in the public sphere but also within the 'private' sphere of domestic and family life. The orthodox terrain of class theory and analysis seemed to have little to contribute as far as an analysis of the position of women was concerned. The increase in women's employment also served to highlight major weaknesses as far as occupational class schemes were concerned. Such schemes had been devised in relation to a model of predominantly male employment. The persistence of occupational segregation by sex, despite the increase in the employment of women, meant that such schemes could no longer be implicitly treated as gender-neutral. The persistence of the gendered division of labour, however, continues to create apparently insuperable obstacles to the development of a single classification which would encompass both men and women.

Some authors have argued that contemporary transformations signify a significant shift in the nature of society itself. Globalization and the growth of postmodern culture, it is suggested, have swept away the last vestiges of traditionalism, and are in the process of eroding the powers of the state itself. In the West corporatist bargains are crumbling; state socialism has collapsed in the East. The whittling away of state and employment-related structures are leading, some have argued, to the emergence of systems of stratification that are primarily *cultural* in their origins, as individuals select and are drawn to, on the basis of their personal qualities and accomplishments, the symbols and lifestyles expressing their needs and preferences. Thus Waters (1996; see also Pakulski and Waters 1996b) argues that stratification in contemporary societies, in which tastes and interests are constantly shifting, is 'status-conventional'. Indeed they argue that the 'class' basis of stratification has more or less disappeared. It is as consumers that many individuals express their environmental concerns; another example of this reasoning would be the supposed increase in significance of the 'gay' pound and dollar. In short, people's identities are being increasingly expressed and manifest through consumption, rather than production.

It has also been argued that consumption is providing the basis for new social cleavages. Saunders (1987), for example, has argued that the major social cleavage in contemporary societies is that between those whose consumption needs are largely met through the market, on the one hand, and those largely dependent on state benefits on the other. Similar arguments have developed in the debate concerning the emergence of a putative underclass in the United States (these arguments will be examined in more depth in chapter 7).

The kinds of criticism reviewed above have focused upon the question of whether 'classes' should still be regarded as actual or potential significant social forces in the late twentieth century. They do not suggest, however, that capitalist societies are not still highly unequal. Following from this point, it may be suggested that, although 'work' as employment *may* possibly have declined as a significant source of social identity, work is still the most significant determinant of the material well-being of the majority of the population. Thus descriptive class indexes continue to demonstrate the persisting structure of inequality in contemporary societies. It still makes sense to describe late capitalist society as being dominated by a 'ruling class' which is economically dominant, and has the capacity to influence crucially political and social life (Scott 1991).

In chapter 4, criticisms of class analysis will be examined in some detail. Chapter 5 will evaluate the response to these criticisms from the varying perpectives which class analysis encompasses. We will also critically examine arguments that, by the end of the twentieth century, the forces of individualization and globalization have brought about a societal shift from industrial capitalist to 'postmodern' societies. It will also develop an argument to the effect that despite the economic and political changes and developments which have indeed taken place during the turbulent 1970s and 1980s, class and stratification theory does *not* have to be fundamentally recast in order to accommodate them. One general criticism will, however, be accepted. Recent debates *have* been hampered by an excessive focus on 'class' to the exclusion of other sources of structured social inequality. Much of the fire and brimstone, however, has been occasioned by people talking past, rather than to, each other. In a classic commentary on postwar sociology, Merton had observed that: 'In sociology as in other disciplines, pseudofacts have a way of inducing pseudoproblems, which cannot be solved because matters are not as they purport to be' (1959: xv). The lack of agreement relating to a number of basic concepts – particularly 'class' – within stratification theory and research, it may be suggested, has tended to generate a number of 'pseudo-debates'. Nevertheless, the rich tradition of stratification theory and research can still supply essential concepts through which to analyse our rapidly changing times.

- One of these concepts is that of social status (or prestige), briefly described above. In chapter 7, the development of citizenship will be explored as an example of a particular application of the status concept. In all advanced industrial nation states, citizens have become entitled to a guaranteed – if modest – level of material support whether or not they are engaged in market activities. As Esping-Andersen (1990) has put it, certain services – for example in the areas of health and education – have to varying extents been 'decommodified'. Marshall has described these as the rights of social citizenship, which he views as extensions of the rights of civil and political citizenship acquired from the eighteenth century onwards. Civil and political citizenship rights were initially granted to white adult males only, but the universalistic ideologies of liberal democracy have made it difficult to resist the sustained claims of excluded groups. Thus women and ethnic groups have made successful claims to citizenship status. Class struggles, it may be argued, were significant in the extension of citizenship rights, but the struggles of feminists, and ethnic minorities, to achieve these rights should be distinguished from those of class. Indeed, white male 'class' interests have often been seen as being at variance with those of other, non-class, groups within the stratification order. A further twist to the development of social citizenship in the twentieth century is that some commentators of the right have asserted that the state provision of non-market supports has contributed to the development of a permanent underclass in advanced industrial societies.

One feature of the underclass debate is that it has been argued that within this grouping there has developed a particular culture, or set of moral perspectives, which serves to perpetuate its disadvantaged situation. We will examine this somewhat dubious argument, and although it will be argued that it should not be accepted, it does serve to highlight the significance of the non-economic determinants of the stratification order. It has been stressed that, even in capitalist market societies, status claims have been of continuing significance in determining the distribution of material rewards and resources. The renewed emphasis on the significance of consumption, however, has brought to prominence the role of status, as expressed in 'lifestyles' and consumption practices, in the structuring of inequalities. For example Bourdieu (1973, 1986) has argued that cultural capital should be considered as playing a similar role to that of economic capital in the production and reproduction of inequalities.

Culture has been argued to play an increasingly significant role in the changing circumstances of 'consumer capitalism'. In particular, it has been suggested that cultural producers are a significant element within the 'new middle class', a grouping which, along with the 'underclass', has been identified by numerous commentators as a significant new stratification development associated with late twentieth-century industrialism. The 'new middle class' incorporates not just the symbol producers, but also the 'need merchants' who exist to prepare the labour inputs for the new service economy. This economy increasingly demands social, rather than technical or practical, skills, and with these demands there develops the providers – therapists, fitness experts, counsellors, and so on. These debates on the new middle class are examined in chapter 6, together with more general arguments as to the significance of *consumption* in contemporary societies.

Concluding summary

From the first, 'class' has always been a term with a variety of meanings. It has served to describe, in a relatively straightforward fashion, structures of material and symbolic inequality, as well as to describe social forces which have a capacity to act upon the world. Over the last two decades, however, research and theorizing in the area of class and stratification has undergone further fragmentation in response to economic and political changes, as well as changes in the perceptions of social scientists as to how the social world may best be investigated. This fragmentation has given rise to a proliferation of approaches to class and stratification analysis.

This book, therefore, has a relatively modest purpose. It does not seek to draw a new 'class map', or to develop a further original (and final?) approach to the analysis of social stratification. Rather, it attempts to provide a map of class and stratification analysis for the undergraduate student. This will involve the identification of weaknesses, as well as strengths, but it will nevertheless be argued consistently that the investigation and exploration of structured social inequality should remain as one of the central problem areas of sociology.

Notes

1 The 'ideological' origins and nature of the caste system have been challenged, particularly by Marxist anthropologists (Meillassoux 1973). It is argued that in reality caste differentiation reflected degrees of material power and domination, rather than ritual purity.

2 As we shall see in ch. 7, some categories of human beings, notably women, were initially excluded from this 'fraternal social contract'. See Pateman (1988, 1989).

3 As we shall see in ch. 2, Marx argued that feudal societies, like capitalist societies, were class-stratified. However, it may be suggested that the discourse of 'class' is peculiarly modern, and this is the major reason why the term will be restricted to modern industrial societies in the subsequent discussion.

4 An obvious counter-argument to this view is that many of the goods and services created by innovators have not benefited either the environment or society in general. Tobacco and Thalidomide might be cited as examples.

5 In this argument, there was an echo of the election campaign of 1963. The then Conservative Cabinet was largely composed of Old Etonians, and the Labour leader (Harold Wilson) made much in his challenge of his own humble origins, stressing the contrast with the social backgrounds of the Conservative leadership. The Labour Party won the election.

6 Goldthorpe has recently claimed that his class scheme is not related to any particular theory (Goldthorpe and Marshall 1992). Others, however, have located its origins in Weber's analysis (Morris and Scott 1996). This issue will be discussed at some length in ch. 4.

2 Class Analysis: The Classic Inheritance and its Development

Introduction

As described in chapter 1, the term 'class' is widely used as a general label to describe structures of inequality in modern societies. Such descriptive accounts of inequality, however, will incorporate implicit or explicit assumptions as to why a particular individual, occupation or social category should be located in a particular class. 'Class' has also been used in more abstract terms to describe a social force – most particularly by Marx, who described all history as 'the history of class struggles'. The notion that 'classes' can have transformative capacities is not limited to Marxism. The social forces (or 'actors') identified by class theorists such as Marx and Weber, however, do not correspond neatly to the class categories identified in descriptive accounts of the 'class structure'. Nevertheless, as we shall see in this chapter, both Marx's and Weber's theoretical accounts of social class have generated insights which have guided the particular allocation of individuals, occupations or social categories within specific class schemes. As a consequence of this practice, the 'classes' produced by the application of class schemes to the structure of employment have often been treated, implicitly, as if they also constituted actual or potential class actors. It will be argued that there are many difficulties with this assumption.

Social class and inequality have been amongst the central topic areas within sociology. It is not surprising, therefore, that the investigation of these topics over the last half-century should have been significantly shaped by debates taking place within sociology itself. Thus debates in social theory, as well as the specific theoretical contributions of Marx and Weber, have also had an important impact on class analysis. Our primary objective in this chapter, besides giving an account of Marx's and Weber's classic contributions, will also be to explore the impact of these varying theoretical inputs on the developing project of class and stratification analysis.

The ideas of both Marx (1818–83) and Weber (1864–1920) continue to shape debates in class theory in the late twentieth century. However, their contributions have been extensively reinterpreted and reformulated by successive generations. Of these two 'founding fathers', Marx was primarily a political activist, rather than an academic social theorist. From the 1960s however, there was a revival of academic interest in Marx's work which ran in parallel with the theoretical debates in sociology which were then current – in particular, the developing critique of normative functionalism or the 'consensus' perspective (Lockwood 1964). As noted in chapter 1, the dominant paradigm in Anglo-American sociology in the 1950s and early 1960s was essentially positivist – that is, it held to the view that sociology was the study of observable and objective *facts* about the social world (rather than being concerned with *a priori* 'theories' concerning the nature of the world as in theological or metaphysical speculation). It had a primary emphasis on the study of social structures or systems, rather than individuals. As the conflict theorists claimed, it was also concerned mainly with the functional coherence and normative integration of these systems, rather than with any conflicts or underlying tensions (Smelser 1988: 10). These kinds of sociological assumptions had also shaped the 'industrial society' thesis – that is, the idea that all industrial societies have a tendency to converge in a similar, non-conflictual, direction (Kerr et al. 1973).

However, critics of positivism argued that social facts cannot be objectively located but are theory-dependent – that is, they are not simply 'out there' but are socially *constructed*. Thus even apparently objective facts such as census data are gathered with regard to theoretical assumptions which may not always be explicit (Hindess, 1973). The emphasis on social structures or systems was criticized (Wrong 1966) for its 'oversocialized' conception of human nature. The recasting of social theory was associated with an increasing emphasis on the significance of human *action*; it was emphasized that human beings are neither (to paraphrase Garfinkel) structural nor cultural 'dopes' but act reflexively with the social world. The emphasis on stability and integration characteristic of normative functionalism was increasingly rejected in favour of perspectives that emphasized conflict rather than consensus, domination rather than integration (Rex 1961).

As a consequence of these theoretical debates, sociology has fragmented into a number of separate paradigms, and it would be difficult, if not impossible, to describe a 'dominant paradigm' in contemporary sociology. These divisions have also been reflected in its sub-fields. Despite a common origin in Marx's and Weber's work, therefore, class theory in sociology has developed in a number of different directions. However, these differences have not always been recognized explicitly by the many contributors to debates on 'class'.

Marx

Marx's aim was to provide a comprehensive analysis of capitalist society with a view to effecting its transformation; he was a committed revolutionary as well as a social theorist. In the *Communist Manifesto*, Marx and Engels (1962: 34) describe the course of human history in terms of the struggle between classes:

> Free man and slave, patrician and plebeian, lord and serf, guild-master and journeyman, in a word, oppressor and oppressed, stood in constant opposition to each other, carried on an uninterrupted, now hidden, now open fight, a fight that each time ended, either in a revolutionary reconstitution of society at large, or in the common ruin of the contending classes.

There can be little doubt, therefore, as to the centrality of class in Marx's work, but, although the theme is constant, he nowhere gives a precise definition of the class concept. Indeed, it is somewhat poignant that his last manuscript breaks off just at the moment at which he appeared to be on the point of giving such a definition, in a passage beginning: 'The first question to be answered is this: What constitutes a class? – and the reply to this follows naturally from the reply to another question, namely: What makes wage-labourers, capitalists and landlords constitute the three great social classes?' (Marx 1974: 886).

For Marx, class relationships are embedded in production relationships; more specifically, in the patterns of ownership and control which characterize these relationships. Thus the 'two great classes' of capitalist society are bourgeoisie and proletariat, the former being the owners and controllers of the material means of production, the latter owning only their labour power, which they are forced to sell to the bourgeoisie in order to survive. However, Marx did not have, as has sometimes been suggested, a 'two-class' model of society. It is true that he saw the bourgeoisie and proletariat as the major historic role-players in the capitalist epoch, but his analyses of contemporary events made it clear that he saw actual societies as composed of a multiplicity of classes. That is, Marx used the term 'class' both as an analytical concept in the development of his theory of society, and as a descriptive, historical concept. For example, in his account of the (1852) Bonapartist coup d'état in France, 'The Eighteenth Brumaire of Louis Bonaparte' (1962a), a variety of social groupings are identified including the landed aristocracy, financiers, the industrial bourgeoisie, the middle class, the petty bourgeoisie, the industrial proletariat, the lumpenproletariat and the peasantry.

Marx's account of antagonistic class relationships did not rest upon ownership and non-ownership alone. Rather, ownership of the material forces of production is the means to the exploitation of the proletariat by the bourgeoisie within the very process of production itself. The key to Marx's understanding of this process lies in the labour theory of value, a concept which Engels described as one of Marx's major theoretical achievements. In a capitalist society, argues Marx, labour has become a commodity like any other, but it is unique in that human labour alone has the capacity to create *new* values. Raw materials (commodities) such as wood, iron or cotton cannot by themselves create value; rather, value is added when they are worked on by human labour to create new commodities which are then realized in the market. The labour which is purchased (and therefore owned) by the capitalist will spend only a part of the working day in the creation of values equivalent to its price (that is, wages); the rest of the working day is spent in the creation of surplus value, which is retained by the capitalist. (Surplus value does not simply describe profit, but is distributed to a number of sources including taxes, payments to 'unproductive' labourers and new capital investment, as well as profits or dividends.) Thus even though the labourer may be paid a wage that is entirely 'fair', that is, it represents the value of this labour in the market, and the worker has not been cheated or swindled in any legal sense (cheating and swindling *may* occur, of course) – he or she has nevertheless been exploited.

It has been emphasized that Marx was not just concerned to

provide a description of the nature of exploitation in class societies, but also to give an account of the role of social classes in the transformation of societies themselves. Thus, for Marx, classes are social forces, historical actors. For Marx, men (and, it should be said, women) *make* their own history, although not necessarily in the *circumstances* of their own choosing. Some commentators have suggested that for Marx a class only existed when it was conscious of itself as such. However, in *The Poverty of Philosophy* he appears to make an unambiguous distinction between a 'class in itself' and a (conscious) 'class for itself', when he writes of the proletariat that 'this mass is already a class in opposition to capital, but not yet a class for itself' (1955: 195). This ambiguity in Marx's work has been of considerable significance in the development of sociological analyses of class.

Marx's account of the generation of human consciousness is central to his theory of historical materialism, the social-scientific core of Marxist theory. This is summarized in the Preface to *A Contribution to the Critique of Political Economy*:

> In the social production of their life, men enter into definite relations that are indispensable and independent of their will, relations of production which correspond to a definite stage of development of their material productive forces. The sum total of these relations of production constitutes the economic structure of society, the real foundation, on which rises a legal and political superstructure and to which correspond definite forms of social consciousness. The mode of production of material life conditions the social, political, and intellectual life process in general. It is not the consciousness of men that determines their being, but, on the contrary, their social being that determines their consciousness. (Marx 1962b: 362–3)

Two related – and contentious – insights may be drawn from this account. First, that it is the economic 'base' that determines the political and ideological 'superstructure' of human societies; and second, that it is material being that determines human consciousness, rather than vice versa. These arguments may be illustrated via a summary of the account of the transition from feudalism to capitalist industrialism, as outlined by Marx and Engels in the *Communist Manifesto*. The relations of production in feudal society – the system of manorial estates held by right rather than purchase, with an unfree peasantry bound to labour on the land through feudal obligations, were the material basis of an ideological superstructure in which the existing social order was given divine justification through the Catholic Church. Feudal society was static and technologically underdeveloped, and the network of customary rights and obligations which underpinned it acted as a hindrance to the development of the dynamic capitalist order. The feudal aristocracy was, however, ultimately unable to resist the power of the rising bourgeoisie, the 'revolutionary class' in the feudal context. Thus after centuries of feudal stagnation the transition to capitalism was nevertheless achieved – often accompanied by more or less violent events (such as, for example, the French Revolution). The triumphant bourgeoisie may have broken with feudal restrictions and consolidated their rights in the ownership of the means of production (that is, capital), but in creating the class that had only its labour to sell as its means of subsistence – that is, the proletariat – the bourgeoisie had created their own 'grave diggers': 'Society as a whole is more and more splitting up into two great hostile camps, into two great classes directly facing each other: Bourgeoisie and Proletariat' (Marx and Engels 1962: 35). The proletariat would constitute the revolutionary class within capitalist society, and through its struggles would usher in first socialism and eventually true communism.

Marx's distinction between base and superstructure has been the subject of extensive debate. He has been widely accused of economic reductionism – the assertion that the economic base *determines* social, political and intellectual development. Such a mechanistic model would, indeed, constitute a gross oversimplification of the complexities of human behaviour, and in a letter written after Marx's death his collaborator Engels emphasized that the theory of historical materialism should not be interpreted as claiming that the economic situation was the *sole* cause of human behaviour. Rather, he argued that although it might be 'ultimately' determinant, at any particular moment, other social relations – political, ideological – would also be affecting human actions. The base/superstructure debate, however, was not closed as a consequence of Engels's intervention.

Marxist theory has developed in a number of different directions. By the 1970s two broad strands within Marxism relating to the base/superstructure debate had emerged: 'humanist' and 'scientific'. As Urry (1981: 8) has noted, these perspectives incorporated 'the reproduction of certain of the problems which have already been encountered within orthodox sociology'. This was the structure/action debate; the contrast between, on the one hand, sociological perspectives which emphasize above all the significance of human action in explanations of social institutions and behaviour, and, on the other, the functionalist or structurally deterministic accounts of society which such 'action' approaches criticized. Thus, humanist Marxism – as in, for example, the work of Gramsci – tends to treat the base/superstructure distinction as a metaphor which can all too easily be interpreted in a deterministic fashion. Gramsci emphasizes the value of Marx's analysis as a means of developing a critique of the dehumanizing aspects of modern capitalism, a critique which will ultimately enable the actor to transcend his or her 'alienation'. As with the action approach within sociology, therefore, a central role is given to the human actor.

'Scientific' Marxism was the self-assigned label of French structural Marxists such as Althusser (1969) and Poulantzas (1975). Althusser argued that ideology and politics were not determined by the economy in a mechanistic fashion, as some simplistic interpretations of Marx had assumed. Rather, they should be seen as conditions of its existence and are therefore 'relatively autonomous' – although, echoing Engels, Althusser held that the economic was determinant in 'the last instance'. The work of Althusser and Poulantzas was also characterized by a distinctive (rationalist) epistemology, or view of how knowledge about the world is acquired. Knowledge about the social world, they argued, does not proceed by observation but through theoretical practice or 'science' – of which Marxism was an example. Thus we do not 'know' classes by observing them but rather through the theoretical identification and exploration of the class structure, and individuals are the 'bearers' or 'agents' of these structures of social relations. This approach, therefore, emphasizes above all the primacy of the identification and description of class *structures* . The manner in which individuals are distributed within these structures is, from their perspective, of comparatively minor importance; the important task for the 'scientist' is to identify the structure itself, and thus the 'real interests' of the individuals located within it. It is not difficult to see the parallels here with functionalism and structural over-determinism in sociology (Connell 1982). Different classes are being identified according to their 'functional' relationship to the capitalist mode of production as a whole, which is described in Marx's account of the exploitation of workers within the labour process and the way in which different groups in society are related to this process.

As we have seen, Marx had drawn a distinction between a 'class in itself' and a 'class for itself'; this has been described as a distinction between a set of 'objective' conditions which define the class, and the 'subjective' consciousness which this class possesses (Braverman

1974). However, what is the nature of this subjective consciousness? It has been argued (Abercrombie and Turner 1978) that Marx's work provides two, conflicting, accounts of the generation of class consciousness. On the one hand, the passage cited above from the *Critique of Political Economy* could be used to argue that each class develops its 'own' consciousness: that factory workers, for example, will develop a common understanding of their exploited position. On the other hand, the same passage could be used to argue that the dominant class has the capacity to generate a dominant ideology – that the employers, for example, will have the capacity to generate amongst factory workers a belief that the prevailing arrangements are beneficial for all concerned. Thus in *The German Ideology*, Marx and Engels state: 'The ruling class are in every epoch the ruling ideas, i.e. the class which is the ruling *material* force of society, is at the same time its ruling *intellectual* force' (1970: 64). Thus a subordinate class may, as a consequence, hold to views which are at variance with its own 'objective' interests – a phenomenon which has been described by later Marxists as a 'false consciousness' of their true class situation.

Throughout the 1980s, the debate on class continued amongst Marxist theorists. Structural Marxism no longer has the influence it once had – at least in part, it may be suggested, because of the electoral failure of the left during this period (see Preface in Benton 1984). The collapse of 'state socialism' has also been widely interpreted as an empirical refutation of Marxist theory. The revival of Marxist scholarship in the 1960s was accompanied by an optimism of the left which persisted throughout much of the 1970s; the 1980s, however, witnessed the electoral rise of the 'New Right' – Thatcherism in Britain, Reaganomics in the United States. Political theorists including Przeworski (1985), Laclau and Mouffe (1985), and Wood (1986) have examined the possibilities of the development of socialism in these changing circumstances. Much of this discussion has involved a fundamental revision of some basic Marxist political ideas. In particular, the central place which the proletariat or working class occupied within Marx's original writings has increasingly been called into question. Wood (1986: 3–4) has summarized these revisions (which she describes, somewhat scathingly, as the 'New True Socialism') as follows: first, the absence of revolutionary politics amongst the working class reflects the fact that there is no necessary correspondence between economics and politics (that is, the link between base and superstructure is regarded as tenuous, even non-existent). Second, there is no necessary or privileged relation between the working class and socialism, and so a socialist movement can be constituted independently of class (thus dissolving the link between 'class' and 'consciousness'). Third, socialism is in any case concerned with universal human goals which transcend the narrowness of material class interests and may therefore address a broader public, irrespective of class. Thus the struggle for socialism can be conceived as a plurality of democratic struggles, bringing together a variety of resistances to many forms of inequality and oppression (for example, those associated with gender and race).

These arguments amongst Marxist theoreticians have not been directly concerned with class and stratification research in sociology, but they have nevertheless had a considerable impact. The American sociologist Erik Wright (1989) has systematically developed both his 'class map' and his strategy of analysis in response to inputs from these sources. More generally, however, it may be suggested that contemporary debates within theoretical Marxism have contributed to more general arguments to the effect that 'class' is no longer a relevant analytical concept as far as late twentieth-century societies are concerned.

Marx, therefore, saw classes as real social forces with the capacity to transform society. His class analysis did not simply describe the patterning of structured social inequality – although an explanation of this structuring can be found in the relationships to the means of production through which classes are to be identified. His theories have been enormously influential and are open to a number of different interpretations. Two major problems have been identified which are still the focus of considerable debate within sociology: first, the relative significance of the 'economy' (or class forces) as compared to other sources of social differentiation in the shaping of human activities; and second, whether or not consciousness is integral to the identification of a class. As we shall see, the position of Max Weber, the other major theorist whose ideas have been central to the development of sociological perspectives on class, was rather different on both of these issues.

Weber

The contrast between Marx's and Weber's analysis of class may at times have been overdrawn, but it cannot be doubted that their approaches to social science were very different. Marx was a committed revolutionary, Weber a promoter of 'value-free' social science; and although Weber could not be described as an idealist, he was highly critical of Marx's historical materialism. Marx claimed to have identified abstract social forces (classes) which shaped human history – although, as we have seen, the extent to which Marx considered such structures *can* be identified independently of human action is itself a topic of much debate. Weber, in contrast, was an explicit methodological individualist. That is, he argued that all social collectivities and human phenomena have to be reducible to their individual constituents, and explained in these terms. As far as class is concerned, for Weber:

> We may speak of a 'class' when (1) a number of people have in com-mon a specific causal component of their life chances, in so far as (2) this component is represented exclusively by economic interests in the possession of goods and opportunities for income, and (3) is represen-ted under the conditions of the commodity or labour markets. (Gerth and Mills 1948: 181)

Thus 'class situation' reflects market-determined 'life chances'. The causal components contributing to such life chances include prop-erty, giving rise to both positively and negatively privileged property classes (that is, owners and non-owners), and skills and education, giving rise to positively and negatively privileged 'acquisition' or 'commercial' classes. Weber was aware of the (almost) infinite vari-ability of 'market situations' and thus of the difficulty of identifying a 'class', and his discussion in *Economy and Society* incorporates the listing of over twenty positively and negatively privileged, property and acquisition, classes. This empirical plurality is resolved by Weber's description of a *'social* class', which 'makes up the totality of those class situations within which individual and generational mobility is easy and typical' (Giddens and Held 1982: 69). He identi-fied as 'social classes' (a) the working class as a whole; (b) the petty bourgeoisie; (c) technicians, specialists and lower-level manage-ment, and (d) 'the classes privileged through property and educa-tion' – that is, those at the top of the hierarchy of occupation and ownership. In short, at the descriptive level, Weber's account of the 'class structure' of capitalist society is not too different from that of Marx, despite the fact that their identification of the *sources* of class structuring (production relationships on the one hand, market rela-tionships on the other) *are* very different.

Marx and Weber, however, differed profoundly as far as the ques-tion of class action was concerned. For Weber: ' "classes" are not communities; they merely represent possible, and frequent, bases for communal action' (Gerth and Mills 1948: 181). 'Associations of class members – class organizations – may arise on the basis of all ... classes. However, this does not necessarily happen ... The mere differentiation of property classes is not "dynamic", that is, it need not result in class struggles and revolutions' (Giddens and Held 1982: 69–70). Indeed, in a passage which clearly refers to the Marxist notion of 'false consciousness' Weber writes that:

> every class may be the carrier of any one of the innumerable possible forms of class action, but this is not necessarily so. . . . That men in the same class situation regularly react in mass actions to such tangible situations as economic ones in the direction of those interests that are most adequate to their average number is an important ... fact for the understanding of historical events. However, this fact must not lead to that kind of pseudo-scientific operation which has found its most classic expression in the statement of a talented author, that the individual may be in error concerning his interests but that the class is infallible about its interests. (Gerth and Mills 1948: 184–5)

Weber's historical sociology, therefore, was developed in conscious opposition to Marxist theories of historical development – at least in its more economistic versions – as in Weber's analysis of the genesis of modern capitalism in *The Protestant Ethic and the Spirit of Capitalism*. In this book, he explored the unintended consequences of Calvinist ideology, and its impact on historical development, through an examination of the 'elective affinity' between Protestantism and the 'spirit of capitalism', which affected the development of capitalism itself. Weber argued that rational, ascetic Protestantism, as developed within a number of Calvinist churches and Pietistic sects in Europe and America during the seventeenth century, provided, through its rules for daily living (diligence in work, asceticism, and systematic time use) a particularly fruitful seedbed for the development of capitalism. It would be misleading to argue that Weber had developed his argument in order to advance an alternative, 'idealist', interpretation of history; he did not seek 'to substitute for a one-sided materialistic an equally one-sided spiritualistic causal interpretation of culture and of history' (Weber 1976: 183). However, as Marshall (1982: 150) has argued, the question as to whether Marx's materialist or Weber's pluralistic account of the rise and development of capitalism is to be preferred is not, ultimately, an empirical one but, rather, a question of the 'validity of competing frameworks for the interpretation of social reality'. Although Weber's account of the rise of capitalism cannot be described as 'idealist', therefore, it does lead, inevitably, to an account of the relationship between the 'ideological' and 'material' realms of human activity which would be in conflict with Marx's analysis.

Weber's analysis is also to be distinguished from Marx's in that he not only denies the inevitability of class action and conflict, but also the identification of class as a primary source of differentiation in complex societies. For Weber, ' "classes", and "status groups" are phenomena of the distribution of power within a community' (Gerth and Mills 1948: 181), and in certain circumstances status may be the predominant source which regulates entitlements to material rewards. Status is associated with honour and prestige and, indeed, may often come into conflict with the demands of the market, where, to use an old phrase suitably adapted: 'every man (and woman) has his (or her) price'. In contrast: 'in most instances', wrote Weber, 'the notion of honour peculiar to status absolutely abhors that which is essential to the market: higgling' (Gerth and Mills 1948: 193). Thus in Weber's analysis the feudal lord or abbot, for example, would belong not to a dominant class but to a status group. 'Status', in Weber's writings, is a complex concept. First, there is the meaning which has already been described: that which reflects the etymological link with 'estate' or *'Stände'* and describes positions which represent particular life chances or fates for the status group in question. Second, status groups have been identified as 'consciousness communities', as when, for example, Collins (1971: 1009) describes status groups as 'associational groups sharing common cultures ... Participation in such groups gives individuals their fundamental sense of identity.' Third, as we have seen in the previous chapter, status has been used to describe consumption categories or 'lifestyle', as 'the totality of cultural practices such as dress, speech, outlook and bodily dispositions (Turner 1988: 66).

The crucial differences between Marx's and Weber's accounts of class may be summarized as follows: first, for Marx, class relationships are grounded in exploitation and domination within *production* relations, whereas, for Weber, class situations reflect differing 'life chances' in the *market*; second, Marx's historical materialism gives a primacy to 'class' in historical evolution which is at odds with Weber's perspective on historical explanation; and finally (and following from this point), whereas for Marx class action is seen as inevitable, for Weber classes 'merely represent possible, and frequent, bases for communal action' (Gerth and Mills 1948: 181).

Class and sociology after the Second World War

Sociology had been well established in the United States before the Second World War, and 'At the beginning of the 1950's ... one could find large numbers of studies dealing with almost every aspect of behaviour in the United States. No other society had ever been subjected to such detailed examination' (Bendix and Lipset 1967a: 6). A strong tradition of empirical investigation, therefore, was well established. This included research into social stratification, which, as in studies such as Warner's (1963) anthropologically inspired *Yankee City* series, first published in the 1940s, had a focus on occupational inequality and social mobility, often in small communities. As has frequently been noted, in such studies 'class' was in practice operationalized as a particular dimension of the Weberian concept of *status* in that it was mainly concerned with social prestige rankings within the community. The pre-eminenent sociological theorist in the United States was Talcott Parsons; as we have seen, the structural functionalism which characterized his approach had a tendency to emphasize order rather than conflict, and thus to direct attention away from the conflict and tensions in society which are the focus of *class* (rather than status) analyses.

Sociology in Britain was relatively underdeveloped in the 1950s, and had been much influenced by the Fabian tradition of social improvement and reform. Thus a preoccupation with structured social inequality had always been present. An example of this tradition of British 'political arithmetic' would be Glass's *Social Mobility in Britain* (1954), which had used an occupational (class) scale in its statistical analyses of social mobility. In Continental Europe, sociology was more deeply rooted in established traditions of philosophy and social theory. The intellectual diaspora which was a consequence of the rise of fascism brought many European scholars to the United States and Britain, and with it an increasing emphasis on the significance of 'theory' in sociology.

The first major reader in the field of class and stratification to be published in English after the Second World War – *Class, Status, and Power* (1953; 2nd edn 1967), edited by Reinhard Bendix and S. M. Lipset – reflected this mingling of influences. The title was itself a deliberate play on a section of Weber's *Economy and Society*, 'Class, Status, and Party', which had been of considerable significance in shaping sociological thinking about 'social class'. The importance of the distinction between economic 'classes' and 'status rankings' (the latter describes the conceptualization of class in Warner's research) was increasingly emphasized. However, the use of the 'class' concept by the different contributors to the volume reflected the variety of definitions of the term which has been noted in chapter 1. Thus there were a number of papers on class theory, in which class was discussed as an abstract force, whereas other contributions used the same word – class – to describe the occupational aggregates used in, for example, empirical analyses of residential segregation. Bendix and Lipset's article – 'Karl Marx's theory of social classes' (1967b) – provided a guide to 'Marx on Class' for a whole generation of sociology students in Britain and America.

They identified a 'basic ambiguity', which has already been noted, in Marx's theory concerning class action:

> on the one hand, he felt quite certain that the contradictions engendered by capitalism would inevitably lead to a class-conscious proletariat and hence to a proletarian revolution. But on the other hand, he assigned to class-consciousness, to political action, and to his scientific theory of history a major role in bringing about this result. (1967b: 11)

In other words, is class consciouness and therefore conflict inevitable, or not? As Bendix and Lipset demonstrated, Marx's own work provided an extensive discussion of the circumstances in which class consciousness *might* develop (conflicts over the distribution of material resources, alienation and deskilling within the labour process, concentration of workers within factories, combinations to raise wages, increasing polarization within society, and so on), but, they argued, ambiguity still remained as to whether it *would* develop. However, if the question of class consciousness is viewed as contingent rather than inevitable (and this, it will be remembered, was Weber's position), then the question becomes an empirical one – in what circumstances does class consciouness develop? As Lockwood has noted: 'once shorn of its deterministic assumptions, the Marxian problem of the relationship between class position and class consciousness could become a subject of far-reaching and systematic sociological inquiry' (1958; 1989: 217).

The development of theoretical accounts of the 'class structure'

The way was laid open, therefore, for the analytical and empirical separation of the specification of the class structure from the question of consciousness, between the 'objective' and 'subjective' dimensions of class. Within this emerging sociological perspective, a central problem is that of the identification of the class structure itself – that is, a structure of positions which may or may not give rise to consciousness. The structure of employment became the major focus of such attempts. Dahrendorf's work was extremely influential in this regard. In *Class and Class Conflict in an Industrial Society* (1959: 151), he drew upon the work of both Marx and Weber in deriving the class structure from 'positions in associations (i.e. occupations) co-ordinated by authority and defin[ing] them by the "characteristic" of participation in or exclusion from the exercise of authority'. In a similar vein to Bendix and Lipset, he argued that: 'The general theory of class consists of two analytically separable elements: the theory of class formation and the theory of class action, or class conflict' (1959: 153). This analytical separation of 'structure' and 'action', as we have seen, assumed considerable significance in sociology and has had an important effect on the development of 'class analysis'.

Like Dahrendorf, Lockwood in *The Blackcoated Worker* drew upon the theoretical analyses of both Marx and Weber in his now-classic 1958 account of a 'socioeconomic group that had long been a discomfort to Marxist theory: the growing mass of lower non-manual or white-collar employees' (1958; 1989: 218). (In fact, Lockwood's research focused entirely on clerical occupations.) He described 'class position' as including three factors: 'market situation', that is 'the economic position narrowly conceived, consisting of source and size of income, degree of job-security, and opportunity for upward occupational mobility'; secondly, 'work situation', or 'the set of social relationships in which the individual is involved at work by virtue of his position in the division of labour'; and finally, 'status situation', or the position of the individual in the hierarchy of prestige in the society at large. Experiences originating in these three spheres were seen as the principal determinants of class consciousness (1989: 15–16). It must be emphasized that Lockwood was not merely concerned descriptively to locate clerks in the class structure. A central issue in his work is the question of class consciousness and action, and he explored the differentiation of 'class situation' within the clerical category which gave rise to variations in the level and type of trade union activity amongst clerical workers – trade unionism is here being viewed as an expression of class consciousness. Nevertheless, in maintaining, like Dahrendorf, an analytical separation between structure (formation) and action, Lockwood's work left open the possibility that 'class analysis' might come to have a primary focus on one or the other. Although, therefore, his original work was concerned as much with the question of class consciousness and action as it was with class structure, it might be suggested that one of its enduring legacies has been that it provided, within a neo-Weberian framework, the means to locate empirically particular groups of occupations within the 'class structure'. In particular, Lockwood's concepts of 'work' and 'market' situation were key elements in Goldthorpe's (1980; 1987) development of a theoretical class scheme, based on the occupational structure, which has been widely employed in empirical research (as we shall see in the next chapter, Goldthorpe now uses the term 'employment relations', rather than Lockwood's concepts).

Another sociologist who has devoted considerable effort to the theoretical identification of a 'class structure' within the structure of employment relationships is the American Marxist Erik Wright. Wright's initial development of his Marxist 'class map', which was to become the basis of his own theoretical class scheme, was carried out in a conscious dialogue with structural Marxism (Wright 1976). Thus although Wright's theoretical perspectives are clearly very different from those of Lockwood, Dahrendorf, Goldthorpe and other 'left Weberians', his work is, like theirs, an attempt to identify sets of 'class positions' within the structure of employment. Wright's earlier work was much influenced by Braverman, whose *Labor and Monopoly Capital* (1974) was modelled on Marx's analysis of the labour process in *Capital,* vol. 1. Braverman argued that with the development of mass production, work had become increasingly routinized and, as a consequence, there had been a continuing 'proletarianization' of the labour force – despite the apparent increase in 'white-collar' or 'middle-class' employment. Braverman's account of the 'deskilling' of craft work and the rationalization of the labour process had a considerable impact on industrial sociology. In respect of class analysis, however, his work had the effect of driving a further wedge between structure and action: 'No attempt will be made to deal with the modern working class on the level of its consciousness, organization, or activities. This is a book about the working class as a class *in itself*, not as a class *for itself*' (1974: 26–7; emphasis in original).[1] His account, therefore, focused entirely on developments within the labour process and did not discuss the possibility of class resistance or action. Thus although it is highly unlikely that Braverman would have had any sympathy with structural Marxism, his work had a similar impact. The 'analytical separation between class formation and class action' (Dahrendorf) was increasingly coming to represent distinct areas of theoretical and empirical activity (Crompton and Gubbay 1977).

Since the Second World War, therefore, we can trace the emergence of a distinctive sociological strand of 'class analysis'. Marxist and Weberian theories of social class are employed, as in the work of authors such as Lockwood, Dahrendorf and Braverman, to generate theoretical accounts of how particular jobs and occupations might be located within a structure of class positions. Increasingly, these accounts are used to elaborate and refine a predominant empirical approach within social stratification as a whole, in which employment aggregates are described as 'classes'. That is, 'classes' are identified theoretically within the structure of employment. Following from Bendix and Lipset's appropriation of Marx's distinction between a class 'in itself' and 'for itself', class structure and class action are regarded as analytically separable. Thus these theoretically identified employment aggregates may be regarded as 'classes' – although the question of class action is contingent, rather than inevitable. This strategy, therefore, brings together within a single framework theoretical analyses of social class with empirical analyses of inequality. It is an approach with tremendous explanatory and analytical promise but, as we shall see, it also embodies a number of serious, and probably irresolvable, difficulties.

Culture, class and history

We have summarized above a number of sustained attempts, deriving from different theoretical perspectives, to identify *a priori* a 'class structure' located within the structure of work and employment. A number of different factors served to push class analysis in this direction, including the established convention in American and British sociology of identifying 'classes' as occupational aggregates, the influence of both structural-functionalism and structural Marxism, and the revival of sociological interest in the labour process. However, these developments ran in parallel with other approaches to the study of social class, which tended to be associated with a humanistic, rather than a structuralist, Marxist perspective, and a methodological approach which drew primarily upon history and anthropology.

A broadly historical approach to the topic of social class, similar to that found in the work of Weber and Marx, has been a constant theme in the work of sociologists. In Britain, the work of Bottomore (1991) and Bauman (1982) might be cited as examples. From the 1960s there has been a continuing dialogue between sociology and history, much of which has been concerned with the concept of 'class' (Stedman Jones 1976; Neale 1983, Abrams 1980). A major example is E. P. Thompson's *Making of the English Working Class*, first published in 1963. In this book, and in his other work, Thompson argues explicitly against the more determinist versions of the model of economic 'base' and ideological 'superstructure' which had been developed from Marx's work. As Kaye (1984: 172) has argued: 'In his historical studies ... Thompson has persistently pursued an intellectual struggle against those varieties of Marxism and social science which are characterized by economic determinism and the denial of human agency.' A rejection of determinism and emphasis on human agency might suggest the possibility of close parallels with Weber, but Thompson has from the first been associated with a tradition of Marxist history which, in Britain, has a lengthy pedigree. This tradition includes authors such as Maurice Dobb, Christopher Hill and Eric Hobsbawm, who have written extensively on the development of capitalism and the transition from feudalism, the English Revolution, rural protest, and the development of Empire. The concept of 'class', and class struggle, has a central place in all of their writings, but Thompson's account of the 'making' of the English working class in the eighteenth and nineteenth centuries develops a distinctive perspective on 'class' which has had a major impact. Although his work is focused on the British case, it has been extremely influential in other countries.[2]

Thompson defines 'class' in the manner of an abstract force which nevertheless has real consequences: 'By class I understand a historical phenomenon, unifying a number of disparate and seemingly unconnected events ... I emphasize that it is a *historical* phenomenon. I do not see class as a 'structure', nor even as a 'category', but as something which in fact happens' (Thompson 1968: 9). Like Marx, Thompson sees class as embedded in relations of production, but he is emphatic that classes cannot be discussed or identified independently of class *consciousness*: 'class experience is largely determined by the productive relations into which men are born – or enter involuntarily. Class-consciousness is the way in which these experiences are handled in cultural terms: embodied in traditions, value-systems, ideas, and institutional forms' (1968: 10). Thompson's emphasis on the significance of experience and conciousness has led to criticisms from other historians that his work is excessively culturalist – that is, it represents a shift away from the investigation of *economic* structures and relations which, it may be argued, should occupy a central place in any Marxist historical investigation (Johnson 1979). This specific point relating to Thompson's work will not be pursued here – although the interrelationship between the 'economic' and the 'cultural' will be explored in some depth in chapter 6. For the moment, however, we will explore a topic of some relevance to class analysis in sociology, and which assumes a central place in Thompson's work – that is, the possibility (or otherwise) of identifying a class 'structure' independent of class consciousness.

Kaye has argued, following Wood, that Thompson has 'reformulat[ed] class analysis as class-struggle analysis' (1984: 201), but nevertheless Thompson does not claim that there are no 'objective' class relations. As we have seen, Thompson is explicit that the productive relations which determine class experience have an existence apart from the individual, but he *does* insist that 'class is a relationship, and not a thing ... "It" does not exist, either to have an ideal interest or consciousness, or to lie as a patient on the Adjustor's table' (1968: 11). In taking up this position, Thompson was arguing against what he perceived to be the dominant sociological approach to 'class analysis', which was briefly described in the previous section of this chapter. He was equally critical of the structural-functional approach of Parsons and Smelser as well as the 'conflict' approach of Dahrendorf (1959). Smelser (1959) had carried out a detailed historical study of the Lancashire cotton industry which had used Parsons's 'general theory of action' in order to construct a set of empty theoretical 'boxes' to be filled by empirical research. This was informed by the principle that structural differentiation created new roles which then functioned more effectively in the new circumstances. On an extreme reading of this approach, human actors are thereby reduced to puppets. Dahrendorf had developed a model of the 'class structure' in which 'classes are ... based on a structural arrangement of social roles' (1959: 148). Thus Dahrendorf's analysis focuses on the structuring of these roles, rather than on their incumbents: 'Classes are based on the differences in legitimate power associated with certain *positions*, i.e. on the structure of social roles with respect to their authority expectations. It follows from this that an individual becomes a member of a class by playing a social role' (Dahrendorf 1959: 149; my emphasis). It is not difficult to see how this approach would be at variance with that of Thompson, who describes Dahrendorf's work as 'obsessively concerned with methodology', and as excluding 'the examination of a single real class situation in a real historical context' (Thompson 1968: 11).

Besides its impact on the development of social history, Thompson's work has also been influential in the area of cultural studies, within which there has developed an approach to 'class analysis' very different from that of those who have concentrated upon the identification and investigation of the macro-level class structure. Much of this work has been influenced by Gramsci's humanist Marxism. As we have indicated above, Gramsci rejected the base/superstructure dichotomy of economistic Marxism, and emphasized the pervasive importance of culture and ideology to the persistence of structures of class domination. Culture, he argued, is neither apolitical, nor a mere reflection of the ideology of the dominant class. Central to Gramsci's thought is the concept of *hegemony*, that is, the manner in which the active *consent* of the subordinate classes to their domination is achieved. Thus 'every struggle between classes is always also a struggle between cultural modalities' (Hall 1981); winning the struggle of ideas is as important to the 'class struggle' as are economic and political struggles.

Thus within cultural studies there have been developed ethnographic accounts of the manner in which individuals in different classes both resist and reproduce their class situations. An influential example of this genre is Willis's *Learning to Labour* (1977), a study of working-class male adolescents. Willis illustrated how, in his terms, the explicitly oppositional working-class culture (that is, opposed to 'middle-class' values, including conformity, an emphasis on the importance of formal education, and so on) which was developed within the school context nevertheless reflected that within the working-class world of work which these youths were about to enter, and thus, paradoxically, reinforced their subordination. It is a feature of this cultural approach to class analysis, therefore, that no distinction is made between 'structure' and 'action', and that 'culture' is defined as encompassing both the meanings and the values which arise amongst distinctive social groups and classes, as well as the lived traditions and practices through which these meanings are expressed and in which they are embodied (Hall 1981: 26).

Much of the work stimulated by Thompson has focused on the working class, but in recent years the lifestyles of the 'new middle classes' have become objects of intense scrutiny, following the work of Bourdieu (1986). This dimension of the ongoing analysis of the relationship between class structures and cultural developments will be reviewed in chapter 6 of this book.[3]

Once again, the indivisibility of structure and action

Methodologically speaking, the development of 'theoretical' or 'relational' employment-based class schemes, on the one hand, and historico-cultural ethnographies, on the other, represent opposite poles in the development of 'class analysis'. However, these are by no means the only direction that class analysis has taken in sociology. The development of theoretical class schemes, focused on the structure of employment, depends on the analytical separation of the study of class structure from that of class action, of 'subjective' and 'objective' dimensions, but the validity of this separation has always been contested – and not only by those committed to an ethnographic approach. For example, Stark (1980) has been highly critical of Braverman's separation of the investigation of a class 'in itself' from a class 'for itself'. He argues against the type of class analysis which 'proceeds by identifying the members who "make up" the class; this aggregate is then given the properties of a purposive actor' (1980: 96–7). As a consequence of this separation, he argues, Braverman's history was empirically inadequate in that it did not examine either worker resistance or the purposive strategies of the emergent managerial class. Rather than simply identifying classes as aggregates of 'places', Stark argues, in a manner reminiscent of Thompson, for a 'relational' approach:

> a class is not 'composed of' individuals; it is not a collection or aggregation of individuals. *Classes*, like the social relations from which they arise, exist in an antagonistic and dependent relation to each other. Classes are constituted by these mutually antagonistic relations. In this sense ... the object of study is not the elements themselves but the relations between them. (1980: 97)

Thus the transformation of method, he argues, must also be accompanied by a shift in the level of abstraction of class analysis, away from an obsessive over-concern with the 'mode of production' to the study of the interaction of organizations and groups.

Stark's arguments, therefore, may be seen as an example of the ongoing parallel between debates in Marxist theory and those in mainstream sociology during the 1960s and 1970s. Giddens, whose work was influential in developing the critique of positivism, first developed his ideas on 'structuration', which has become the core of his social theory, in his book *The Class Structure of the Advanced Societies* (1973; 1981). He introduced the concept of 'structuration' as a means of focusing upon '*the modes in which* "economic" relationships become translated into "non-economic" social structures' (1981: 105) that is, *social* classes.[4] Two types of structuration were identified. First, mediate structuration, which describes the links between particular market capacities – the ownership of productive property; the posscsion of educational and technical qualifications; and manual labour power and identifiable groups in society. Mediate structuration is governed by the extent of social mobility. Second, proximate structuration points to the factors which shape local class formation, including relationships of allocation and authority within the enterprise (here his discussion has close parallels with Dahrendorf's), and the impact of 'distributive groupings' in the community and neighbourhood. Thus Giddens's initial identification of a 'social class' incorporates both structure and agency. On the question of class consciousness, Giddens extends the original Marxist concept to a number of levels. He argues that 'structuration' will result in a common class *awareness*, but not necessarily class *consciousness* – that is, any sense of opposition to other social classes. He argues that, in contrast to Marx's analysis, a *revolutionary* consciousness which might lead to the transformation of society is most likely to develop at the historical moment of the emergence of the capitalist order, when material disparities are at their greatest and the imposition of authoritative control most rigorous. In mature capitalism, in contrast, the working class is characterized merely by *conflict* consciousness, and social democracy is the characteristic form of developed capitalist society.

Giddens's account of the 'class structure', therefore, reflected the developing critique of positivism and structural over-determination within sociology itself, in that class relationships were presented as being *actively* structured, rather than simply being taken as given. The introduction of the notion of 'structuration' has led his subsequent work in a more methodological direction, and he has not returned to a further substantial treatment of class analysis. He notes that the book has today a 'somewhat "archaic" feel', and 'if I were to go over the same ground again today, the book would need thoroughgoing revision, and I would modify parts of it substantially' (Giddens 1990: 298). Some indication of the direction such revisions might take are given in later essays which explore the interrelationship of class and 'citizenship' (see chapter 7 below), and the significance of the labour process to the nature of exploitation within capitalism (Giddens and Mackenzie 1982). It may be noted that the question of action arises at two points in his analysis; first, that which relates to the 'structuration' of the different classes, and second, the nature and possibilities of class action once 'structuration' has occurred.

Given this emphasis on the active structuring of class relationships, it is not surprising that Giddens's approach to class analysis struck a resonant chord with historians influenced by Thompson's work.[5] The possibilities of the development of class consciousness and action consequent upon class formation have also been a continuing focus of empirical research in British sociology. Much of this work was stimulated by Lockwood's influential article 'Sources of variation in working class images of society' (1966). For the most part, Lockwood argued individuals 'visualise the ... structure of their society from the vantage points of their own particular *milieus* and their perceptions of the larger society will vary according to their experiences ... in the smaller societies in which they live out their daily lives' (1966: 249). He thus developed a typology of working-class images of society ('traditional proletarian', 'traditional deferential', and 'privatised'), which corresponded to variations in the characteristic 'work' and 'community' situations experienced within the working class. Thus particular structural locations are seen as corresponding to particular societal images.

Lockwood's work stimulated a number of empirical studies which explored the link between particular occupational groups, structural locations, and social imagery – for example, Newby's (1977) study of agricultural workers, Brown and Brannen's study of shipbuilders (1970), as well as wide-ranging review and debate (Bulmer 1975). This work makes no empirical separation between the investigation of structure and action, and was often consciously related to the 'action' perspective which developed within sociology from the 1960s (Willener 1970). Thus within sociology there has been a continuing exploration of the origins and significance of class action. This kind of research, however, has more usually taken the form of the case study, rather than relying primarily on the large-scale sample survey (Marshall 1988).

A major response, therefore, to the break-up of the 'orthodox consensus' in sociology from the 1960s onwards was a renewed emphasis on the significance of human *action* for sociological investigations and explanations. Empirical studies of social class influenced by this perspective have often taken the form of micro-level studies of particular groups and occupations, within their specific social context. Much of this work has overlapped with the sociology of work and occupations, in particular that stimulated by the 'labour process' debate (Crompton and Jones 1984; Smith 1987). Another perspective which developed during the 1970s, and which has been particularly influential within human geography and urban sociology, was a return to *political economy*. As the label implies, this strand of analysis tends to be interdisciplinary, and has often been informed by Marx's work. In the next section, therefore, we will discuss the applications of the class concept within social geography and urban sociology, where it has been employed in a somewhat eclectic manner, and has incorporated both objective and subjective, aggregational and relational, dimensions of class analysis.

Social class, urban sociology and the turn to 'realism'

The concept of social class has occupied a central position in both urban sociology and radical geography. These sub-disciplines have been highly responsive to current developments in social thought, and have been much influenced, in succession, by structuralist Marxism (Castells 1977), political economy, the rediscovery of the labour process and the 'deskilling' debate (Massey 1984), philosophical realism (Sayer 1984) and, most recently, debates about 'postmodernism' (Harvey 1990). There has also been a continuing focus on the interpretation of contemporary social developments; in particular the debates relating to the restructuring of Western economies following the recession of the late 1970s and early 1980s have loomed large in empirical and theoretical discussions in Britain. This flexibility and openness of approach have been a source of both strength and weakness. On the one hand, they have encouraged a theoretical pluralism which appropriately reflects the complexity of the issues under investigation. On the other, the somewhat eclectic approach to be found within the New Human Geography has resulted in a tendency to borrow and mix concepts developed within rather different theoretical traditions, and a failure to appreciate that the confusions thus imported have resulted in a number of pseudo-debates which have not proved particularly fruitful.[6]

The influence of Marxism within urban sociology has meant that there has been a continuing emphasis within it on the significance of class *structure*. This has often been taken, in an unproblematic fashion, to be represented by the occupational structure. As a consequence, radical urban sociology has made extensive use of occupational class schemes – in all their variety (Sarre 1989). Thrift and Williams (1987: 5) distinguish five major concepts which are 'fairly consistently used in a class analysis, namely class structure, the formation of classes, class conflict, class capacity and class consciousness'. These concepts are more or less appropriate at different levels of analysis, which they describe as both spatial – cross-national, regional, individual communities – as well as temporal. Class structure, which is defined as 'a system of places generated by the prevailing social relations of production' (p. 6) is 'the most abstract' of the five concepts, and Thrift and Williams emphasize that class structure 'is only one element of class and it is unfortunate that in the literature it has all too often become an end in itself' (p. 7) – a comment which may be taken as a criticism of structural Marxism. Thus they do not claim that the class structure alone determines action, and stress that other social forces such as 'race, religion, ethnicity and gender, family and various state apparatuses' will 'not only blur the basic class divides but also generate their own divisions' (1987: 7).

The formation of classes, class conflict, class capacity and consciousness, they argue, demands a relational approach, as these processes can only be studied in the context of action, that is, actions (struggles) which shape the very emergence of 'classes' themselves. Here we have in their discussion of 'class' aspects which have close parallels with E. P. Thompson's Marxist humanism, but these are used in combination with a 'class structural' approach.

Urban sociology has also been much influenced by the 'realist' theoretical approach. Philosophical realism became influential as a possible solution to the theoretical problems raised by the critique of positivism (Keat and Urry 1975; 1981). Thus realism does not reject the natural science model out of hand, but argues that empirical regularities do not, in themselves, establish the full extent of our knowledge. Rather than mere constant conjunction, a 'realist' causal explanation must answer the question of why these realities exist in terms of the causal mechanisms that generate them (Layder 1990). Thus 'realism' directs attention not just at events, but at the underlying processes or mechanisms which produce them. These relatively enduring social entities are held to have causal properties which give rise to events – but the mere existence of a causal property does not mean that an event *will* occur. The realization of particular causal properties often depends on the blocking, or realization, of others, and empirical investigations guided by 'realist' principles have reflected this complexity (Bagguley et al. 1989). 'Realist' accounts have tended to focus on class *formation*, which has many parallels with Giddens's account of 'structuration'. In the 'realist' approach, therefore, class structure and class action would not be separated.

Thus for example Keat and Urry claim that:

> The term 'class' is used by Marx in a realist manner. It refers to social entities which are not directly observable, yet which are historically present, and the members of which are potentially aware of their common interests and consciousness. The existence of classes is not to be identified with the existence of inequalities of income, wealth, status or educational opportunity. For Marx, and generally for realists, class structures are taken to cause such social inequalities. The meaning of the term, 'class', is not given by these inequalities. Rather it is the structure of class relationships which determines the patterns of inequality. (1975: 94–5)[7]

Keat and Urry are particularly critical of what they describe as the 'positivisation' of class in American stratification studies, that is the identification of 'classes' as aggregates of individuals without reference to 'causal properties' but 'in terms of various kinds of demographic, social, and psychological criteria' (1975: 95). Thus in his subsequent work (Abercrombie and Urry 1983; Lash and Urry 1987), Urry has taken a socio-historical approach in his empirical investigations of the class structure. In particular, he has devoted considerable attention to exploring the emergence of the 'service class', and its 'causal powers' in contemporary capitalism.

Theoretical 'realism' within urban sociology, therefore, sees classes as having 'causal powers' which are 'realized' in the struggle with other classes. Thus empirical analyses informed by this approach are often sociohistorical in their approach. Savage et al.'s (1992) work on the middle classes in Britain provides a clear statement of this approach to 'class analysis'. As indicated above, the major focus of the 'realist' approach is upon class *formation*, and this is reflected in their work. They argue that the 'middle classes' have access, to varying degrees, to three assets – or potential 'causal powers'. These are, first, property; second, organizational assets (that is, access to positions in organizational hierarchies, and the power that goes with them); and third, cultural assets, that is, the 'styles of life', or 'habitus', which serve to buttress and perpetuate structures of power and advantage (there are obvious parallels between cultural assets and the Weberian concept of status). Savage et al. draw upon a wide range of empirical material to suggest how relatively stable social collectivities have emerged on the basis of these 'causal powers'.

The 'realist' approach, therefore, may be characterized as having its major empirical focus upon processes of class formation, rather than upon descriptions of the class structure. The emphasis upon the contingency of the realization of particular 'causal powers' means that, in practice, empirical accounts of the processes of class structuring carried out within this framework are multidimensional. The stress upon contingency and multidimensionality within the realist approach is a source of both strength and weakness. In particular, it is difficult to provide empirical tests of association and causal relationships – as, for example, those who have developed theoretical class schemes (such as Goldthorpe and Wright) have attempted to do. However, this weakness may also be seen as a strength, in that the 'realist' approach is a flexible one and has provided a number of important insights into contemporary social developments.[8]

Conclusions

Marx and Weber, despite their very real theoretical differences, both conceptualized social classes as groups structured out of *economic* relationships, and both saw classes as significant social 'actors' in the context of capitalist industrialism. For Marx, class struggle would have a central role in the ultimate transformation of capitalism. Weber did not hold to this view, but there can be little doubt that he saw class conflict as a major phenomenon in capitalist society. In the late twentieth century, a criticism that is increasingly made of both authors (particularly Marx), and indeed, of 'class analysis' in general is that such arguments place too much emphasis on the significance of economically determined classes at the expense of other, competing sources of social identity such as nationality, gender, locality, or ethnic group. In short, it is argued, nineteenth-century sociology cannot adequately grasp the complexities of late twentieth-century society.

This chapter has not discussed these arguments in any detail (they will be examined in chapters 4 and 5), but as we have seen there has developed within Marxism theoretical approaches to class which have modified considerably – indeed, abandoned – the economism of earlier theoretical conceptualizations. The discussion above has been mainly concerned with the fate of the class concept itself, particularly in relation to the ongoing debates relating to structure and action in sociology. Weber's rejection of the inevitability of the development of class consciousness and thus action was an element in his overall rejection of Marxist economism and determinism. In sociology (and history), however, the question of class consciousness has been incorporated into a more general debate concerning the nature of social reality, which has crucially shaped the perspectives of a number of different authors who would all claim to be doing 'class analysis' – although the diversity of their work belies the common label.

In the course of this chapter, there have emerged a series of dichotomies relating to both sociology and class analysis, some of which may be summarized as follows:

Sociology
structure   action

Class analysis
class in itself   class for itself (Marx)
objective   subjective (Braverman)
class formation   class action (Dahrendorf)
aggregational   relational (Stark)

The persistence of such dichotomies in the social sciences has often been criticized, as when, for example, Bourdieu writes that:

> One can and must transcend the opposition between the vision which we can indifferently label realist, objectivist or structuralist on the one hand and the constructivist, subjectivist, spontaneist vision on the other. Any theory of the social universe must include the representation that agents have of the social world and, more precisely, the contribution they make to the construction of the vision of that world, and consequently, to the very construction of that world. (1987: 10)[9]

It might be argued, however, that although Bourdieu has described the essence of sociological 'good practice', the overarching theory that would succesfully achieve this integration has not yet been developed or rather, there is certainly no consensus that it has been. Giddens's theory of 'structuration', as well as the development of philosophical 'realism', have both been offered as theoretical solutions,[10] but neither has gained universal acceptance; there is no dominant theoretical paradigm in sociology. In the light of these constraints two, rather different, emphases on the question of 'action' have been identified within discussions relating to class. These are, first, an insistence upon the active construction of classes themselves (class formation or 'structuration'), as when, for example, Therborn writes that: 'Classes must be seen, not as veritable geological formations once they have acquired their original shape, but as phenomena in a constant process of formation, reproduction, re-formation and de-formation' (1983: 39) – that is, the role of action in the constitution of 'classes' *in* themselves. Theories of class formation can be distinguished from theories of class action – the question of whether a 'class' acts *for* itself. Weber, as we have seen, would regard such a possibility as contingent, and this would also be Bendix and Lipset's position. To adopt the first position, some may suggest, renders the second redundant – a class 'in itself' is simultaneously a class 'for itself'. In contrast, the second position assumes that the examination of class structure may be undertaken independently of the examination of class action.

These debates are not mere abstractions. They have not only crucially affected perceptions of class, but also the way in which research into social class has been carried out. In the next chapter, therefore, we will focus on the work of class analysts whose starting point is the class *structure* – that is, attempts to measure 'social class'.

Notes

1   It has to be said that, whatever Braverman's other strengths, his understanding of class analysis in sociology was rudimentary. His description of 'class analysis' in sociology was confined to a discussion of self-rated class which he took to represent the investigation of class consciousness, and his discussion of Lockwood's work treats it as a historical, rather than a sociological, account of clerical work.
2   See, for example, Dawley (1979).
3   Contemporary social history has moved beyond Thompson towards a rejection of materialist explanations, and has been much influenced by post-structuralism. For an extensive discussion see Joyce (1995).
4   It is of interest that Giddens uses Willis (1977), a 'cultural' investigation of the 'class structure', as an example of the empirical application of 'structuration' (Giddens 1984: 289).
5   See Kaye (1984: 23–5); also Gregory (1982).
6   For example, some of the arguments surrounding the relative significance of class and consumption sector. This became a debate as to the relative significance of employment class vs. house ownership in determining political attitudes and behaviour. Employment class remains most significant. See Hamnett (1989).
7   Note that Pawson (1989) has argued convincingly that although their critique may be valid, Keat and Urry's methodological prescriptions are essentially structuralist.
8   Urry's work, and the work of those influenced by him, has been taken as a representative example of the way in which 'realism' has been employed in British sociology. However, it should be recognized that there are many 'realisms' (Wacquant 1989), and indeed, that Wright, whose methodology is clearly very different from Urry's, would also claim to be a 'realist'. However, as Burawoy (1989) has remarked: 'the realist view of science is strong in stating its ontological premises but weak in dealing

with the epistemological problems it raises'; thus a plurality of method might be anticipated.

9 To avoid confusion, it should be pointed out that Bourdieu is here using the term 'realist' to describe those who, having determined empirically the properties and boundaries of the class structure, argue that these are 'real' classes. These approaches will be discussed at length in ch. 3.

10 These are not the only offerings; see Archer (1982) on 'morphogenesis'. The diversity of theoretical approaches serves to emphasize the point that there exists no dominant theoretical paradigm.

3 Measuring the 'Class Structure': Goldthorpe and Wright

Introduction

In this chapter, our discussion will focus primarily on empirical accounts of class *structures*. In chapter 1, it was noted that the division of the population into unequally rewarded groups is commonly described as a 'class structure', and in modern industrial societies this usually means a focus on the structure of employment. The division of the occupational order into economic 'classes' is probably the most frequent 'taken-for-granted' use of the class concept in contemporary sociology (Westergaard and Resler 1975). However, it is important to distinguish between, on the one hand, class schemes which simply *describe* the broad contours of occupational inequality and, on the other, theoretically derived class schemes which purport to incorporate, at the empirical level, the actualities of class *relations*. There are a wide variety of employment-based class schemes, constructed for a variety of different purposes. A simple but important point – which is all too often overlooked – is that all class schemes are social constructs, or rather, the constructs of social scientists. Therefore different class schemes, when applied to the same occupational structure, can produce quite different 'class maps'. For example, it is a feature of Wright's scheme, which will be discussed later in this chapter, that it produces more 'proletarians' than other classifications.

In this chapter, different class schemes will be discussed in relation to three broad analytical categories. These are (a) occupational class schemes which have been devised primarily for use as commonsense descriptive measures in social policy research; (b) subjective scales of occupational prestige or social ranking; and (c) 'theoretical' occupational class schemes, constructed with explicit reference to the theoretical approaches of Marx and Weber. It may be objected that no system of classification can be said to be independent of 'theoretical' assumptions, even if they are not overt (Hindess 1973). Nevertheless, the differentiation between class schemes on the basis of their theoretical claims is commonplace (Nichols 1979; Marshall et al. 1988), and, as we shall see, the development of particular theoretical schemes has been associated with the development of distinctive research programmes of 'class analysis' using the scheme in question.

In previous chapters, the diversity both of definitions of the 'class' concept, as well as of approaches to 'class analysis', has been described. Thus although the 'employment aggregate' approach to class analysis, which is the main focus of this chapter, is certainly a very important development in the field of class analysis, it is not the only way in which class has been investigated empirically. In particular, we have drawn attention to socio-historical and case study research which has explored the processes through which classes are structured, not only through patterns of ownership and control, but also as a consequence of technical change and development, political struggles, etc. Explorations of class formation have often focused upon changes in the labour market and structures of employment – as in, for example, Braverman's (1974) influential account of the 'deskilling' of the labour process. As we shall see in the next two chapters, changes in the nature of work and employment have been linked to arguments that contemporary societies have been transformed in a more fundamental sense, and that we are moving towards a 'postmodern' society in which theories developed to analyse 'modern' societies – including class theories – have become redundant. We will argue that, notwithstanding these kinds of criticism, occupation still provides a useful measure of structured social inequality. This does not mean, however, that the 'employment aggregate' approach to class analysis is itself beyond criticism. These issues, however, will be taken up in later chapters; for the moment, we will consider some basic issues raised by the strategy of using occupation as a proxy for 'class'.

Occupations

The economic, technical and social changes brought about by the development of capitalist industrialism have been accompanied by a continuing division of labour and differentiation of occupations. The point need not be laboured that 'occupation' has become, for the majority of the population, probably the most powerful single indicator of levels of material reward, social standing, and 'life chances' in general in modern societies (Blau and Duncan 1967: 6–7). Thus throughout the twentieth century it has become commonplace for social researchers of all kinds (in academia, government and commercial agencies, and so on) to divide up the occupational structure into aggregates corresponding to different levels of social and material inequalities, which are commonly known as 'social classes'. Reid (1981: 6), for example, defines a 'social class [as] a grouping of people into categories on the basis of occupation', and Parkin has asserted that: 'The backbone of the class structure, and indeed of the entire reward system of modern Western society, is the occupational order' (1972: 18).

However, despite its acknowledged usefulness as a social indicator, there are a number of difficulties in using occupation as a measure of 'class'. Four major areas of difficulty may be identified. First, there is the fact that only a minority of members of an industrialized society will be 'economically active', and therefore have or be seeking an occupation, at any time. A variety of strategies are available for allocating the 'economically inactive' (children, old people), or those without an occupation, to an occupational class. These include giving all household members the same 'class' as that of the 'head of household' or 'main breadwinner'; locating the retired in the 'class' indicated by their last occupation, and so on. It has been argued that this strategy has been a reasonably successful one (Marshall et al. 1996). However, the growing minority of the long-term unemployed, including people who have never had a job at all, present a continuing problem for employment-based class schemes.

Secondly, although 'class processes' – that is, the structures of production and market relationships – will obviously have an important impact on the occupational structure, there are also other factors, in particular the ascriptive (or status) differences associated with gender, race and age, which are of considerable significance in structuring the division of labour. It is important also to recognize that many of the claims made by occupational groups in the constant jockeying for material advantage which is a feature of the activities of trade unions and professional groupings are in fact *status* claims, for example, those related to established relativities which have been fiercely protected by skilled-craft groupings. The occupational structure, therefore, will also bear the imprint of these other factors which are not, strictly speaking, the outcome of capitalist *class* processes. Sayer and Walker (1992) have taken these kinds of argument even further, arguing the division of labour should be seen as an independent axis of occupational structuring, whose effects are often confused with 'class' processes.

Thirdly, occupational title does not give any indication of capital or wealth holdings, that is, property relations (this point has been extensively argued by Westergaard 1995). As Nichols has argued, 'in the ... "social classes" of the census the owners of capital are lost to sight' (1979: 159).[1]

The fourth area of difficulty relates to the capacity of occupational class schemes to describe class relations in a theoretical sense. The Marxist distinction between the 'technical' and the 'social' division of labour has been used to argue that 'occupation' does not grasp the essential components of the Marxist class concept: 'Occupation typically refers primarily to sets of job tasks, that is, it refers to positions within the technical division of labour ... the concept of class refers primarily to the social relations at work, or positions within the social division of labour' (Abercrombie and Urry 1983: 109). An entire strategy of class analysis – Wright's Marxist model – has been based on this conceptual division. Although Weber's approach to social class was very different from that of Marx, he too regarded social classes as something more than occupational aggregates. For Weber, a social class is made up of the 'totality of those class situations within which individual and generational mobility is easy and typical'. Thus Goldthorpe, a leading neo-Weberian class analyst, initially identified mobility boundaries as crucial to the identification of 'social classes' (however, in recent years his position on this issue has been substantially modified).

'Commonsense' occupational class schemes (category (a) above) invariably reflect some kind of hierarchical ordering of occupations, although the assumptions underlying the hierarchy are not always made explicit. These can include income or other material benefits, social status, 'cultural level', and so on. Subjective scales of occupational rankings are similarly hierarchical, 'gradational' classifications. In contrast what are here described as theoretical schemes or approaches attempt to encompass in their construction the actualities of class *relationships*.

The investigation and analysis of occupational *hierarchies* – particularly subjective rankings – has been closely associated with models of society which have stressed the importance of the social solidarity and functional interdependence associated with the division of labour in complex societies, whereas the development of theoretical class analysis and 'relational' class schemes has had more of an emphasis on cleavage and conflict. Thus the dominant paradigm in sociology (normative functionalism) established in the United States after the Second World War was associated with a view of the occupational structure as a hierarchy of rewards and prestige into which the population was sorted according to its capabilities. In Davis and Moore's (1945) functional theory of stratification, the structure of social inequality was seen as a mechanism through which the most appropriate and best-qualified persons were allocated to the functionally most important positions in society, and, as a consequence, the question of individual 'status attainment' has been a key topic in stratification research in the United States (Blau and Duncan 1967).

In contrast, 'conflict' theories of stratification considered the division of labour and the development of 'classes' to be likely to be a non-resolvable source of conflict and tension in society. This difference is reflected in the class schemes of those authors, such as Goldthorpe and Wright, whose analysis has been grounded in Marx's and Weber's theoretical arguments. Davis and Moore's theory has also been criticized from within a modified functionalist perspective which incorporates aspects of a 'conflict' view. How can some occupations, it was argued, be regarded as functionally 'more important' when, in a highly complex society, *all* occupations are necessary in respect of the whole? (Consider the chaos when public service workers go on strike.) The 'sacrifices' made by those undergoing training (in terms of earnings forgone) are usually made by others (parents) and, in any case, are massively over-compensated by the subsequent level of reward. Systems of stratification can also bring with them rigidities, and levels of social conflict, which are positively *dysfunctional* as far as the social order is concerned (Tumin 1964).

'Commonsense' occupational hierarchies and the analysis of 'social classes'

In Britain, the most frequently used class scheme has been that of the Registrar-General – for example, most of the empirical material in Reid's (1981) comprehensive summary of occupational class differences in employment, mortality, family arrangements, education, politics and so on is organized using the Registrar-General's classification. It was first developed in 1913 by a medical statistician (Stevenson), who was engaged in a wider debate concerning levels of infant mortality. As Szreter (1984) has demonstrated, Stevenson, although no eugenist himself, initially developed the scale in the context of a debate with eugenists such as Francis Galton, who believed that the social and occupational structure more or less reflected a natural hierarchy of ability and morality in society. From the first, therefore, the Registrar-General's scheme has been hierarchical.

The Registrar-General's social-class classification has been devised with the aim of including within each category unit groups:

> so as to secure that, as far as is possible, each category is homogeneous in relation to the general standing within the community of the occupations concerned. This criterion is naturally correlated with ... other factors such as education and economic environment, but it has no direct relationship to the average level of remuneration of particular occupations. (HMSO 1966: xiii)

It has been through a number of revisions since its inception (Hakim 1980), but the most commonly used version, devised for the 1971 census, is:

I	Professional etc. occupations
II	Intermediate occupations
III (N)	Skilled non-manual occupations
III (M)	Skilled manual occupations
IV	Partly skilled occupations
V	Unskilled occupations

As Reid's (1981) compendium *Social Class Differences in Britain* demonstrates, these occupational groupings correlated with a wide range of inequalities in income, health and education. Indeed, given the origins of the index, a somewhat salutary indication of its staying power can be drawn from the fact that, although rates of infant mortality have of course declined considerably since the early years of this century, considerable social-class differences in infant mortality rates still persist. In 1981, for example, the infant mortality rate per 1,000 live births in England and Wales was 7.7 for Social Class I, but 18.8 for Social Class V (McPherson and Coleman 1988: 427). Nevertheless, the Registrar-General's scale contains a number of anomalies and difficulties in the classification of particular occupations

(Nichols 1979). In older versions of the scale, the category of 'manager' presented particular problems, and drawing the boundary between manual and non-manual employment has been a constant source of contention. These and other classification difficulties resulted, from the 1951 census onwards, in the creation of a more detailed classification of socio-economic groups (SEGs). The seventeen-point SEG scale includes details such as size of establishment in relation to 'managerial' occupations, and collapsed versions have been widely used in government surveys such as the General Household Survey.

The Registrar-General's class index was devised and has been developed by the Office of Population and Census Statistics (OPCS),[2] but this is not the only government department in Britain collecting details of occupations. In particular, the Department of Employment (DE)[3] developed in the 1960s and 1970s a detailed classification of occupations (Classification of Occupations and Directory of Occupational Titles: CODOT), which was integrated into the 1980 census Occupational Classifications. It was felt that the combination of OPCS and DE categorizations had not been particularly successful and, from the 1991 census, these should be replaced by a new classification, the Standard Occupational Classification (SOC). This hierarchical classification assumes that occupations involve a set of typical work activities, which are then classified into major, minor and unit groups according to, first, the level of skill and qualifications involved, and second, the nature of the work activities (Thomas and Elias 1989). At the time of writing, a further revision of the Registrar-General's index is under way, which will be used in the 2001 census. It is likely that it will be closer to the SEG classification than the present class scheme, and will be collapsible into a shortened version which will have many similarities with Goldthorpe's scheme (Rose and O'Reilly 1997).

Despite the fact that they have been subject to a process of almost constant revision, occupational class schemes used by government departments have nevertheless remained remarkably similar in their broad outlines – managerial and professional occupations at the top, unskilled workers at the bottom. Other industrial countries have also developed very similar hierarchical scales – for example, the Nordic Occupational scale developed in the Scandinavian countries, and Blau and Duncan (1967), as well as devising their own socio-economic index, utilized a scale of socio-economic status devised by the United States Bureau of the Census which closely resembles the Registrar-General's SEG scale. Another scale in wide commercial use is Social Grade, developed first for the National Readership Survey and commonly used by market research agencies. This divides the population into A, B, C1, C2, D and E – corresponding to upper middle, middle, lower middle, skilled, semi-skilled and unskilled working classes (there are separate categories for the self-employed and unemployed). Again, the occupations comprising the different 'classes' closely resemble those of the other hierarchical scales in general use.

Scales of occupational prestige or 'status'

Marsh (1986) has described the Registrar-General's and other, similar scales as describing 'groups differentiated by lifestyle'; this label would be particularly appropriate to market research, where occupational coding is often carried out on the doorstep (an excellent source of information concerning 'lifestyle'!) by the interviewer concerned. The Registrar-General's and market researcher's 'class' categories have also often been described as status or prestige scales (Weber described status groups as being differentiated 'above all, by different styles of life'). However, the 'prestige' label is probably more appropriate for occupational scales which have been deliberately constructed according to the reputed prestige or desirability of occupations.

Occupational prestige scales have often been described as 'subjectivist'; that is, as reflecting the subjective assessment of the relative prestige of occupations within a population. One of the earliest and best-known of such scales is that of North and Hatt, constructed in 1947 in the United States for the National Opinion Research Center (NORC) in Chicago, where a cross-section of ninety occupations were ranked by a national sample of the population on a scale ranging from 'excellent' to 'poor' standing (see Reiss 1961). The resulting scale of occupational prestige closely resembles that of the socio-economic classifications reviewed earlier: higher professional and powerful occupations such as physician or Supreme Court justice being ranked at the top, and low-skilled occupations such as street sweeper and garbage collector at the bottom. There proved to be a very high statistical correlation between the results of the earlier and later scaling exercises, and a comparison of similar 'subjectivist' rankings carried out in a number of other countries suggested that there was also a high level of cross-national consensus on occupational prestige rankings (Hodge et al. 1967).

These empirical findings supplied a justification for two, closely related, functionalist arguments concerning social stratification. First, the wide measure of recorded agreement concerning the relative prestige of different occupations corresponded to the distribution of material rewards and power attached to the occupations in question. It was therefore argued that the results of this 'moral referendum' (Parkin 1972) concerning occupational prestige suggested that the distribution of occupational inequality was, indeed, regarded as legitimate by the population at large, and that, as Davis and Moore had argued, the actual pattern of material rewards and status rankings reflected the functional importance of different occupations for the society, as well as being a measure of the training and talent required to fill these positions (Davis and Moore 1945). Second, the cross-national similarity of the prestige rankings of particular occupations was argued by Hodge et al. to reflect an underlying 'logic of industrialism', a theoretical argument which Giddens (1982a) has identified as a central component of the 1960s 'orthodox consensus'. All industrial societies, it was argued, required a similar division of labour and associated structure of occupational prestige (or 'classes'). These two conclusions are brought together in the following extract:

> Development hinges in part upon the recruitment and training of persons for the skilled, clerical, managerial, and professional positions necessary to support an industrial economy. Thus, aquisition of a 'modern' system of occupational evaluation would seem to be a necessary precondition to rapid industrialisation, insofar as such an evaluation of occupations insures that resources and personnel in sufficient numbers and of sufficient quality are allocated to those occupational positions most crucial to the industrial development of a nation. (Hodge et al. 1967: 320)

Similar scales of occupational ranking have also been constructed in Britain – for example, the Hall–Jones scale which was developed as part of a major investigation of social mobility in Britain immediately after the Second World War (Glass 1954). More recently, Goldthorpe and Hope (1974) constructed a new scale for the Oxford Mobility Study where respondents were asked to rank a set of twenty occupations in terms of their 'perceived social desirability' (rather than scoring individual occupations, as in the construction of the NORC scale). Respondents then nominated twenty of their 'own' occupations for inclusion in the ranking.

However, Goldthorpe has been highly critical of both functionalist theories of stratification and inequality, as well as the associated 'logic of industrialism' arguments, which have developed out of work relating to the NORC scale. His approach shares much in common with those authors, such as Lockwood, Dahrendorf, Rex and Collins, who emphasized not interdependence and integration, but the significance of persisting economic and political inequalities, and the social conflicts and competition associated with them, in the shaping of the stratification order. The conflict perspective was highly critical of the capacity of hierarchical scales of prestige or lifestyle to render any account of *class* conflicts. Such scales, it was asserted, measured social status, rather than class, and the apparent agreement on matters such as prestige rankings was an indication not of any moral consensus, but rather, simply represented a general awareness of the empirical distribution of material and symbolic rewards to particular occupations (Parkin 1972: 40–1). The relative distribution of rewards described in hierarchical schemes reflected, it was argued, the *outcome* of class processes, rather than giving any account of the underlying structure of class *relations* which had brought them about.

A parallel argument has been developed by Wright (1979), who built upon Ossowski's distinction between *gradational* and *relational* class theories in his critique of existing empirical approaches to 'class analysis'. Gradational class schemes – such as prestige or income hierarchies – describe but do not explain. Gradational differences, he emphasized, are the *outcome* of class relations. Wright divided relational conceptions of class into two categories: (a) those deriving primarily from Weber's work, where 'class' is seen as deriving from social relations of exchange; and (b) those deriving primarily from Marx's theories, where 'class' is seen as grounded in production relationships.

Thus these kinds of criticism of empirical 'class analyses' using commonsense and hierarchical scales have led to the development of 'theoretical' (or 'sociological') class schemes (Crompton 1991); that is, class schemes which attempt to divide the population into 'social classes' which correspond to the kinds of groupings described by Marx and Weber. As has been noted in chapter 1, this strategy attempts to bring within a single framework of analysis theoretical approaches to social class and the detailed empirical investigation of the 'classes' themselves. Two such programmes of class analysis, associated with particular 'relational' class schemes, have achieved particular prominence since the 1970s: that devised by John Goldthorpe, which has often been described as 'Weberian', and Erik Wright's explicitly Marxist class scheme.

Both of these class schemes have been used and developed by cross-national research programmes which have been in progress for nearly two decades. These are the CASMIN (Comparative Analysis of Social Mobility in Industrial Societies: Goldthorpe) and the Comparative Project on Class Structure and Class Consciousness (Wright: more usually known as the Comparative Class Project). Not surprisingly, therefore, both schemes have been revised and clarified during this period, in response to both theoretical criticisms and practical exigencies. Therefore, although we are reserving our comprehensive examination of current critiques of 'class analysis' until the next chapter, we will nevertheless be incorporating some of them in our exposition of the two sociological schemes in question.

Theoretical ('relational') class schemes: I   Goldthorpe

Goldthorpe's class scheme is constructed via the aggregation of occupational categories within the Hope–Goldthorpe scale of 'general desirability' (described above) into a set of 'class' categories. The key concepts guiding the allocation of occupations to classes were initially 'market' and 'work' situation; two of Lockwood's three factors comprising 'class situation' (see chapter 2 above):

> we ... bring together, within the classes we distinguish, occupations whose incumbents share in broadly similar *market* and *work* situations ... That is to say, we combine occupational categories whose members would appear, in the light of the available evidence, to be typically comparable, on the one hand, in terms of their sources and levels of income and other conditions of employment, in their degree of economic security and in their chances of economic advancement; and, on the other hand, in their location within the systems of authority and control governing the processes of production in which they are engaged. (Goldthorpe 1980; 1987: 40)

The Hope–Goldthorpe categories which formed the basis of the scheme also incorporated employment status: 'Thus, for example, "self-employed plumber" is a different occupation from "foreman plumber" as from "rank-and-file employee" plumber' (1987: 40). The seven categories of the original Goldthorpe class scheme have often been aggregated into threefold service/intermediate/working class categories in empirical discussions of the British material.

The use of Lockwood's concepts of 'work' and 'market' situation ('market' situation being taken directly from Weber's work) has meant that Goldthorpe's class scheme has often been described as 'neo-Weberian'.[4] Lockwood's concepts had originally been developed in his study of clerical workers (1958); and his description of 'work situation' identified elements such as proximity to authority, level of work autonomy, nature of workplace supervision etc. in describing a clerk's 'class situation'. Thus Goldthorpe's initial descriptions of the derivation of his class scheme included references to monographs describing the 'work situation' of various occupations. Later descriptions of the class scheme, however, do not include any reference to 'work situation', and indeed Goldthorpe now rejects any notion that work tasks and roles play any part in the construction of the scheme (Erikson and Goldthorpe 1993: 42). He now describes his scheme as being constituted in terms of *employment relations*. This would still include employment status, but the notion of employment relations draws upon the distinction between a 'service' and a 'labour' contract of employment. In a labour contract, the exchange of wages for effort is specific, whereas a service contract includes important *prospective* elements including salary increments and promotion prospects. 'Intermediate' classes lie between the groupings distinguished by 'service' or 'labour' contracts.

The publication in Britain (in 1980) of Goldthorpe's work on social mobility was subject to considerable criticism, particularly from feminists (for example, Stacey 1981; Stanworth 1984). The Nuffield mobility survey had sampled only men; women were only included in the study as wives. Goldthorpe's class scheme itself was moulded to the contours of men's employment and did not differentiate very well between the kinds of jobs held by women. In particular, the scheme tends to crowd women into a single 'class' category – III (routine non-manual employment). Not only, however, did the scheme appear to be a rather crude instrument as far as women's employment was concerned, but the placing of lower-level clerical jobs in the 'Intermediate' (class III) category seemed to make little sense as far as women were concerned. Whereas for a man (until fairly recently) a clerical job was usually but a stepping-stone to a managerial position, for most women, these were dead-end jobs with few prospects of promotion (Crompton and Jones 1984). Goldthorpe's practice of allocating all members of the household to the class of the 'male breadwinner' was also extensively criticized, particularly given the increasing number of married women in employment.

Although Goldthorpe has at times appeared to be very resistant to feminist criticisms (e.g. Goldthorpe 1983), nevertheless, his work has incorporated important changes. The class position of the household is now inferred from that of the 'dominant' breadwinner, who might be male or female. More importantly, class III has been divided into two categories (a and b), reflecting the concentration of women into low-level white-collar work. When the class scheme is applied to women, class IIIb is treated as class VII. The class scheme has been further elaborated by dividing class IV (a and b) into self-employed with, and without, employees. A further modification, following participation in the CASMIN project, has been to identify farmers and employees in agriculture separately (the agricultural sector is substantial in some of the countries – e.g. Ireland – taking part in the CASMIN project).

Table 1 brings together and describes the 'original' and 'expanded' versions of the Goldthorpe class scheme (original version in roman type; later modifications in italic). The final column indicates Goldthorpe's current characterization of his classes in terms of their 'employment relations'.

This arrangement of occupations into 'classes' in the Goldthorpe scheme closely resembles that of conventional hierarchical schemes reflecting prestige and/or lifestyle, such as the ABC scheme used by market researchers, or that of the Registrar-General. However, Goldthorpe is adamant that his class scheme does not have a hierarchical form but, rather, reflects the structure of class (employment) *relations* (1980; 1987: 43). Goldthorpe's scheme has been subject to a wide range of criticisms. Its 'relational' (and therefore non-hierarchical) nature has been questioned (Marsh 1986; Prandy 1991). The allocation of occupations to particular class categories has been disputed; in particular, its seeming endorsement of the manual/non-manual distinction as a *class* boundary, even in the case of routine white-collar workers.

Although Goldthorpe's scheme has often been described as neo-Weberian, his recent work has stressed that the measure should not be regarded as deriving from any particular theory; rather, it should simply be seen as a 'research instrument'. In recent clarifications of his position, Goldthorpe has made it clear that the scheme is to be judged on the basis of the empirical findings it generates, rather than on any 'theoretical' basis:

> its [i.e. the scheme's] construction and adaptation have indeed been guided by theoretical ideas – but *also* by more practical considerations of the context in which, and the purposes for which, it is to be used and the nature of the data to which it is to be applied. In turn, the crucial test of the schema, as of any other conceptual device, must lie in its performance: it must be judged by the value that it proves to have in enquiry and analysis. (Erikson and Goldthorpe 1993: 46)

Table 1   The Goldthorpe (CASMIN) class scheme

			Employment relation
Service	I	Higher-grade professionals, administrators and officials; managers in large industrial establishments; large proprietors.	*Employer or service relationship*
	II	Lower-grade professionals, administrators and officials; higher-grade technicians; managers in small business and industrial establishments; supervisors of non-manual employees.	*Service relationship*
Intermediate	III	Routine non-manual – largely clerical – employees in administration and commerce; rank-and-file employees in services.	*Intermediate*
	IIIb	*Routine non-manual employees, lower grade (sales and services).*	*Intermediate (men), labour contract (women)*
	IV	Small proprietors and self-employed artisans.	*Employer*
	IVb	*Small proprietors, artisans, etc, without employees.*	*Self-employed*
	IVc	*Farmers and smallholders, other self-employed agricultural.*	*Employer or self-employed*
	V	Lower-grade technicians, supervisors of manual workers.	*Intermediate*
Working	VI	Skilled manual workers.	*Labour contract*
	VII	Semi-skilled and unskilled manual workers.	*Labour contract*
	VIIb	*Agricultural workers.*	*Labour contract*

Thus in Goldthorpe's early work, on social mobility in Britain, the construction of a class scheme is only the starting point of his overall strategy of 'class analysis'. It divides the occupied population according to their employment relations, but it must then be established to what extent actual 'classes' have been formed within this structure; or, to use Goldthorpe's phrase, the extent to which a class can be said to have a 'demographic identity'; that is, whether classes have emerged as 'specific social collectivities ... collectivities that are identifiable through the degree of continuity with which, in consequence of patterns of class mobility and immobility, their members are associated with particular sets of positions over time' (1983: 467). Thus patterns of social mobility are crucial to the identification of a 'class'. Once the extent of demographic identity has been established, the further question may be pursued as to the extent to which 'sociopolitical class formation' has also taken place; that is, 'the degree of distinctiveness of members of identifiable classes in terms of their life-chances, their life-styles and patterns of association, and their sociopolitical orientations and modes of action' (1983: 467). For example, Goldthorpe suggests that, in Britain, the extent of mobility associated with classes III and V of his scheme implies that these 'classes' are inchoate and unformed and thus highly unlikely to generate class-based socio-political action (1980; 1987: 335). In contrast, he argues, Britain posseses a 'demographically mature' working class which might be expected to generate systematic socio-political action, as well as an emerging 'service class' which, although not as stable as the working class, is nevertheless in the process of development as a significant social force.

Goldthorpe's approach to class analysis, therefore, follows a systematic structure → consciousness → action model which, as we shall see in the next chapter, has occasioned much criticism. Goldthorpe does not ignore the question of class action but he draws an analytical separation between class formation and class action and treats them empirically as quite separate phenomena. The scheme itself is not seen as drawing upon any systematic theoretical position, and Goldthorpe has argued that (1983: 467): 'class analysis begins with a structure of positions, associated with a specific historical form of the social division of labour.... It is ... in no way the aim of class analysis to account for either a structure of class positions or for the degree of class formation that exists within it in functional terms.' Here he was distancing himself from functionalist accounts of the social structure and, as we shall see, he has later developed a similar argument in respect of Wright's Marxist account.

Goldthorpe's work on the CASMIN project (Erikson and Goldthorpe 1993) has moved away somewhat from some of the considerations which informed his original work on social mobility in Britain. It may be suggested that in his comparative work there is less of an emphasis on the processes of demographic class formation, as described above. Rather, Erikson and Goldthorpe's major concern has been to explore cross-national continuities in the relative social mobility experiences of occupational groups (or 'classes'). Erikson and Goldthorpe have used this work to criticize Liberal theories of 'Industrial Society'. Liberal theorists of Industrial Society had suggested that, as industrialism developed, the technical 'logic of industrialism' would mean that opportunity structures would become more open and class differences would be eroded (Kerr et al. 1973; Blau and Duncan 1967). This equalization of opportunities would mean that rates of social mobility would increase. However, Erikson and Goldthorpe argue that, although there may have been an increase in *absolute* rates of social mobility, the class difference in *relative* mobility rates persists, that is, that there is 'constant social fluidity' across different societies. In our last chapter, we will be examining these debates (and their implications) at greater length. For the moment, however, we would merely wish to note that Goldthorpe's apparent move away from the problematics of class formation has been much criticized as being a move away from his Weberian 'roots' (Scott 1996), as we shall see in the next chapter.

Theoretical ('relational') class schemes: II Wright

Goldthorpe has been described as a 'neo-Weberian' or 'left Weberian' sociologist. In contrast, Wright has, since the middle of the 1970s, been following a self-consciously *Marxist* project, a central feature of which has been his efforts to develop a Marxist class scheme; as he has put it, one of the central objectives of his work has been 'to generate a concept capable of mapping in a nuanced way concrete variations in class structures across capitalist societies' (1989: 274). His project has been developed in constant dialogue with other Marxist theoreticians, and in the light of empirical research findings generated by the Comparative Project of Class Structure and Class Consciousness, the international research project co-ordinated by Wright. Wright is quite frank that his goal of generating an adequate Marxist 'class map' has not, as yet, been achieved. However, in his efforts to move towards an adequate measure, his class scheme has been through a series of transformations.

Like Goldthorpe, Wright is critical of orthodox sociological strategies for measuring the 'class structure'. He dismisses hierarchical or gradational schemes as 'static taxonomies': 'While it might be the case that most of the participants in the storming of the Bastille had status scores of under 40, and most of the French aristocracy had scores above 70, such labels do not capture the underlying dynamics at work in the revolutionary process' (1979: 8). Thus we have, yet again, the criticism that such schemes do not tap the dynamics of class *relationships*. Wright also draws a sharp distinction between 'class' and 'occupation' (1980). Occupations, he argues, are understood as positions defined within the *technical* relations of production; classes, on the other hand, are defined by the *social* relations of production.

> a carpenter transforms lumber into buildings; a doctor transforms sick people into healthy people; a typist transforms blank paper into paper with words on it, etc. Classes, on the other hand, can only be defined in terms of their social relationship to other classes, or in more precise terms, by their location within the social relations of production. (1980: 177)

Thus, he argues, occupational aggregations cannot produce 'classes', and his own empirical work has used especially gathered survey data to locate individuals within his successive class schemes: 'The basic strategy I have used ... has been to elaborate the ways in which class relations are embodied in specific *jobs*, since jobs are the essential "empty places" filled by individuals within the system of production' (Wright 1989: 277).[5]

Individual jobs are then located within Wright's class scheme, which has been derived from explicitly Marxist principles. Notions of control and exploitation within the social relations of *production* are central to Wright's analysis (it should be noted that he has consistently maintained a distinction between his own approach and Weberian approaches to the measurement of social class, which he characterizes as being grounded in *market* relationships). In developing the first version of his scheme, he argued that the social relations of production can be broken down into three interdependent dimensions: (a) social relations of control over money capital, (b) social relations of control over physical capital, and (c) social relations of authority – that is, control over supervision and discipline within the labour process (1980: 24). One of Wright's major preoccupations has been to give an empirical account of the 'middle class', or 'nonproletarian employees', in contemporary capitalist societies. Braverman (1974) had argued that the growing stratum of employees such as supervisors, or lower managerial and administrative workers, had a 'foot in both camps' (that is, bourgeois and proletarian), in that it both 'receives its petty share in the prerogatives and rewards of capital, but ... also bears the mark of the proletarian condition' (1974: 407). Wright's initial solution to this paradox was to develop the concept of 'contradictory class locations'. Such jobs were said to represent positions which are 'torn between the basic class relations of capitalist society'.

Wright's first starting-point was from the three basic positions within class relations in capitalism; the bourgeoisie, who are characterized by their economic ownership, and exercise social control over both the physical means of production and the labour power of others; the proletariat, who are characterized by neither ownership nor control – even of their own labour-power – which is in fact purchased by the bourgeoisie; and the petty bourgeoisie, who own and control their means of production even though they do not control the labour-power of others. To these basic class positions Wright added three contradictory locations: (a) managers and supervisors, who, even if they do not legally own the means of production, nevertheless exercise *de facto* control over both the material means of production and labour-power; (b) semi-autonomous employees who, even if they do not own or control the material means of production, nevertheless retain control over their own labour-power; and (c) small employers. This set of class positions is brought together in figure 1,

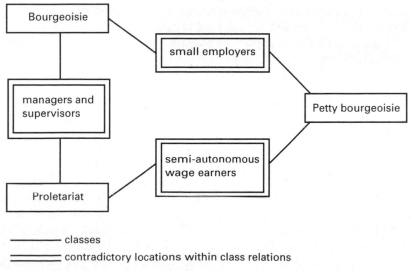

—————— classes

═══════ contradictory locations within class relations

Figure 1   Wright's first Marxist class map: relations of domination

which shows that individuals are located within the 'class map' according to the extent to which they possess economic ownership, control, autonomy – or lack of it – within the process of production. Specific information on these topics has been gathered via large-scale sample surveys carried out by Wright and his collaborators (Wright 1985, appendix II).

Wright's first class scheme was subject to a number of theoretical criticisms which eventually resulted in a recasting of his original model. Most fundamentally, Wright came to the opinion that his original class map had not, as he had argued, provided an analysis of the Marxist account of *exploitation* within capitalist relations of production but, rather, had merely given a descriptive account of *domination* (Wright 1985: 56–7). Domination is, of course, a significant aspect of class relations but it may be viewed as essentially epiphenomenal – that is, as being a consequence of exploitative class relationships, rather than their cause.

Wright's solution to this theoretical problem was to develop the work of John Roemer, who had applied game-theoretic principles to Marx's analysis in order to give an account of exploitation. Wright summarizes Roemer's basic strategy as follows:

> The basic idea of this approach is to compare different systems of exploitation by treating the organization of production as a 'game'. The actors in this game have various kinds of productive assets (i.e. resources such as skills and capital) which they bring into production and which they use to generate incomes on the basis of a specific set of rules. The essential strategy adopted for the analysis of exploitation is to ask if particular coalitions of players would be better off if they withdrew from this game under certain specified procedures in order to play a different one. (Wright 1985: 68)

If a group would be better off by withdrawing from the first game, and entering into an alternative game (and their previous partner would be worse off as a consequence), then exploitation can be said to be taking place under the conditions of the original game.

In his development of the analysis of exploitation (rather than domination), Wright distinguishes four types of assets, the unequal ownership or control of each of which forms the basis of different types of exploitation. These are: labour-power assets (feudal exploitation), capital assets (capitalist exploitation), organization assets (statist exploitation) and skill or credential assets (socialist exploitation). No actually existing society ever consists of a single form of exploitation, and thus, empirically, classes with particular

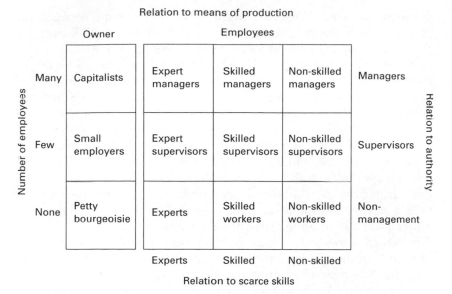

Figure 2   Wright's second class scheme: relations of exploitation
Source: E. O. Wright *Class Counts*, Cambridge University Press, 1997, fig. 1.3

assets may be simultaneously exploited through one mechanism of exploitation but exploiters through another mechanism. Through this complex chain of abstract reasoning, therefore, Wright develops a further 'class map' reflecting relations of exploitation, rather than domination (see figure 2).

As can be seen from figure 2, the number of Wright's classes has increased from six to twelve. The major difference between Wright's earlier and later approaches, however, is that whereas the presence or absence of work autonomy was central to the identification of significant 'contradictory' class groupings in Wright's first scheme, this element is absent from the second version. Rather, such groupings are now identified through their possession of expertise and skills, as well as their position in organizational hierarchies. It has been pointed out that this development of Wright's analysis has a close parallel in Weberian approaches to the identification of the individual's 'class situation'; as such assets clearly differentiate groups 'according to the kind of services that can be offered on the market ... and will thus have an impact on individual "life-chances"' (Rose and Marshall 1986). As we shall see, Wright would not necessarily reject such suggestions, but nevertheless argues that 'The pivotal difference [i.e.

between Marx and Weber] is captured by the contrast between the favourite buzz-words of each theoretical tradition: *life chances* for Weberians, and *exploitation* for Marxists' (Wright 1997: 31).

Rather like Goldthorpe's, Wright's class scheme has to be evaluated in the context of his work as a whole – although the theoretical elaboration of his scheme has occupied a significant place within this corpus. Besides the empirical evaluation of his own approach to social class against other strategies of operationalizing the 'class structure',[6] Wright's aim has been to test empirically a number of basic Marxist assumptions. Thus, for example, he has, like Goldthorpe, been highly critical of liberal analyses concerning the class trajectory of 'industrial societies'. Wright and Singlemann (1982) have used empirical data classified by Wright's class categories (mark I) in an analysis of the American occupational structure which appeared to demonstrate that, contrary to Blau and Duncan's optimistic assumptions, relating to occupational 'upgrading', the American class structure was undergoing a process of 'proletarianization'. Their evidence suggested that Braverman's thesis of the 'deskilling' of the labour force could be sustained at the macro-level. Within given economic sectors there was 'a systematic tendency for those positions with relatively little control over their labor processes to expand during the 1960s and for those positions with high levels of autonomy to decline' (1982: 198). These tendencies had been to some extent masked by the growth of semi-autonomous employment, particularly in the state sector, but they predicted that this would be checked by a decline in state employment given the growing 'fiscal crisis' of the state.

However, in a later paper (Wright and Martin 1987) which draws upon further evidence (and uses class categories mark II), Wright argues that, contrary to the predictions of his earlier argument: 'In terms of the working class . . . the 1970s were a period of relative deproletarianization . . . In no case is there any evidence that the prolonged stagnation of the 1970s generated a tendency for the proportion of managers, supervisors and experts within sectors to decline . . . these results [run] consistently counter to our theoretical predictions' (1987: 16). Indeed, all of the evidence points in the *opposite* direction: 'The implication of these analyses, then, is unmistakable: the results are more consistent with what we construe to be the post-industrial society thesis than the traditional Marxist proletarianization thesis' (1987: 18). Wright does not as a consequence reject Marxist analysis. The globalization of capitalist relations, he argues, suggests that national units of capitalism are not necessarily representative of capitalism as a whole and, in any case, such internationalization means that there will be a tendency for managerial class locations to expand more rapidly in the core capitalist countries and proletarian positions to expand more rapidly in the Third World. In any case, he suggests that the extent of the incompatibility between Marxist and liberal theories of industrial development may have been overdrawn; as the effects of the material conditions posited in postindustrial theory can, using his revised class framework, be described in class terms.

Wright also uses comparative data drawn from Sweden and the United States to develop his arguments relating to class structure and politics. The long tradition of left-corporatist social democracy in Sweden has shaped not only the 'class' (that is, occupational) structure, as compared to the United States, but has also, perhaps paradoxically, resulted in a heightened salience of 'class thinking' and thus class attitudes which are more polarized. Thus he is careful always to stress that the effects of class structure are mediated by politics. To the extent that Wright indulges in political prescription, it is perhaps paradoxical that his comments are very similar to those of Goldthorpe. Goldthorpe (1987: 350) suggests that the interests of the 'mature' working class in Britain would be best served by some version of 'left democracy'. Similarly, Wright states that 'the heart of the positive struggle for socialism is radical democracy' (Wright 1985: 287). Thus, despite their very different theoretical orientations and strategies of analysis, it would seem that Wright and Goldthorpe might be in broad political agreement on a number of contemporary issues.

The empirical questions that Wright addresses have, not surprisingly, been shaped by his broader theoretical interests – hence, for example, the extensive attention he has given to the question of class consciousness (see Wright 1997, Part IV). However, he has also used his comparative material to explore topics similar to the major concerns of the CASMIN project – most notably, the question of the permeability of class boundaries and inter-generational mobility. Rather to his surprise, he found that an analysis of the permeability of class boundaries (as measured by class mobility, friendships, and cross-class marriages) revealed that the authority boundary was always more permeable than the skill boundary (Wright 1997: 230). From a Marxist standpoint this was unexpected, as the control of the labour of others would be considered more significant than the possession of individual skills – indeed, this finding might be considered as confirming a 'Weberian' view of class.

However, notwithstanding such negative (or surprising) findings, Wright has always been explicit that his continuing commitment to a Marxist class scheme stems from his primary commitment to Marxist theory as an organizing theoretical framework, which he claims is still 'the most coherent general approach to radical, emancipatory social theory' (Wright 1989: 322). Ultimately, his choice 'remains crucially bound up with commitments to the socialist tradition and its aspirations for an emancipatory, egalitarian, alternative to capitalism' (1997: 37).

Conclusions

This chapter has reviewed a number of different strategies (or classification schemes) through which the structure of employment in industrial societies may be divided in order to produce statistical aggregates which are then labelled 'social classes'. Many such schemes are largely descriptive in their intentions – that is, they provide a convenient measure of the broad contours of structured social inequality in late twentieth-century capitalism. They also supply a (somewhat rough and ready) indication of 'lifestyle' and associated social attitudes. Different schemes have been used in a wide variety of social science and other contexts – for example, research on social policy, market research, research on voting behaviour and social mobility. The range of different theoretical and practical applications for which different class schemes are utilized suggests that it is not possible to identify particular schemes which are 'right' or 'wrong'; rather, different schemes are more or less appropriate for particular tasks. Nevertheless, sociologists have at times appeared to be reluctant to accept such theoretical and methodological plurality, and there have been extensive arguments about which particular scheme is 'superior' – arguments which extend across a range of different issue areas. For example, Marshall et al. (1988) have compared in some detail the Registrar-General's, Goldthorpe's, and Wright's class schemes. It is difficult, however, to see what is actually gained from this exercise, as the class schemes in question were devised for different purposes and on the basis of different (implicit and explicit) theoretical assumptions.

Employment-derived class schemes have also been used to provide evidence for theoretical debates – for example concerning the nature and future trajectory of 'industrial societies' (Wright and Singlemann 1982; Wright and Martin 1987), or to test Marx's and Braverman's arguments concerning 'proletarianization' (Rose et al.

1987). This chapter has drawn particular attention to the class schemes associated with the development of the theoretical programmes of class analysis of Goldthorpe and Wright. These programmes were generated as part of a widespread critique within sociology of approaches to the study of society which emphasized order, rather than conflict, within the stratification system and employed subjective and/or intuitive occupational rankings in its 'class' analyses. Relational schemes, in contrast, attempted to capture the underlying divisions and conflicts associated with class in capitalist industrial societies.

Both Goldthorpe and Wright have been engaged, in the 1970s and 1980s, in extensive programmes of empirical research to which their (rather different) definitions of 'class' are central. Their respective energies have produced a considerable quantity of published materials, and associated debates, which merit separate books in themselves (indeed, such volumes have appeared: Clark et al. 1990; Wright 1989). Nevertheless, however distinguished these sociologists (and the research teams associated with them) are, the point must be emphasized that neither Wright nor Goldthorpe, nor the 'employment aggregate' approach in general, represents 'class analysis' in its entirety. In our outline of the work of the two authors in this chapter, we have drawn attention to the points of difference between them – differences which they, too, have emphasized in recent commentaries (see in particular Goldthorpe and Marshall 1992, to be discussed in the next chapter). Nevertheless, Goldthorpe and Wright also share in a broad similarity of approach to 'class analysis' in that both locate the 'class structure' in the employment structure, and both have adopted the technique of the large-scale sample survey. This approach has produced a number of important empirical findings. However, national-level sample surveys are not sufficient to explore many of the topics within the field of 'class analysis' as a whole. In particular, the national-level survey approach is not suitable for the exploration of the actual *processes* of class formation. These take place in organizations, localities and other associations such as political parties, and are more usually investigated via a holistic, case study, approach. As we shall see in subsequent chapters, the 'employment aggregate' approach to class analysis is in fact quite narrowly focused, a fact which has become increasingly apparent in the process of its recent clarification.

Nevertheless, there is a widespread assumption within the social sciences that 'class' is described by the occupational structure – indeed, 'class structure' and 'occupational structure' are often taken to be synonymous. This convention stems from the practice established by turn-of-the-century statisticians such as Stevenson of dividing up the population into unequally-rewarded occupational orders or 'classes'. Stevenson was engaged in a debate with eugenists, not Marx or Weber. It is not surprising, therefore, that 'class' schemes such as the Registrar-General's should correspond only fortuitously to the theoretical concerns of these classic sociologists. The convenient assumption that class structure = occupational structure can cause problems for the unwary, or those not versed in the finer details of relational class schemes and/or sociological theory. In the next chapter, therefore, we will examine these and other criticisms of the diverse project of 'class analysis' as a whole.

Notes

1   As an illustration of this anomaly, Nichols points out that in the British *Classification of Occupations*, 1951, the 'capitalist', the 'business speculator', and the 'landowner' were lumped into the same residual category as the 'expert' (undefined) and the 'lunatic (trade not stated)'!
2   The title of this agency has been changed to the Office of National Statistics (ONS).
3   Now the Department for Education and Employment (DfEE).
4   This impression will have been reinforced by the fact that Goldthorpe had worked closely with Lockwood on the 'Affluent Worker' project: see Goldthorpe et al. 1969.
5   In fact, Wright's distinction between 'occupation' and 'class' as reflecting the distinction between 'technical' and 'social' relations of production cannot be sustained, as many occupational titles encompass 'social' relationships. For example, 'managers and administrators' constitute a Major Group within the Standard Occupational Classification (UK).
6   Particularly the 'productive labour' definition employed by Poulantzas. Wright's conceptualization, unsurprisingly, proved to be superior.

4 Problems of Class Analysis

Introduction

Chapter 3 has considered a range of different strategies developed within sociology and the social sciences for the measurement of the 'class structure' via the structure of employment. A feature of all such approaches is that the identification of the class structure may be treated as analytically and empirically separable from the question of class action. Many such measures (for example, the Registrar-General's social class classification) are descriptive schemes originally devised for social policy purposes rather than as a contribution to theoretical debates in class analysis. However, the question of the most appropriate measure of social 'class' became a central issue for an important debate within postwar Anglo-American sociology: 'consensus' versus 'conflict' approaches. It was argued that normative functionalism had laid an unwarranted emphasis on integration and consensus, thus obscuring the very real conflicts that characterized industrial capitalist society. The stability and (apparent) cross-national similarity of occupational rankings had been interpreted as a manifestation of this supposed consensus, as well as providing an empirical demonstration of the 'industrial society' thesis. In contrast, those sociologists who stressed the significance of social conflict emphasized the need to develop measures of social *class*, rather than descriptive measures of occupational inequality. Thus in the 1970s and 1980s there were developed sociological measures of the structure of employment which, in contrast to 'gradational', status or 'commonsense' schemes, purported to reflect, theoretically, the structure of actual class *relations* in capitalist societies. Two major empirical programmes of 'class analysis' – those of Goldthorpe and Wright – have been developed using such schemes.

Debates relating to class, and class analysis more generally, continue to reflect the various understandings of the class concept (as discussed in chapter 1), as well as differences in methodology and theoretical orientation amongst sociologists themselves. Because the concept has always been seen as central within the social sciences, debates have also continued to reflect recent developments in social theory, including post-structuralism and postmodernism. These academic discussions have been ongoing against the extensive and rapid social, economic and political changes taking place in the world. Indeed, some have argued that these changes have fundamentally transformed late industrialism; that there has been a fundamental shift in the nature of society itself and that postmodern theories reflect our globalized, postmodern, present reality. Thus the field of class analysis is characterized by extensive fragmentation (Crompton 1996a). This fragmentation has been paralleled by extensive 'pseudo-debates' within class analysis, in which, given their very different definitions and theoretical approaches, different academics argue past, rather than with, each other. As we shall see, this has been no more the case than in recent commentaries on the 'end' or 'death' of social class.

Within the domain of class theory and analysis, a number of contrasts, and different academic strands, may be identified. One major *de facto* division (which has become very apparent during recent commentaries), is between the 'employment aggregate' approach (as described in the last chapter) on the one hand, and debates relating to the significance of class for broader theories of society, and societal change, on the other. Another contrast may be drawn between the exploration of the *consequences* of class structuring (which has become the major focus of Goldthorpe's and Wright's work), and the investigation of the *processes* of class formation. This contrast also corresponds to a broad difference of methodological approach. The employment aggregate approach has used national level sample surveys and attempts to draw a sharp distinction between 'class' and other factors, whereas empirical studies of class processes have used variants of the case study method. In these studies, the interaction of class with other factors (including status) is often very apparent.

One important reason for the continuing confusion between 'employment aggregate' and 'societal shift' debates in class analysis,

however, is that one of the major employment aggregate practitioners, Erik Wright, has continued to link the two (as we shall see, this
is also true of other commentators, both critics and defenders, of
'class analysis'). These debates *are* linked in that the kinds of topic
investigated within the employment aggregate approach are and
have been generated through theoretical debates concerning both
the nature of society and the best concepts through which to analyse
it. Wright has made an important contribution to debates in Marxism (which, as we have seen, has been a major theory of societal
change) as well as developing his explicitly 'Marxist' version of the
employment aggregate approach. However, a crucial question,
which has not been satisfactorily resolved, is whether either
Goldthorpe or Wright have successfully operationalized class in
either the 'Marxist' or the 'Weberian' sense (as we shall see,
Goldthorpe has now rejected the 'Weberian' label). Another source
of confusion lies in the fact that, although Goldthorpe and Wright
have often been presented as theoretical and sociological opposites,
the similarity of their methods of analysis means that their positions
have converged over the years.

We will conclude this chapter by arguing that debates about
whether employment-derived measures are useful social indicators
should be considered separately from debates about whether modern societies are undergoing some kind of fundamental transformation or 'societal shift'. However, these societal changes have
contributed to a mounting tide of criticism of the employment-
aggregate approach. In the next section of this chapter, therefore,
we will examine three major developments in the late industrial
world which have been important in this respect. These are: first,
changes in the nature of work and employment; second, shifts in the
gender division of labour, in particular the growth of married
women's employment; and third, the apparent lack of significance of
employment 'class' for politics, identity and action. In chapter 5, we
will focus on the broader questions raised by arguments that we are
experiencing a fundamental transformation in the nature of society
itself.

Changes in the structure of work and employment

Since the end of the Second World War, the expansion of capitalist
industrialism has had important consequences for the international
division of labour. The industrialization of South East Asia has been

accompanied by the decline of heavy manufacturing in the West, the United States 'steel belt' has become a 'rust belt' and in Britain, once dependent single-industry localities in South Wales and the North-East have ceased to manufacture this most basic commodity of 'industrial society'. Other major industries, such as shipbuilding, have suffered a precipitate decline in the level of worldwide demand, whilst that construction which remains is predominantly in countries such as Korea. Post-Second World War expansion in the West had seen the rapid growth of manufacturing to meet the demand for consumer goods – notably vehicles – but increasing competition and the saturation of home markets has also led to a marked decline, particularly in Britain, in these industries. The post-war boom was already coming to an end by the 1960s, but the worsening of the economic crisis, exacerbated by the world oil price rises of the early 1970s, led to a further collapse of manufacturing industry in the West.

Throughout the 1970s, governments in Britain had attempted to grapple with the worsening economic situation through a further extension of the broadly 'corporatist' bargain which had been con-solidated during the period of postwar expansion. This had involved the adoption of Keynesian policies of state economic management – a policy of full employment, which governments attempted to main-tain by controlling demand through taxation and other fiscal policies – in combination with increased levels of state provision of educa-tion, health, and welfare.[1] In 1974, the Labour government in Britain entered into a 'social contract' with the trade union move-ment, in which the unions agreed to regulate the wage demands of their members in exchange for an increased right to participate in the shaping of government policies. These policies were not success-ful in stabilizing the economy, and inflation continued to rise, as did rates of unemployment – a phenomenon which was given the suit-ably unpleasant title of 'stagflation'.[2] They culminated in the 1979 'winter of discontent', during which public-sector workers, whose wages had declined sharply as a consequence of the 'social contract', went on strike.[3] The Conservative government which was then elected pursued policies in sharp contrast with those of the 'social contract'. Industries in decline were no longer protected, and government 'intervention' in the economy was restricted to attempts to control the money supply. Trade unions were excluded from access to state power – indeed a full-frontal attack was mounted on their position, and legal rights (such as those embodied in the Trade Unions and Labour Relations Act 1976) they had achieved during the 1970s were simply removed. Under the influence of neo-liberal economic theories the Conservative government spearheaded a return to 'market forces' in the regulation of economic affairs, which involved the selling of state monopolies such as gas, telecommunications, electricity and water, the increasing 'privatization' of welfare, the application of 'quasi-market' principles to those areas remaining within the state's orbit (such as schools, universities and hospitals), and the promotion of individual entrepreneurship.

The impact of this attempt to move away from the 'welfare state deal' in Britain in the 1980s will be further examined in chapters 7 and 8. For the moment, the significant fact to note is that these policies contributed further to the headlong collapse of manufacturing, and there was a sharp rise in unemployment. Employment in manufacturing declined by 3 million between 1971 and 1988, from 8 to 5 million employees. New jobs were created during the economic restructuring of the 1980s, but these were largely in the service economy, and in the UK service employment increased from 53 per cent to 73 per cent between 1973 and 1993. This decline in employment in manufacturing, which has taken place in all late industrial economies, has resulted in a further decline in those occupations which have by convention been described as 'working-class'. The decline in working-class employment has also been associated with the erosion of working-class communities (for example, in coalmining areas), and increasing individuation.

The labour market has been progressively fragmented, with a growth of flexible and non-standard employment such as part-time work, short-term contracts, and self-employment (see Beatson 1995). Between 1993 and 1997, only 38 per cent of new jobs created in the UK were for full-time, 'standard', employees. These developments have been associated with increasing insecurity of employment and the decline of the long-term career, as a consequence of organizational restructuring and 'downsizing'. According to Beck (1992: 143), these kinds of change have resulted in the development of an 'individualized society of employees' in a 'risk-fraught system of flexible, pluralized, decentralized underemployment'. In these new forms of employment (which include homeworking, casual work, and so on), the boundaries between work and non-work are, it is argued, becoming increasingly fluid. 'Work' in the sense of an occupation once provided a focus for the development of class-based identities in industrial societies, but as a consequence of increasing insecurity and flexibility in the labour market, Beck argues, both 'class' and 'status' are losing their significance.

These changes have been described as a move from prevailing 'Fordist' to 'post-Fordist' techniques of production and labour organization (R. Murray 1989; Sabel 1982). 'Fordism', it is argued, was characterized by large-scale mass production of cheap, uniform commodities, the detailed division of labour, and extensive hierarchical organization of productive activity. Hence the label 'Fordist', which describes the system of mass, assembly-line production of cars developed by Henry Ford in the United States during the early decades of this century. It is the system of production in manufacturing which Braverman described as the 'degradation of work in monopoly capitalism'. 'Post-Fordism', in contrast, is supposedly characterized by flexible production techniques on smaller, dispersed sites. The emphasis is on product variety and rapid response to consumer demand – in contrast to Henry Ford's famous statement that customers could have any colour car they wanted – as long as it was black.

Changes in the nature of work itself, particularly those associated with the expansion of service work and the growth and application of Information Technology, have, it is argued, changed the *meaning* of work for employees. Lash and Urry (1994) have argued that technological developments have meant that production systems have themselves become expert systems, and that 'reflexive modernities' are becoming 'economies of signs and space'. The growth of interactive service work (that is, work requiring regular interaction with the consumer), as well as new styles of management such as Total Quality Management (TQM), with its emphasis on workforce 'empowerment' and the generalization of the service relationship within the organization (i.e. every department becomes a 'customer' of another department), have progressively blurred the distinction between 'producers' and 'consumers'. Another simple (but telling) point is that people simply spend less of their lifetimes in paid work. School-leaving ages have risen, more people are going into further education, retirement ages are falling, and long-term unemployment is rising. Thus Offe has argued that 'work' is no longer a 'key sociological concept'; it no longer has 'a relatively privileged power to determine social consciousness and action' (1985: 133).

The expansion of women's employment

The 'industrial society' which was consolidated from the second half of the nineteenth century onwards was developed on the 'male breadwinner' model of the gender division of labour. Married women were excluded from paid work (i.e. became 'housewives') on the assumption that the male 'breadwinner' was paid a 'family wage' (see Glucksmann 1995).[4] As a consequence, the 'Fordist' occupational hierarchy became increasingly masculine. As we have seen, the growth of male-dominated industrial employment was also paralleled by the increasing development of social protections, notably those associated with the welfare state. Welfare state institutions, such as occupational pensions and other social benefits, were explicitly created on the assumption that the male breadwinner model was the norm. Thus women received many social benefits via their 'breadwinner' (Esping-Andersen 1990; Pateman 1989).

Paradoxically, however, the expansion of welfare state-led service provision (as well as the expansion of other state-provided services such as education and health) was a major source of employment growth for women. Thus the basis of the male breadwinner model was being eroded even as its principles were being consolidated in national institutions and policies. Other factors were also leading to the growth of women's employment, including 'push' factors such as rising levels of education, effective fertility controls and the growth of 'second-wave' feminism, as well as 'pull' factors including the buoyant labour markets of the 1950s and 1960s. Service expansion was fuelled not only by state expenditure and job creation, but also the growth of financial, leisure and business services.

Thus for a significant category of people – women – paid employment is becoming considerably *more* important in their lives. In all of the OECD countries, women's employment has grown rapidly since the Second World War – particularly since the 1960s (Paukert 1984). This rise was almost entirely accounted for by an increase in the employment of *married* women. The recession of the 1970s and 1980s was not accompanied by any great decline in women's employment – indeed, many of the service-industry jobs which were created as a consequence of economic restructuring were low-level 'women's jobs'. Women's continuing participation in the formal economy has also been accompanied by both the rise of 'second-wave' feminism and an improvement in their levels of academic and work-related qualifications, and women are increasingly achieving higher-level positions within employment. The emerging structure of employment in the West at the end of the twentieth century, therefore, is not only service-based but increasingly feminized. The increasing employment of women presents a number of problems for employment aggregate class schemes, as we shall see in a later section of this chapter.

Class, politics and action

'Class' is a central concept within the Marxist theoretical framework; it has, therefore, always had a central place in the political discourse of socialists and Marxists. From the beginning of the 1980s, left-leaning parties suffered successive electoral defeats in both Britain and the United States, and there was a neo-liberal 'return to the market' in government policies ('Reaganomics' in the US, 'Thatcherism' in Britain). Towards the end of the 1980s, government regimes in the self-proclaimed state 'socialist' countries in the Eastern bloc progressively collapsed.[5] They have been replaced by governments which have, with varying degrees of enthusiasm, embraced the doctrine of market forces.

A powerful subtext in these debates is that the 'failure of the left' is also a failure of socialist theory; that socialists have remained encumbered for too long by the trappings of outdated ideologies which required revision and updating in the light of 'New Times'.[6] The major thesis associated with such arguments, which reflects the economic changes discussed above, is that the decline of mass production, and with it a mass labour force, has led to the declining significance of the (mass, male) 'working class' and thus of class *politics*. The political parallel of mass production was Keynesian economics in combination with varying degrees of centralized planning and organization; when such political accommodations finally collapsed at the end of the 1970s the vacuum was filled by the neo-liberal 'return to the market' which has further fragmented class politics. Thus 'class', at least in its now obsolete mass manual, male working-class dimensions, is of declining significance in 'New Times', and must be replaced by a new emphasis on ecological and feminist issues, a concern for internationalism together with a move away from authoritarian centralism, and a recognition of the centrality of consumption, rather than outdated 'productivism' (Hall and Jaques 1989: 11–12).

This apparent decline of 'class politics' seemed also to signify the unravelling of yet another element of the 'industrial society' thesis which, as has been described in previous chapters (chapter 1, p. 9), was a significant element of the 'orthodox consensus' which prevailed in postwar sociology in Britain and America. This was the

Lipset–Rokkan thesis concerning the institutionalization of class politics (1967). It argued that as nation states mature, political divisions (parties) come to reflect relatively stable class cleavages in society. Thus political representation allows for the expression of class interests within the framework of democratic politics. This model was extensively criticized, but the British case, in broad outline, did correspond to the bipartisan 'class containment' model; with the middle and upper classes tending to vote Conservative, the lower and working classes for Labour. Nevertheless, as we have noted, both parties gave broad support to 'welfarist' policies such as increased educational provision, the development of public housing, and support for the National Health Service. However, from the 1960s onwards, the link between class and voting has apparently become increasingly tenuous – that is, a process of 'dealignment' (between employment class and voting behaviour) would seem to be under way. One measure of dealignment is the Alford index, in which the percentage of non-manual votes for left parties is subtracted from the percentage of manual votes (thus the larger the index, the closer the alignment of class with vote). Since the 1960s, the Alford index has been in decline across a wide range of Western societies (Pakulski and Waters 1996b: 134).

Within left-oriented political debates, some have dismissed a concern with 'class' as 'outdated productivism'; others still maintain its historical centrality. In political sociology, contemporary debates have also emphasized the significance of the development of the 'New Social Movements' which, according to Offe (1985a) have 'transformed the boundaries of institutional politics'. Offe describes the 'old politics' – that is, the major political issues in Western Europe from the immediate postwar years until the early 1970s – as being centrally concerned with issues of economic growth, distribution and security. In 'New Times' language, the 'old politics' corresponded to the politics of Fordism. As described by the Lipset–Rokkan thesis, old politics was also marked by a considerable degree of consensus – on the desirability of economic growth, of welfare provision, and so on – and distributive conflict organized politics along broadly 'class' lines; parties of the unionized working class competing with bourgeois parties which included both the old and elements of the 'new' (that is, lower-level white-collar) middle class. However, the accommodative basis of the old politics has been challenged by both the New Right, as well as by the growth of New Social Movements, which include the peace movement, ecological movements, human rights and feminist movements.

The neo-liberal New Right is highly critical of the extent of state involvement characteristic of the 'old politics', which it saw both as acting as a brake upon economic recovery and as eroding the base of individual responsibilities and undermining civil society. New Social Movements are similarly critical of the state's capacity to resolve the major problems which they identify, but, Offe argues, they seek not to 'roll back' the state, or 'reprivatize' civil society but to *transform* political action through the development of a non-institutional politics which will bring about permanent changes. The feminist slogan 'the personal is political' may be used to describe this approach to political action, which is also characterized by relatively non-hierarchical modes of organization, mass protests and, often, direct action.

New Social Movements, Offe argues, represent a significant break with class politics. The bases of their organization do not correspond to socio-economic classes, or their corresponding left/right ideologies, but '[are] rather coded in *categories* taken from the movements' issues, such as gender, age, locality etc., or, in the case of environmental and pacifist movements, the human race as a whole' (Offe 1985a: 831; my emphasis). Class, in the sense of socio-economic status, is related to New Social Movements, however, in that much of their membership is drawn from the 'new' new middle class – that is the educated, socially aware elements of the middle class who grew up within the economic security of the old politics and found employment within the institutions it created (that is, in administration, health, education, etc.). The 'new' new middle class may be distinguished from the 'old' new middle class of lower-level white-collar workers. Such groupings have politicized, not on behalf of a class, but around the wider issues addressed by New Social Movements: 'New middle class politics, in contrast to most working class politics, as well as old middle class politics, is typically the politics *of* a class but not *on behalf of* a class' (1985a: 833).

These academic debates relating to politics, it must be remembered, were taking place at a time in which (particularly in Britain), left-of-centre political parties endured successive electoral defeats (the Conservative government was in power from 1979 to 1997). The election of 'New Labour' might seem to have reversed this trend. However, a major feature of 'New Labour' is its conscious attempt to distance itself from 'old politics', in particular the major representatives of 'class politics' such as the trade unions. Indeed the transformation of Labour politics might itself be seen as yet another instance of the increasing lack of relevance of 'class' in contemporary political debates.

The failure of class action

The decline of the linkage between employment class and voting behaviour might be seen as a manifestation of a more general tendency which has always been a feature of critical commentaries on class – that is, the absence of a link between 'classes' and consciousness and action of a class nature (where voting is considered as an expression of a 'class' identity). The identification of a class structure has often been associated with the (implicit or explicit) assumption that class interests may be identified corresponding to their structural location, and likely class action then derived from these interests. This reasoning, therefore, moves from structure → consciousness → action (Pahl 1989). It might be thought to be a characteristically Marxist progression, but it is *not* specific to Marxist authors. For example, Erikson and Goldthorpe (1988) have written of the need to investigate the conditions under which a 'class in itself' becomes a 'class for itself', that is, 'the conditions under which individuals who hold similar class positions do actually come to define their interests in class terms and to act collectively – for example, through class-based movements and organizations – in their pursuit' (cited in Muller 1990). Goldthorpe's analytical reasoning from class structure → demographic class formation → sociopolitical class formation reflects this linkage of structure → consciousness → action, but he regards this linkage as contingent, rather than inevitable.

In chapter 2, we saw how establishing the linkages between 'structure' and 'action' was not just a problem for class analysis in sociology, but for the social sciences more generally. One of the most influential critiques of the failure of class action, however, has been directed specifically at Marxist class theory and its development within sociology. Lockwood (1981) argues that Marxism's 'weakest link in the chain' (a phrase borrowed from Lenin's dictum that a chain is only as strong as its weakest link) lies in the inadequacy of Marx's theory of action, which, he argues, is basically utilitarian in inspiration. Thus in the Marxist account the capitalist is a 'rational miser', but the proletariat is expected to achieve a 'higher-order' rationality or reason – that is, to perceive that short-term advantage (for example, gains achieved in competition with other proletarians) will not necessarily lead to the long-term objective of socialism.

Marxism explains proletarian deviations from rational action as being either 'irrational' – that is, due to ignorance, or error, as in the case of 'false consciousness'; or 'non-rational' – that is, as a consequence of ideological domination which results in the dominance of 'inappropriate' alternatives (for example, religion or nationalism) to socialist beliefs. Marxism, argues Lockwood, lacks the conceptual tools with which to consider non-rational beliefs and action systematically. Far from recognizing this as a problem, recent Marxist theorists have gone in the *other* direction. Here Lockwood is extremely critical of French structural Marxism as well as sociologists, such as Wright, who were influenced by it. Such debates, Lockwood argues, have not addressed the question of action at all but have instead become a controversy over objective 'places' in the class structure.

Similar criticisms of the Marxists' failure to give an account of action had already been developed in Pickvance's (1977) critique of the application of structuralist Marxist concepts in the field of urban sociology, in which 'the social force appears from the social base at a wave of the magic wand of organization' (p. 179). However, these criticisms, which are well taken, have been directed at a particular variant of Marxist analysis. There are also those who would consider themselves 'Marxists' – such as, for example, E. P. Thompson (discussed in chapter 2) – to whom it would be very difficult to apply these strictures.

Both Lockwood and Pickvance have directed their criticisms at the deficiencies of the structuralist-Marxist account of action, at the failure to make the links in the structure → consciousness → action chain. Both argue that insights drawn from Weber's work are appropriate for making these links, as Weber places value-orientations at the *centre* of his account of social action. The status order is a central element in a Weberian approach to social stratification. It might seem paradoxical, therefore, that non-Marxist sociologists have also been criticized for their failure to treat adequately the question of class action.

Pahl's polemical account developed a critique of 'class analysis', both 'Marxist' and 'Weberian'. He argued that in sociology 'class' has been used unproblematically to give an account of 'structure' in the structure → consciousness → action chain, but as the 'links in the chain' between structure, consciousness and action have not been identified, then 'class as a concept is ceasing to do any useful work for sociology' (1989: 710). However, it may be argued that the force of Pahl's argument is undermined by the fact that he fails to take account of the complexity of the different approaches to 'class analysis'. Pahl's rejection of the use of 'class' to describe an abstract force which explains political and social change rests uneasily alongside his enthusiastic endorsement of E. P. Thompson's approach to class analysis (1989: 717), given that Thompson's objective has been to demonstrate the relevance of class for our understanding of history. In fact, it may be suggested that Pahl's major target, which his early discussion did not specifically identify, was the development of the tradition of 'class analysis' based upon the application of theoretical, relational class schemes – that is, the work of Goldthorpe and Wright (Crompton 1991). As has been described above, these authors do begin with the presumption that the starting point of 'class analysis' lies in the identification of the class structure. Consciousness and action are then assumed to derive from this. Wright asserts that such progression is systematic, Goldthorpe, following Weber, makes no such assumptions and treats class action as contingent. Goldthorpe may therefore defend his approach from critics such as Hindess (1987) and Pahl on the grounds that they have imputed a determinism to his arguments which is simply not there (Goldthorpe and Marshall 1992).

However, neither Marxists nor non-Marxists working in the field of class analysis have provided a theoretically robust account of the analytical move between class 'structure' and consciousness/action. As another contributor to the debate sparked off by Pahl's polemic has argued (and as we have seen in chapter 2), such arguments reveal a much more deep-seated malaise in sociology – and the social sciences in general. Mullins (1991) argues that the sociological analysis of the social forces producing change – whatever these might be – are themselves seriously underdeveloped: 'there is little understanding of various social forces, such as class and consumption ... [there] are gross deficiencies in sociological theory, since most of what is called theory is not theory, but a mix of critique, philosophy, history and taxonomies' (1991: 119). A 'general theory of action' has not yet been achieved. There is no dominant theoretical paradigm in sociology which might provide a comfortable prop (as did, briefly, normative functionalism in the 1950s), for the sociologist's analysis and explanation of social structure and action.

We have discussed three major sets of factors which have contributed to arguments relating to the 'death' of class. These are first, changes in the nature and structure of employment (particularly the growth of women's employment); second, what seems to be the increasing irrelevance of 'class' for politics – in particular, the decline of class-associated voting; and third, the related failure or absence of the structure–action linkage. All of these points may be used to argue against the employment aggregate approach. Changes in the nature and structure of work as employment mean that it no longer provides a useful proxy for 'class', as the kind of 'work' which predominates at the end of the twentieth century no longer provides a source of social identity. The widespread entry of women into paid employment has not only led to problems of classification, but has also served to further highlight the inadequacy of employment-derived class schemes, which are based on a 'masculine' model. Finally (and this is obviously linked to changes in the employment structure), the link between occupational location and vote is in decline, a fact which underlines the already tenuous link between class structure and class action.

Gender and class

It is simply not possible to separate the question of the class position of women from the feminist critique which was developed within sociology following the growth of 'second-wave' feminism in the 1960s. As feminists have argued, sociology, in common with the other social sciences, treated the social world – in particular, the 'public' sphere of paid employment, class and politics – as if it were gender-neutral, whereas it is, in fact, profoundly structured by gender differences. Thus much of the early feminist critique was concerned to retrieve the 'invisible woman', who, it was argued, had been largely ignored in accounts of the *processes* of class formation.

In particular, some Marxist theorists appeared to suggest that women's subordination could be reduced to the workings of the 'class' (economic) structure. Feminists argued that the focus on paid employment in debates on 'class' did not take into account the unpaid domestic labour of women. Thus women's contribution to production (and thus their consequent 'exploitation') was not examined or analysed (Stacey 1981, Walby 1986). Indeed, feminists argued that 'patriarchy' – the domination of women by men – was more significant than 'class' in shaping women's situation. Other feminist writers have argued that the bases of patriarchy are largely ideological, rather than material. Mitchell (1975) used psychoanalytic concepts in combination with those of structuralist anthropology in order to argue that patriarchal ideology is deeply rooted in human culture. However, much of the feminist debate during the 1970s and 1980s was conducted in a dialogue with Marxism, and the question of the relationship between gender and class was seen as of central significance.

For example, the 'domestic labour debate' (Seccombe 1974) was an attempt to locate women's labour, and thus the nature of their exploitation, within a Marxist analysis of the capitalist mode of production. Engels (1940) had differentiated between the bourgeois family, where the wife received board and lodging in return for the production of legitimate heirs to bourgeois property, and the proletarian family, where both husband and wife were exploited through wage labour. This materialist analysis was widely interpreted (particularly in the former state-socialist countries) to imply that the 'liberation' of women lay in drawing them into wage-labour relationships, whence both men and women could subsequently transform their proletarian condition. However, as feminists argued, this analysis ignored women's domestic work, as well as the social and ideological domination of women. Marxist theorists of 'domestic labour' attempted to demonstrate that women's labour in the domestic sphere made a contribution to the generation of surplus value, and thus the exploitation of women could be identified as an element in specifically *capitalist* production relationships.

These debates have not proved particularly persuasive or long-lasting (Molyneux 1979). However, a broadly materialist account of women's oppression within capitalism is still influential (Barrett 1980; 1988), but it is not one which attempts to reduce the nature of women's oppression to the workings of the capitalist system (as the 'domestic labour' analysis had done). Rather, the object of these authors has been to identify a material system of patriarchy which articulates with capitalism. Hartmann's (1981) initial statement of 'dual systems' theory has been extremely influential in setting the terms of this debate: 'Capitalist development creates the places for a hierarchy of workers, but traditional Marxist categories cannot tell us who will fill which places. Gender and racial hierarchies determine who fills the empty places.' Thus 'patriarchy' is being described as a system equivalent or similar to 'class' in shaping the occupational structure, and women are seen as suffering a double disadvantage – by virtue of their sex, as well as in their employment.

The material disadvantages of women in respect of employment are not too difficult to summarize: women have been concentrated in less well-paid, sex-typed occupations; disadvantaged in the labour market as a consequence of their domestic and child-rearing obligations; and, until relatively recently, excluded by men from access to many of the better-paying and more prestigious occupational roles

(Walby 1986; Crompton and Sanderson 1990). The material *conse-quences* of the social position of women are so great that they cannot be denied; an important question for class analysis, however, is whether male/female differentiation is also a significant *source* of collective, and persisting, social identity and action.

Lockwood has argued that it is not. As gender relations are usually heterosexual, they are cross-cut by class and status relations; thus the economic and associational relationships between men and women are highly fragmented. There are thus 'powerful objections to the claim that gender relations are macrosocial phenomena of the same order as classes and status groups' (1986: 15). These kinds of argument would be disputed by many feminists (Walby 1988, 1990). The introduction of Equal Opportunities legislation in many industrialized countries has furnished a context in which women, as women, may pursue the material advantage of their sex, and they have not been reluctant to do so (Equal Opportunities Commission 1990). National campaigns such as those associated with the women's refuge movement, and abortion legislation, have also united women as a whole – although it must be conceded that these issues have divided, as well as united, them. In the changing circumstances of late twentieth-century capitalist industrialism, gender and sexuality are emerging as coherent foci of social organization.

It has been argued that ethnicity and 'race' are similar phenomena to gender in that the patterns of social discrimination and disadvantage with which they are associated are *socially*, rather than biologically, constructed (Barrett 1980, 1988). The persistence of discrimination on racial grounds has been extensively documented, and the point need not be laboured here (Jenkins 1988). However (and in some contrast to gender), race and ethnic organization *has* for long been a significant focus of organized social identity. Ethnic divisions may at times have been advantageous to capital – for example, in the creation and maintenance of a supply of cheap and flexible labour – but capital did not create these divisions. They cannot be simply regarded as epiphenomena of class processes.

Gender and the 'employment aggregate' approach

Our discussion (in chapter 3) of difficulties associated with employment aggregate class analysis has identified two which are particularly germane to the 'woman question'. These are first, the difficulties of separating and identifying the mechanisms of 'class' from the large number of other factors structuring the labour market. These include ascriptive properties associated with gender, race and age, as well as other status factors such as the traditional or customary prestige and advantages associated with particular occupations. As a consequence of these processes, women and men tend to be concentrated into different occupations – the phenomenon of occupational segregation. The second difficulty is how to categorize the 'economically inactive' – and in the case of women 'housewives' present a particular problem.

Occupational-class schemes (both 'commonsense' and 'theoretical') have been developed with reference to the structure of *male* employment. Thus they differentiate only poorly between women's jobs – a late 1980s study of the British occupational class structure, for example, revealed that 39 per cent of women, but only 6 per cent of men, were in Goldthorpe's class III. Men were much more evenly distributed through the 'class' structure, the greatest concentration being the 23 per cent in class VII (Marshall et al. 1988: 74). There is also the problem of occupational sex-typing. The status, rewards, association with authority and so on (the 'work' and 'market' situation) of particular occupations has been determined historically (and in a downward direction) by the fact that they are 'women's' occupations, that is, according to presumptions about the nature of the likely incumbent, rather than according to the class processes structuring the occupation, its job content in a 'technicist' sense, and so on. A classic example of this process of sex-typing is to be found in the example of the secretary or 'office wife' (Pringle 1988). In Britain, the all-female profession of speech therapy is paid less than professions requiring a similar level of qualification and experience (Crompton and Sanderson 1990). The reality of occupational sex-typing has recently been legally recognized in 'equal-value' legislation. Thus it is just not the case, as Lockwood has argued, that 'it is the position of an occupation within some hierarchy of authority that is decisive for its status and not the sex of the person who happens to be in it' (1986: 21).

Men and women in the same occupations may have very different occupational prospects: that is, that the 'class outcomes' of particular occupations are different for men and women. The most oft-cited example here is clerical work, which occupies a crucial position on the boundary between 'working' and 'middle' classes in most class schemes. However, historically, whereas for men clerical work was often a stepping stone to a managerial career (see Lockwood 1958; Stewart et al. 1980), for women it has more usually been a dead-end occupation (see Crompton and Jones 1984). It may be suggested that recent changes in the structure of employment have reduced the salience of these issues. 'Clerical' was in any case a catch-all label for a wide range of lower-level 'white-collar' occupations. In Britain, the category is in decline (Rubery and Fagan 1994), but this is probably also a consequence of the re-labelling of occupations as a result of technical and organizational change. The category of 'management' is particularly suspect here.

Within the employment aggregate approach, an empirical convention had long been established where a woman was allocated the same class position as that of the male 'head of household'. This convention reflected the predominant division of market and domestic labour between the sexes characteristic of the mid-twentieth century, where the male 'breadwinner' went 'out to work' whilst women retained the primary responsibility for the domestic sphere. It might be argued, therefore, that the conventional 'male model' of the occupational class structure simply reflected the *de facto* predominance of men within the structure of employment. For example Giddens wrote that: 'Given that women still have to await their liberation from the family, it remains the case in the capitalist societies that female workers are largely peripheral to the class system' (1973; 1981: 288). This convention, however, was difficult to sustain, given the continuing increase in women's employment which has taken place since the Second World War.

Both Goldthorpe and Wright have responded to these criticisms. Goldthorpe's position has developed somewhat over the years. When his major national investigation of the British class structure was published (1980; 2nd edn 1987), it was subjected to extensive criticism on the grounds that it focused entirely on men, women only being included as wives (Goldthorpe 1983, 1984b; Heath and Britten 1984; Stanworth 1984; Crompton 1989b, 1996c). However, Goldthorpe argued that, as the family is the unit of 'class analysis', then the 'class position' of the family can be taken to be that of the head of the household – who will usually be a male. Arguments concerning the extent to which women are disadvantaged within the structure of employment merely serve to prove his point. Far from being a case of intellectual sexism, his approach actually recognizes the discrimination which women suffer. To incorporate women's employment on the same terms as men's, he argued, would lead to confusion. Many women work in lower-level white-collar jobs ('Intermediate' class locations in Goldthorpe's original class scheme), and to incorporate their occupations would result in the generation of 'excessive' amounts of spurious social mobility. He also argued that his empirical evidence had demonstrated that a woman's 'conjugal' class is in general more significant than her 'occupational' class in determining her socio-political attitudes. This finding gives further support to his overall strategy.

However, as we have seen, he has modified his original position in adopting, with Erikson, a 'dominance' strategy, in which the class position of the household is taken as that of the 'dominant' occupation in material terms – whether this occupation is held by a man or a woman (Erikson and Goldthorpe 1988). Furthermore, although Erikson and Goldthorpe still insist that the unit of class analysis (as they see it) is the household, and not the individual, their class scheme has in fact been modified in its application to women as individuals. Class IIIb (routine non-manual) has been categorized as 'intermediate' for men, but 'labour contract' for women. Besides these modifications of his original approach, Goldthorpe (Erikson and Goldthorpe 1993: ch. 7) has demonstrated that, as measured by the Goldthorpe class scheme, the pattern of women's relative rates of social mobility closely parallels that of men. This demonstrates that, when considered separately, the impact of 'class' is similar for men and women, and that the different experiences of men and women in the labour market are a consequence of sex, and not class.

Wright's analysis generally takes the individual, rather than the household, to be the unit of class analysis.[7] However, in respect of economically inactive housewives (and other members of the household, such as children), Wright (1997: 246–7) employs a strategy similar to that of Goldthorpe. Thus he introduces the notion of a 'derived' class location, which provides a 'mediated' linkage to the class structure via the class location of others. Wright is sensitive to the issue of gender, and the fact that gender is a major sorting mechanism within the occupational structure as well as reciprocally interacting with class (as in the 'male breadwinner' model of the gender division of labour; see Wright 1997 ch. 9). Nevertheless, he argues that while gender is indeed highly relevant for understanding and explaining the concrete lived experiences of people, it does not follow that gender should be *incorporated* into the abstract concept of 'class' (Wright 1989: 291). Thus in his empirical work, 'class' and 'gender' are maintained as separate factors.

We can see, therefore, that in responding to feminist criticisms, both Goldthorpe and Wright insist that class and gender should be considered as *distinct* causal processes. This analytical separation of class and gender may be seen as part of a more general strategy within the employment aggregate approach in which the continuing relevance of 'class' is demonstrated by the empirical evidence of 'class effects' (Goldthorpe and Marshall 1992). Although, therefore, Goldthorpe and Wright have apparently developed very different approaches to 'class analysis' (and, as we shall see, Goldthorpe makes much of these differences in his own defence of class analysis as he sees it), their underlying approach to the articulation of gender with class is in fact the same. It may be suggested that this stems from the similarity of the empirical techniques used by the CAS-MIN and Comparative Class projects: that is, the large-scale, cross-nationally comparative, sample survey. This kind of research proceeds by isolating a particular variable – in this case, employment class – and measuring its effects. As we shall see, these common elements in the approaches of both authors are also evident in their broader defence of 'class analysis'.

Are social classes dying?

'Class' has always been a contested concept. It is also a concept with many different meanings. Thus, when announcements are made as to the 'death of class', it is important to be explicit as to what particular version of 'class' is in a terminal condition. In an article that sparked off an extended debate, Clark and Lipset (1991) used the term in a somewhat general sense to describe hierarchical differentiation. Thus their empirical arguments as to the death of class emphasized the decline of hierarchies in production, employment and the family, together with the decline in the association between class and voting behaviour. The decline of the class vote is explained with reference to the decline of hierarchies: 'Political issues shift with more affluence: as wealth increases, people take the basics for granted; they grow more concerned with life-style and amenities. Younger, more educated and more affluent persons in more affluent and less hierarchical societies ... move furthest from traditional class politics (1991: 403). As their critics have noted (Hout et al. 1993), the interchangeable use of 'class' and 'hierarchy' in Clark and Lipset's critique led to some confusion, as it was not clear whether they were discussing the decline of 'class' or 'status' divisions. Hout et al. went on to argue for the continuing significance of class, using both Wright's and Goldthorpe's class schemes in order to demonstrate the persisting association between class and earnings. They were also critical of Clark and Lipset's evidence relating to the decline of class voting, arguing that the measure they employ (the

Alford index) is too crude to describe the complexities of the relationship between class and voting behaviour.

Other commentators have argued that there are further inconsistencies in Clark and Lipset's use of the class concept. Pakulski (1993) distinguishes between the use of the class concept (most usually by Marxists) as a theory of social conflict and social change, as compared to the use of the concept to describe units of stratification and patterns of social inequalities. This distinction corresponds to the difference between 'societal shift' and 'employment aggregate' debates concerning 'class' which were discussed in the Introduction to this chapter (see also chapter 1, p. 11). Pakulski goes on to argue that the 'death of class' identified by Clark and Lipset is actually the death of Marxist class theory of social change, rather than of the 'descriptive', or employment aggregate, use of the concept.[8]

Goldthorpe and Marshall's (1992) much-discussed (Lee and Turner 1996) defence of class analysis also conflates the 'employment aggregate' and 'societal shift' debates, although in a rather different way. Goldthorpe and Marshall mount their defence of class analysis in two stages: first, by distinguishing their approach from that of 'Marxists'; and second, by demonstrating the continuing association of employment class (as defined by Goldthorpe) with a range of empirical phenomena including social mobility, education and voting behaviour.[9] However, Goldthorpe and Marshall's *critique* of Marxist class analysis relates largely to Marx's theory of 'societal shift',[10] whereas their *defence* relates entirely to their own version of the 'employment aggregate' approach. This is somewhat confusing, as it treats as if they were equivalents two very different discourses of 'class analysis'; one a theory of societal change (Marxist class theory), the other a measure of advantage and disadvantage in employment relationships (Goldthorpe class analysis). In this and other chapters, we have emphasized that the 'societal shift' and 'employment aggregate' debates reflect two rather different understandings of the class concept. Defending one (the employment aggregate approach) with reference to the other (Marx's theory of societal change), as Goldthorpe and Marshall have done, serves only to perpetuate the muddle.

As we have already noted in our Introduction, Wright has also contributed to the confusion by continuing to run in tandem Marxist class theory and his own version of employment aggregate class analysis. Much confusion might be avoided if it were recognized that there are in fact two Wrights: Wright I, the Marxist class theoretician, and Wright II, the employment aggregate class analyst. It is true that the theoretical perspectives of Goldthorpe and Marshall on the one hand, and Wright on the other, *are* very different. Wright continues to declare himself a Marxist, Goldthorpe and Marshall argue that they have no particular theoretical allegiance. Nevertheless, their *empirical* approach to employment-aggregate class analysis is very similar. We have already seen that they take identical perspectives on the relationship between gender and class, and in their more general defence of the employment aggregate approach to class analysis, Goldthorpe and Wright again assume very similar positions.

Converging approaches

As noted above, the core of Goldthorpe and Marshall's defence of class analysis describes the persisting association of employment class with a range of other factors such as mobility, educational opportunities etc. Wright (1997) constructs an identical defence of his 'Marxist' version of the employment aggregate approach. He describes class analysis as an 'independent variable' specialty like endocrinology, in which 'you are allowed to study a vast array of problems – sexuality, personality, growth, disease processes etc. . . . so long as you explore the relationship between the endocrine system and those explananda.' (p. 1). Thus, Wright argues, the employment class variable may be explored in relation to a range of other societal phenomena – voting behaviour, income, gender, etc. In short, despite their theoretical differences, both Wright and Goldthorpe defend their versions of the employment aggregate approach in very similar terms. Wright himself has argued that: 'The empirical categories [i.e. Wright's class categories] . . . can be interpreted in a Weberian or hybrid manner. Indeed, as a practical set of operational categories, the class structure matrix used in this book does not dramatically differ from the class typology used by Goldthorpe . . . and Erikson and Goldthorpe' (1997: 37). As has already been argued, this similarity stems from the similarity of method employed by both Goldthorpe and Wright; that is, large-scale sample survey research.[11]

As discussed at some length in chapter 3 and summarized in the opening paragraphs of this chapter, sociological, relational class schemes were originally devised as a supposedly superior alternative to 'commonsense' class schemes as well as the status scales which had been used in status attainment research. In contrast, sociological class schemes purported to operationalize *class*, rather than either a random agglomeration of occupations and/or a prestige scale. Two major sociological contenders have emerged, relating to the two major sociological class theorists of the nineteenth and early twentieth century. Much ink has been spilt and countless arguments have raged, but it would seem that, in practice, the different schemes and scales – commonsense, prestige, Marxist, Weberian – are in fact measuring very similar phenomena. Indeed, that this fact would seem to be accepted by some of the major contributors to the debate. Thus Hout et al.'s defence of 'class analysis' (by which they meant the employment aggregate approach) found that the class ratio of earnings in the US using Wright's class scheme was 4.2:1 for men and 2.5:1 for women using Wright's scheme, and 4.9:1 for men, and 3.6:1 for women, using Erikson and Goldthorpe's. There has been much heated debate about which scheme is the 'best', but the different kinds of scheme are in fact highly correlated with each other, and their categories overlap to a considerable extent, particularly in their collapsed versions which are used with great frequency. (Emmison 1991; see also Jones 1988, Prandy and Blackburn 1997).

Although, therefore, the usefulness of the employment aggregate approach to class analysis may be defended, both Wright and Goldthorpe may be criticized for their relative failure to achieve their original objectives: that is, the development of a theoretical, relational, measure of 'class'. Indeed, both have recently been criticized for abandoning their theoretical 'roots'.

The absence of theory

As we have seen above, the approaches of both Goldthorpe and Wright have undergone a *de facto* convergence, but at some cost to the theoretical insights which contributed to the initial construction of their class schemes. Scott (1996; see also Morris and Scott 1996) has recently argued that Goldthorpe's research (or the 'Nuffield programme', as it has come to be called in recent debates) has lost sight of the Weberian programme of 'class analysis' which was its original starting-point. Following Weber, Scott draws a distinction between an individual's 'class situation' and 'social classes'. As we have seen in chapter 2, for Weber a 'class situation' is indicated by property and market relations; social classes are actual strata as indicated by mobility processes. Mobility processes include not only social mobility as such, but also other demographic processes such as marriage, as well as socially shared activities.

Scott argues that, whilst Goldthorpe's original programme of 'class analysis' did incorporate these Weberian distinctions, the current 'Nuffield programme' does not. As we have seen in chapter 3, Goldthorpe's earlier (1980; 1987) work was indeed concerned to establish the demographic (mobility) boundaries between the different classes (as identified by his class scheme) in Britain. However, Scott argues that in his later work Goldthorpe has not only drastically modified his class scheme in response to the needs of the cross-national (CASMIN) research project, but has also abandoned any systematic attempt to identify 'social classes' (or strata identified by mobility boundaries). Scott argues, therefore, that:

> Despite Goldthorpe's continued use of the phrase 'social class', his new categories are not social classes al all. They are nominally defined economic categories of class situations that have been designed to maximise the predictive powers of the schema in comparative research. If the phrase were not likely to cause confusion, Goldthorpe's new categories could be called 'economic classes' to distinguish them from the social classes that Weber saw as the real collectivities in a class society. (1996: 215–16)

Gubbay (1997: 76) has developed a parallel critique of Wright's Marxist version of employment aggregate class analysis. He argues that although Wright began his class project with a *relational* class scheme – that is, a scheme 'deriving from a theory about society as a totality which identifies relations between "classes" as crucial to its dynamics', the subsequent revisions of the scheme means that it has lost this capacity. Gubbay engages in a detailed critique of Wright's efforts to create a Marxist operationalization of class, and concludes that 'the drive to demonstrate the fruitfulness of his approach in empirical research on the statistical correlation of his class categories with income and consciousness, has moved him far away from Marxist class analysis' (1997: 80).

Scott and Gubbay, therefore, criticize Goldthorpe and Wright for the abandonment of their original theoretical programmes of class analysis. Both Scott and Gubbay sketch out alternative programmes – Weberian and Marxist respectively – which would require the construction of complex alternative empirical measures. Scott describes the need to refine occupational classifications so as to incorporate 'status' and 'command' situations, and also suggests that a comprehensive scheme would incorporate 'racialisation, ageing, and sexualisation' as well (1996: 204). In indicating how a theoretical Marxist class analysis might be developed, Gubbay describes a complex framework which would not only describe flows of surplus value, but would also identify different fractions of capital (including the state), as well as providing 'an opening to historical understanding of the changing forms of social division by gender, "race" and nation' (1997: 86). It is noteworthy, however, that neither of these critics has actually provided a concrete operationalization of their improved theoretical models.

Pahl's (1996) commentary on Goldthorpe and Marshall's defence makes a similar criticism as to the lack of theoretical underpinnings in the latest version of Goldthorpe's employment aggregate approach, as set out in Goldthorpe and Marshall (1992) and Erikson and Goldthorpe (1993). Marshall (Marshall et al. 1997) has defended the Goldthorpe class scheme against these charges on the grounds that it is ultimately grounded in the hypothesis that employment relations are the crucial determinant of the structure of class positions in industrial societies – that is, the scheme incorporates an explanatory thesis which can be empirically tested. In contrast, Wright's (1997: 37) continuing allegiance to Marxist theory is explicitly political, his choice is 'crucially bound up with commitments to the socialist tradition and its aspirations for an emancipatory, egalitarian, alternative to capitalism'.

Nevertheless, it would be difficult to argue that either of the two major protagonists who have developed relational (or sociological) class schemes have been particularly successful in operationalizing the class theories which were their original source of inspiration. Goldthorpe and Wright may be viewed as the leading practitioners of a distinctive sociological approach to class analysis which was developed during the 1960s and 1970s. The impetus for this approach, as has been described in previous chapters, came from the use of theoretical accounts of 'social class', drawn from the work of Marx and Weber in order to develop theoretical, relational employment classifications which described the 'class structure' – as we have seen, it was considered particularly important to distinguish between 'class' and 'status'. These accounts were then operationalized through the large-scale sample survey, a method of research whose capacities were enormously enhanced by the advent of computers and electronic data processing. This approach brings together, within a single framework, the theoretical analysis of social class with the empirical analysis of class inequalities and class structures. It is an approach with tremendous promise, but also severe limitations. There are insoluble difficulties in the identification of 'class' independently of the other factors which structure employment relations, and the nature of the links between class structure and class consciousness or action cannot be sufficiently explored through survey data. Both Goldthorpe and Wright are clear that the concept of 'class' refers to social *relationships*, but these relationships cannot be adequately grasped through approaches which rest, in the last instance, on the aggregation of individual attributes (Ingham 1970).[12] Both Goldthorpe and Wright have revised their class schemes, and attempted to clarify their positions. These clarifications have revealed the inherent limitations of both approaches and, to paraphrase Goldthorpe and Marshall, employment aggregate class analysis appears as a far more limited project, intellectually as well as politically, than it once did (1992: 15).

The continuing relevance of employment aggregates

Both Goldthorpe and Wright, therefore, have been criticized for their failure to successfully incorporate either Marxist or Weberian class theory into their empirical investigations into social class. However, this kind of criticism does not mean *either* that 'class analysis' as a whole may thereby be rejected, *or* that the empirical investigations associated with the employment aggregate approach have not produced useful findings. Our previous discussion has noted their limitations, but their advantages are also considerable.

It has been emphasized throughout this book that 'class' has always been used as a descriptive term in relation to patterns of social inequality, and there can be no question that employment-based measures – of all kinds – remain essential for the investigation of structured social inequality. Empirical research using occupational-class schemes has and continues to be carried out in order to assess the impact of social policy. For example, such research has demonstrated the (relatively) limited impact of government reforms which have been designed to moderate the impact of structured occupational inequality in areas such as education. After the Second World War, the 1944 Education Act instituted free secondary education for all schoolchildren in Britain. However, secondary education was organized in a tripartite system of grammar, technical and secondary modern schools which were not of equal academic standing. It was demonstrated that there were significant occupational (class) biases in the selection of children at the age of eleven (proportionately more middle-class children were selected for grammar schools, more working-class children allocated to secondary moderns), even when measured intelligence was held constant (Douglas 1964). In 1962, the Robbins Report on higher education recommended changes designed to tap the underdeveloped 'pool of ability' in British society, and as a consequence there was a massive expansion of university and post-secondary education. However, as Halsey has argued, empirical research (deriving from the same sample as that used for the Oxford Mobility Survey) demonstrated that: 'The familiar picture ... emerges, as with educational expansion generally, that though the fastest *rates* of growth almost always accrue to the working class, the greatest absolute increments of opportunity go to the service class' (Halsey et al. 1980; Halsey 1988: 188, 291). Thus, whereas the proportion of working-class children at university had tripled as between the 1913–22 and 1943–52 birth cohorts in the sample, this has represented an increase of 0.9 per cent to 3.1 per cent, whereas the proportion of the 'service class' going to university had increased from 7.2 per cent to 26.4 per cent (these data relate to men only). Although the data reveal evidence of a long-term trend in the direction of greater educational opportunity (Halsey 1988; Marsh and Blackburn 1992), the educational reforms committed to increasing the 'openness' of British society seem to have met with only moderate success (we will be returning to this topic in our final chapter).

As we have seen, arguments concerning the political significance of class have been conducted through an examination of the statistical association between occupational class categorizations and voting intentions and behaviour. Trenchant critics of Goldthorpe such as Saunders (1990a) have used this kind of evidence to demonstrate the declining significance of class. Conversely, defenders such as Marshall and his colleagues have argued, on the basis of data which demonstrate a fluctuating, but not consistent, association between occupational class(es) and voting patterns that: 'Social class and social class identities are no less salient today than during earlier periods commonly acknowledged as being characterized by "class voting" ' (1988: 260). The use of the Alford index (described above) to describe 'class dealignment' has been widely criticized (Goldthorpe 1996). It is argued that its simple dichotomy fails to reflect the complexities of the modern occupational structure. Heath and his colleagues have argued for the superiority of the Goldthorpe class scheme over this dichotomous (manual/non-manual) measure in the analysis of patterns of voting behaviour in Britain (Heath et al. 1991; Sarlvik and Crewe 1983). They have also demonstrated that employment class seems to be particularly significant as far as *right-wing* voting is concerned, particularly amongst the self-employed. They argue that the Goldthorpe class categories have greater construct validity – that is, the Goldthorpe class measure is closer to the underlying theoretical term ('class') than the simple manual/non-manual division of the psephologists. These arguments have been reinforced by comparing the strength of the association between the categories identified by the different schemes and the phenomena they purport to explain (voting behaviour).

This demonstration of empirical associations between inequality and occupational-class measures could easily be extended – examples might include evidence relating to infant mortality, children's reading capacities, as well as many others. There can be little doubt, therefore, that occupational class retains its utility as a measure of inequality, as well as likely 'life chances'. The central role of occupational-class analysis in the British 'political-arithmetic' tradition should not be abandoned. Even if, as theorists such as Offe (1985a) have argued, 'work' has become less centrally important in the lives of individuals (and this claim is open to dispute), the work individuals do remains the most significant determinant of the life-fates of the majority of individuals and families in advanced industrial societies.

Conclusion

This chapter has begun to unravel some of the complex arguments relating to the 'end' or 'death' of social class and class analysis. In so doing, we have also developed a critique – as well as a defence – of the employment aggregate approach to class analysis. Within sociology, the employment aggregate approach to 'class analysis' has been described as 'hegemonic' (Savage et al. 1992). The argument of this book is not that this approach should be abandoned, but rather that its limitations should be recognized – a point we will develop in the next chapter.

Over the last twenty years, two major cross-national programmes of employment aggregate class analysis have been developed. We have seen that both of the class schemes used in these programmes have been through extensive modifications, and that neither Wright's nor Goldthorpe's class scheme can be described as 'theoretical' in the sense of having successfully mapped Marxist or Weberian categories on to the structure of employment. The manner in which both Wright and Goldthorpe have approached the issue of gender, as well as the arguments they develop in defence of their approach to 'class analysis', are similar. Thus, in relation to their empirical work, their positions have converged over the lifetimes of the two projects, despite their stated differences of theoretical orientation.

Nevertheless, the two class schemes *are* different, and produce different results when they are mapped on to the same population. Wright's scheme produces more proletarians than Goldthorpe's, for example, as well as having a separate category for capitalist owners. Does this mean, therefore, that a decision can be firmly taken as to which of the two schemes is 'correct'? The answer to this question is 'no'; the two schemes simply reflect two different ways of approaching the same phenomenon. Much of the debate within employment aggregate class analysis in recent years has indeed been taken up with the issue of which scheme is 'best', and Goldthorpe's scheme, in particular, has been subject to extensive validation – which itself has been disputed (Marshall et al. 1988, 1997; Evans 1992; Prandy and Blackburn 1997; Breen and Rottman 1995; Pawson 1989). This debate has become somewhat arcane and of little consequence to the non-specialist, and it will not be described in any detail here. In carrying out empirical research, it *is*, of course important to use the best available measure – it is not for one minute being suggested that the social scientist should simply abdicate any responsibility in this matter. However 'the best' measure will vary, depending on the topic to be investigated.

Thus, as we have seen, Heath and his colleagues have argued that Goldthorpe's class scheme is to be preferred to the simple manual/non-manual dichotomy used in constructing the Alford index in assessing the extent of class dealignment in voting behaviour. Breen and Rottman (1995: 93) prefer Goldthorpe's class scheme to Wright's on the grounds that the large size of Wright's proletariat effectively obscures the very wide range of resources and interests within this grouping. However, Savage and his colleagues (1992; see also Butler and Savage 1996) find Wright's approach more discriminating in researching the 'middle class' – in particular, the distinction drawn by Wright between managers and professionals, who in Goldthorpe's scheme are grouped together into an undifferentiated 'service class'. The choice of measure, therefore, will be shaped by the nature of the task in hand. However, very often the social scientist has little choice in the matter. National statistics are collected on very different bases, and the universal cross-nationally comparable occupational classification (ISCO 68) suffers a number of deficiencies (in particular, its failure to reflect the recent differentiation in and increase of service employment). A number of cross-national data sets are becoming available,[13] and the researcher has little choice but to use the classifications they employ, whatever her or his views on their suitability. There is no single employment-derived class scheme that can be unambiguously declared to be the 'best' which can be used in all circumstances to investigate all cases.

The work of both Goldthorpe and Wright includes substantial empirical achievements. We have already described Goldthorpe's work on social mobility, which, together with that of his colleagues associated with the CASMIN project, has demonstrated conclusively the significance of *structured* occupational inequality, and its persistence through generations. Comparative work using a standard measure of occupational class has enabled sociologists to assert with some confidence the nature of the circumstances which contribute to different mobility experiences; that is, we have now a considerably enhanced understanding of the underlying *causes* of social mobility (Erikson and Goldthorpe 1993). Wright (1997) has recently published his 'final report' on the class project, which incorporates important papers on the permeability of class boundaries, authority and gender in the workplace, and the impact of state employment on attitudes – as well as a number of other topics. As Gubbay (a Marxist critic of Wright) has argued in relation to Goldthorpe's work: 'his project is [not] mindless empiricism and, indeed, there is much in the findings of the research programme of interest to Marxists as well as Weberians' (1997: 77).

However, there are important aspects of class analysis which cannot be explored through the employment aggregate approach. Because of the dominance of Wright's and Goldthorpe's research programmes, arguments about the continuing significance (or otherwise) of 'class' have often taken the form of arguments concerning the continuing strength of the association between occupation (or job) and a variety of attitudinal and behavioural factors. That is, the 'employment aggregate' approach is implicitly taken to represent 'class analysis' as a whole. However, it will be argued in subsequent chapters that 'classes' and class processes cannot be adequately analysed through employment or occupational aggregations alone. The explanatory power of the 'class' concept rests in the assumption that classes are regarded as significant social collectivities. Social collectivities can only be fully investigated in their context, and must therefore be studied in relation to the institutions and organizations which articulate their claims – trade unions, political parties, and so on. This requires a methodological approach extending beyond that of survey analysis.

It is being argued here, therefore, that employment-based measures are useful, but by no means comprehensive, indicators of class inequalities and class relations. One obvious difficulty as far as their utility as a measure of inequality is concerned is that employment is not a reliable indicator of wealth holdings. Gender is another important aspect of inequality which is not adequately captured by existing schemes. The persistence of occupational segregation means that many such schemes, which were initially constructed in relation to the structure of male employment, do not reflect the complex reality of women's paid work. Employment-based class measures cannot encompass all aspects of structured social inequality. Even in their most refined theoretical versions, they cannot distinguish effectively between 'class' and 'non-class' sources of employment structuring. The methodology of employment aggregate class analysis is also not particularly well suited to the exploration of the links between structure and action. It can provide macro-level estimates of attitudes and identities which might be assumed to be associated with 'class' in its broadest sense, but it cannot throw much light on the workings and trajectories of the 'political movements and parties', or 'their ideologies, programmes and strategies' which are the actual bases of political mobilization (Goldthorpe and Marshall 1992).

In relation to these kinds of points, Wright's attitude is rather more flexible than that of Goldthorpe. His general framework of class analysis incorporates the meso- or organizational level which is crucial to the process of class structuring, even though his research programme does not incorporate (case) studies at this level. Goldthorpe's position has appeared to be rather different. His major achievement (Erikson and Goldthorpe 1993) has been to demonstrate that, despite the variations in the employment structures of advanced industrial societies, nevertheless, *relative* rates of social mobility can be fitted to a similar model – that is, that similar processes affect social mobility in a wide range of societies, despite their differences. His vision of 'class analysis', therefore, does *not* include the exploration of change and development in the occupational structure itself. Morris and Scott (1996: 48) have criticized this aspect of Goldthorpe's programme, arguing that: 'A programme of class analysis that has "market situation" as one of its central elements cannot afford to ignore the analysis of labour markets.'[14] One feature of labour markets which may prove problematic is that the labour markets associated with 'service-class' jobs appear to be

changing, as management and administrative jobs become characterized by performance-related pay rather than incremental salaries,
and 'non-standard' forms of employment such as short-term contracts become more common.[15]

In later chapters, we will be further exploring the dynamic and
shifting nature of the occupational structure, and the role of class
and other processes in its structuring. We will conclude, however,
with a restatement of one of the major points that has been developed in this chapter; namely, that the usefulness of occupational and
employment classifications as a sociological indicator (and thus the
utility of 'employment class' and the employment aggregate
approach more generally) is an issue which is logically separate from
the question of whether a societal shift – that is, from a 'class' society to something else – is taking place. Of course, employment
aggregate findings may be used as evidence in these debates, and the
two topics are closely related, but even if we were to agree that
'class is dead' (and it will be argued that it is not), occupational and
employment classifications would still be useful social indicators.

Notes

1   This historical period has been described as one of 'Butskellism'; a term derived from
     the surnames of two 'moderate' party leaders of the contemporary left and right –
     Hugh Gaitskell and R. A. B. Butler.
2   It may be suggested, however, that the legislation which accompanied the 'social con-
     tract' – notably in respect of Equal Pay, and Sex Discrimination and Equal Opportuni-
     ties legislation, has proved to have far-reaching social consequences in extending
     'citizenship' rights to these categories.
3   Private industry had not participated in the corporatist deal, and wages in the private
     sector had risen sharply as a consequence of inflation.
4   Industrialization took place at different periods in different countries, a fact which
     has had important consequences for the development of class relations (see Ingham
     1974, Therborn 1983). Women's employment in agriculture, and family enterprises,
     remained significant for much longer in some countries than others, and thus the
     'male breadwinner' label may not always be appropriate. Indeed, it has been sug-
     gested that in some countries – e.g. Finland – the label may never have been useful:
     see Pfau-Effinger (1993).
5   There were and are, of course, many on the socialist left who had always maintained
     that the centrally planned regimes of the Soviet Union were not in fact 'socialist', but
     nevertheless, even such critical socialist analyses have suffered from 'guilt by associa-
     tion' as discredited regimes crumble apace.
6   An influential political account has been developed by intellectuals associated with
     the journal *Marxism Today*. It should be noted that although *Marxism Today* was
     officially a journal of the Communist Party in Britain, many of the contributors have
     never been members of the Communist Party and the journal was in any case from its
     inception associated with the right-wing, 'Eurocommunist' faction within the party. It

should therefore be seen as a forum for left intellectuals, rather than Communist Party members.

7 At the empirical level, the 'unit of analysis' problem is probably best treated as a practical question (Duke and Edgell 1987; Marshall et al. 1988). In certain situations – for example, in labour-market and employment contexts – a woman's 'own' occupational class situation is probably the most appropriate measure to use. In respect of other factors – such as, for example, voting behaviour and social attitudes – there is a considerable amount of empirical evidence to the effect that 'household class' might be a more useful indicator. To use a simple example, a low-level female clerical worker married to a bricklayer is considerably more likely to vote Labour than a woman in a similar job who is married to an insurance manager.

8 In his later work, Pakulski also rejects the 'employment aggregate' approach. See Pakulski and Waters (1996b).

9 It is of interest that Goldthorpe and Marshall's defence of class analysis contains no reference to Clark and Lipset.

10 Thus they argue that their conception of class analysis 'entails no theory of history according to which class conflict serves as the engine of social change' (p. 99); 'no theory of class exploitation, according to which all class relations must be necessarily and exclusively antagonistic' (p. 100); 'no theory of class-based collective action, according to which individuals holding similar postions in the class structure will thereby automatically develop a shared consciousness of their situation' (pp. 100–1); and finally 'class analysis ... does not embrace a reductionist theory of political action – collective or individual – according to which such action can be understood ... as the unmediated expression of class relations and the pursuit of structurally given class interests (p. 101). (All page references to Goldthorpe and Marshall 1992.)

11 It may be suggested that, although their methodologies are identical, the theoretical differences between Goldthorpe and Wright are reflected in their choices of dependent variables to investigate.

12 Both Goldthorpe and Wright stress that their classifications rest on the attributes of jobs, rather than individual persons. Nevertheless, Ingham's argument still applies, given that individual jobs with similar attributes are being aggregated.

13 For example, the European Labour Force Survey, and the International Social Survey Programme.

14 However, it should be noted that Goldthorpe has removed references to 'work' and 'market situation' from the characterization of his class scheme, as described in ch. 3.

15 In a lengthy defence of the Goldthorpe scheme, Marshall (1997) argues that the 'class analysis' programme is now in a position to construct 'causal narratives' to identify the variables linking 'class' (in the Goldthorpe sense) and outcome. The example he cites relates to the fact that autonomy and control at work are important factors in the aetiology of heart disease (1997: 21). This may well prove to be the case, but such 'autonomy and control' do not actually constitute employment relations, but are rather aspects of the 'work situation'. However, Goldthorpe (1996: 315) has been quite emphatic in his rejection of 'work-centred' categorizations of class.

5 Farewell to Social Class?

Introduction

In developing our account of the employment aggregate approach, we have emphasized the particular social and economic conditions of its sociological origins. It is hardly surprising that debates in sociology should reflect the prevailing circumstances of their times. Economic expansion after the Second World War was associated with rising living standards and increased opportunities, and this was reflected in the liberal 'Industrial Society' thesis (an important part of the 'orthodox consensus', see chapter 1, p. 12) in which the assumption of steadily increasing affluence was also linked to the expectation of long-term social stability. The Industrial Society thesis also gave an account of societal development. It was argued that, because of the constraints imposed by the technology of industrialism, all industrial societies would develop similar institutional structures and stratification systems, characterized by increased equality of opportunity (Kerr et al. 1973). In social theory, the Industrial Society thesis was paralleled by the assumption within normative functionalism that there existed a broad consensus relating to the relative value of the functionally differentiated elements of society, and that this consensus extended to the different rewards offered within the occupational structure. This 'consensus' theory of stratification was countered by 'conflict' theory, which in contrast emphasized the role of power, domination and exploitation in structuring levels of reward in the occupational order. Employment aggregate class analysis was an important strand of empirical research that emerged out of these debates.

In a similar fashion, current debates relating to class and stratification also reflect recent social changes, as well as contemporary developments in social theory. Economic and technological developments have transformed 'industrial societies' into advanced service economies. The increase in, and rapidity of, the movement of information and people around the world has contributed to arguments that a process of 'globalization' is under way. It is argued that the nation state is becoming less significant at the same time as local identities (note, not *class* identities) are supposedly becoming more important. Social theory has moved on from debates relating to consensus and conflict to embrace (in some quarters) a radical deconstructionism which can call into question the very utility of sociological analysis. Increasingly, 'postmodern' is a label used to describe not only cultural fashions and trends but the nature of society itself. In these societies, we are told 'class', and class analysis, is no longer relevant.

The argument which has been developed in this book is that the most fruitful way forward, as far as class and stratification analysis is concerned, is not to attempt to mount a defence of 'class analysis' as a whole, but to begin by recognizing the diversity of the different approaches within it. The major theoretical dichotomy in the field of class analysis has been conventionally viewed as being that between Marxist and Weberian approaches (McNall et al. 1991: 1). However, in the course of the preceding chapters, a number of other dichotomies, methodological as well as theoretical, have emerged. These dichotomies should not be regarded as representing impermeable boundaries between different approaches, but nevertheless, their identification is a useful heuristic device for the exploration of class and stratification analysis.

In chapter 1 a difference was identified between, on the one hand, the use of 'class' as a straightforward descriptive term to indicate the contours of material and social inequality, and, on the other, the use of the term to describe entities which correspond, in some manner, to actual or potential socio-economic actors, reflecting the structures and relations of power and advantage which have produced these inequalities. As far as the latter use of the term is concerned, descriptive employment or occupational aggregates might be held to give some kind of empirical indication of these entities, but not necessarily to describe them in any exact sense. However, at least in their initial formulations, class analysts such as Goldthorpe and Wright attempted to provide theoretically sophisticated measures of the structure of employment which, it was argued, also described 'classes' empirically as structures of power and advantage.

We have seen that both of these authors have moved somewhat from their original positions, and employment aggregate class analysis has become, in practice, a systematic comparison of 'class' – as measured by a class scheme – with a range of other variables. The structure of employment *is* a useful proxy measure of 'class', but it is not possible to construct a single measure which could successfully capture all of the dimensions going to make up social class – or even structured social inequality.[1] Thus the large-scale sample survey does not capture all of the attributes which might be incorporated in a truly comprehensive measure of class. To take the example of private wealth holdings: large capitalist owners are not included as a separate category in Goldthorpe's scheme, on the grounds that the numbers generated in a survey would be too small to be of significance in subsequent statistical manipulations. Wright does identify ownership separately, but is similar to Goldthorpe in emphasizing that his scheme focuses upon the nature of the *job*, rather than on the characteristics of the individuals in these jobs. Thus when either Wright's or Goldthorpe's scheme is applied to the structure of employment, it is an empirical possibility that individuals in 'proletarian' or 'working-class' jobs might possess considerable wealth holdings.

Both Wright and Goldthorpe have worked with the assumption that classes may be identified within the employment structure independently of consciousness or action – that is, individuals do not have to be conscious of belonging to a class in order to be allocated to a class; classes relate to places, rather than to people. This means that neither Goldthorpe nor Wright has studied the actual *processes* of class formation empirically. As Breen and Rottman (practitioners of the 'Nuffield' approach) have argued: 'class analysis is less concerned with the factors that shape the occupational structure than with elucidating the consequences of class position' (1995: 169). Wright's position might seem to be different here, as he is explicitly committed to Marxist theory which, as we have seen in chapter 2, does give a theoretical account of the processes of class formation. However, this Marxist account is grounded in abstract theorizing, rather than with any reference to actual labour market processes. Indeed, it has been suggested that for the sake of clarity it is useful to distinguish Wright I – the Marxist class theorist – from Wright II – the employment aggregate class analyst. A further limitation, therefore, of the chosen methodology of Wright and Goldthorpe is that it does not incorporate the empirical examination of the structuring of employment and labour markets, or of the generation and consolidation of wealth holdings. From the perspective of class analysis as a whole, these are major gaps in their work (although this criticism does not, as was emphasized in the last chapter, invalidate what the survey approach *has* achieved).

Within the broader tradition of stratification research, the significance of non-economic factors for social differentiation has been emphasized to a greater extent than within employment aggregate class analysis. The extent to which social or cultural, as contrasted to economic, factors should be taken into account in the identification of social classes – and, indeed, whether 'economic' and 'social' factors can be analytically separated – is, therefore, a further distinction within class analysis which may be identified. As we shall see, these kinds of argument have gathered considerable force in recent years given 'postmodern' arguments about the increasing significance of *consumption* in shaping social divisions and social identities.

As has been argued in the last chapter, a failure to recognize the *de facto* diversity of approach within class and stratification analysis has often led to pseudo-debates. By 'pseudo-debate' is meant that class theorists may be arguing on the basis of very different definitions of basic concepts, such as 'class'. It can also refer to significant differences between the protagonists in their underlying theoretical and methodological assumptions regarding the nature of social science investigation. A frequent source of pseudo-debate occurs when evidence and data regarded as valid within the context of a particular approach to 'class analysis' are not regarded as legitimate within another. For example, in respect of debates relating to women and class analysis, Goldthorpe would only accept as relevant evidence deriving from large-scale data sets, and ethnographic and/or case-study data, focusing on gender and class *processes* would be rejected as inadequate (see, for example, Erikson and Goldthorpe's debate (1988) with Leiulsfrud and Woodward (1987)).[2] Similarly, Rose et al. (1987) have argued that ethnographic or case-study evidence which apparently demonstrates the 'deskilling' or 'proletarianization' of supervisory employees cannot be accepted in its own right, but has to be assessed against the evidence of large-scale survey data. These arguments assume that the 'class' concept *is* adequately conceptualized through the application of sociological or 'relational' class schemes to the occupational order – an assumption which, as we have seen, is highly problematic.

Debates and disputes within class analysis, therefore, are often characterized by an extensive borrowing and mixing of evidence and arguments from different approaches, with the unfortunate result that the protagonists are often to be found talking past, rather than to, each other. A common feature of pseudo-debates in class analysis has been that they often stem from a major, if unacknowledged, dichotomy within the field – between, on the one hand, approaches which take 'classes' to be occupational or employment aggregates and, on the other, the socio-historical investigation of the processes of class structuring and their consequences. Thus, in a fairly straightforward fashion, a wide range of theoretical debates within class analysis have been treated as capable of being resolved by the correlation of attitudinal and other variables against occupational- or employment-class aggregates. This would be a viable strategy if such aggregates *did* actually represent 'classes' in a theoretical sense, or if there were general agreement as to the empirical definition of the class concept – but neither of these conditions applies. The sociological convention of treating occupational or employment aggregates as 'classes' has had, and continues to have, many fruitful applications, but it has also been a major source of confusion.

This chapter, therefore, will have two broad objectives. First, we will argue that the complexity of theory and research in class and stratification analysis requires a plurality of methodological approaches. Thus the 'employment aggregate' approach should be complemented by research on class processes and, in particular, research which explores the mechanisms through which labour markets and occupational groups are structured. This objective will incorporate the investigation of a wide range of factors, including status, and other ascriptive factors, as well as class processes. Our discussion will focus on status in particular. Second, we will examine recent developments in social theory, such as post-structuralism and postmodernism, which have suggested that contemporary societies have moved beyond 'class' – and indeed, are no longer usefully described as 'class' societies.

Bringing status back in

As we have seen, one of the major objectives of those who have developed sociological, 'relational' approaches to employment-based class analysis has been to distinguish their measures from prestige or status scales. In chapters 2 and 3, an account has been given of the manner in which, after the Second World War, sociologists who were actively developing the 'conflict' approach in the field of class and stratification theory and research sought to distance themselves from the prevailing tradition of stratification research in the United States. This tradition was represented in the many-volume *Yankee City* series, which drew upon anthropologically inspired community research which began in 1930 (Warner 1963). Warner defined 'social class' as follows:

> By social class is meant two or more orders of people who are believed to be, and are accordingly ranked by the members of the community, in socially superior and inferior positions. Members of a class tend to marry within their own order, but the values of the society permit marriage up and down. A class system also provides that children are born into the same status as their parents. A class society distributes rights and privileges, duties and obligations, unequally among its inferior and superior grades. (1963: 36–7)

This description of 'social classes' closely resembles the first meaning of the class concept identified in chapter 1 (p. 11) – that is, 'class' as prestige, status, or 'style'. Warner's study of 'class' had in fact focused largely on the prestige order. Warner's definition emphasizes the cultural, rather than the economic, construction of class and corresponds more closely to the commonsense definition of 'class' in ordinary usage. Theoretically informed sociologists were at considerable pains to dissociate themselves from this approach and, following Bendix and Lipset (1967a), were emphatic as to the importance of the Weberian distinction between 'class' and 'status'.

Thus in his defence of his version of 'class analysis' against feminist critics, Goldthorpe (1983) laid much emphasis on this distinction between the 'American' and the 'European' traditions of class analysis:

> In the mainstream American literature the dominant ... form of stratification [is seen] in terms of *social status*: that is, as resulting from the differential evaluations of family units that are made by 'the community' ... the term 'social class' [is used] where European writers would be more likely to use that of 'status groups'. (Goldthorpe 1983: 466)

Similarly, when he came to develop his Marxist 'class map', Wright also drew a sharp distinction between the status or prestige order and the analysis of occupational *class* (Wright 1979; chapter 3 above). He has argued that as status bears no relation to production, it has no place in class analysis (Wright 1985: 79).

Economic 'class' factors (such as the nature of market demand,

and the extent and nature of control and authority relationships) *are* analytically separable from 'prestige' factors in the structuring of employment patterns, the allocation of people to jobs, and the determination of levels of material reward. However, in practice, it is exceptionally difficult to draw a clear distinction between them. That these two aspects are inextricably intertwined is demonstrated, for example, by the considerable extent of empirical overlap between 'class' and 'status' (or prestige) occupational classifications, as we have seen in the last chapter. However, the sharp distinction drawn between class and status in the development of the employment aggregate approach has had a number of consequences, not all of which have been positive. These arguments have had a tendency to identify status with *prestige* or social ranking. However, prestige is only one dimension of the complex status concept, and it may be suggested that the attention given to this dimension has tended to overshadow the exploration of the other aspects of status. Additionally, the desire to separate class from status empirically has also tended to deflect attention from the investigation of their interrelations.[3] It will be argued that status relates to the overall structuring of inequality along a number of different dimensions.

We have reviewed the practical difficulties, deriving from the many-faceted structuring of employment relations and the labour market, of developing a precise theoretical measure of 'class'. We have also explored some of the limitations of the employment aggregate approach; for example, the problems raised by the increase in women's paid employment, the difficulties imposed by the methodology of the large-scale sample survey in providing any systematic account of class consciousness and action, of class formation, or of the generation of wealth holdings. Within the employment aggregate approach there have been lively academic debates, but those not directly involved in these research programmes might consider that they have made only a modest contribution to important aspects of our understanding of recent social and political changes. For example, arguments relating to 'class dealignment' in the patterns of voting behaviour in Britain may have been effectively critiqued by demonstrating the continuing association between working-class occupations and non-Conservative voting, but these findings do not illuminate what some might consider the larger issue of the long-term diminution of the 'working class' itself. Relatively speaking, as measured by a class scheme, employment effects might be demonstrated to be similar for men and women, but this does not give much of an insight into the broader changes in employment and family life brought about by the increase in women's employment. The employment aggregate approach tells us little about the recent increase in the extent of economic and social polarization. Indeed, Marshall et al. have argued that there is 'little to be gained by incorporating into the [Nuffield] research programme of class analysis those individuals without employment' (1996: 30), a statement which suggests that it is unlikely to be able to do so in the future.

Thus the employment aggregate approach *must* be complemented by approaches to *social* class analysis which, rather than seeking to distance themselves from the status concept, are premised upon the interrelationship of the 'economic' and the 'social'. In addition to the investigation of employment aggregates, and equally significant for the understanding of class and stratification, is the study of the *processes* of the active structuring of occupations and groups. Work in this area has been both 'Marxist' and 'Weberian' in its theoretical inspiration, but has been different from the occupational aggregation approach in respect of its methodology as well as its assumptions about the nature of social reality. Much empirical work in this area has been recently associated with a 'realist' approach. Rather than being based upon the large-scale sample survey, these investigations of class structure and action have utilized, above all, the *case study*. We will return to these arguments at the end of this section, but first we will briefly indicate how an approach which stresses the interrelatedness of class and status might illuminate a number of important issues.

The Weberian concept of status has a number of different dimensions which have not always been clearly identified by those who have used it (see chapter 2 above). The status concept may usefully be considered to have three dimensions: (a) to refer to actual prestige groupings or consciousness communities; (b) more diffuse notions of 'lifestyle' or 'social standing' (these first two aspects will obviously overlap to a considerable extent); and (c) non-market-based claims to material entitlements or 'life chances'. The first aspect of the status concept identified above – prestige groupings – is, as we have seen, the aspect from which 'theoretical', employment-based 'class analysis' sought to differentiate itself most sharply. Such groupings are here described as *consciousness communities*: 'In contrast to classes, *status groups* are normally communities' (Weber in Gerth and Mills 1948: 186; emphasis in original). 'Community' in this sense need not necessarily imply residential propinquity. Not surprisingly, Warner's *Yankee City* provides a good historical example of these kinds of linkages: 'When George Washington made his grand presidential tour of the new nation ... he came not only as the Father of his Country and leader of all his people, but as a visiting Virginia aristocrat ... when he arrived in Yankee City he was entertained in the great houses of the town by people who knew him as an equal' (1963: 15). 'Community' in this sense describes associational groups sharing common cultures (Crompton 1987). The material wealth and power of those in the 'great houses' indicates their dominant *class* situation; such groupings, however, also maintain their dominance through the manner in which they deploy their *cultural* resources. Scott (1991; see also Scott 1996) has documented the manner in which the British ruling class is reproduced through a network of social activities including private London clubs, the residual activities of the London 'season', attendance at major sporting and social events, and so on. The British public schools, as well as Oxbridge, also serve to inculcate the kind of 'correct' behaviour which is likely to facilitate recruitment to superior positions: 'Without any need for a consciously intended bias in recruitment, the established 'old boys' sponsor the recruitment through their networks of contacts of each new generation of old boys' (1991: 117). Status as prestige, therefore, plays a central role in the processes of class formation and reproduction. In the next chapter, we will explore Bourdieu's notion of 'cultural capital', which examines these processes in some detail.

The ruling-class 'consciousness communities' briefly described above are clearly associated with a distinctive lifestyle, as Weber argued: 'In content, status honor is normally expressed by the fact that above all a specific *style of life* can be expected' (Weber in Gerth and Mills 1948: 187; emphasis in original). Whereas 'class' is concerned with the production of goods, status is concerned with their consumption. This has been described by Turner (1988: 66) as including 'the totality of cultural practices such as dress, speech, outlook and bodily dispositions'. 'Lifestyle' categories need not necessarily correspond exactly to consciousness communities (although they might reflect an aspiration to join them), but they are clearly linked to each other. However, the topic of consumption and its relation to class and stratification also raises a broader range of issues. As we have seen in the last chapter, rising living standards in the West have brought issues relating to consumption into sharper focus, and it is increasingly argued that an investigation of consumption-related concerns should replace an outdated 'productivism' in class and stratification analysis. Although these arguments will by no means be taken on board in their entirety, consumption in this broader sense – to include issues such as, for example, the consumption of the environment and the construction of self-identities – may be seen to have an impact on class and stratification systems. Besides the role of specific lifestyles in the reproduction of established groupings, therefore, 'lifestyle' in this broader sense may be seen as contributing to the emergence of newly differentiated groups, and supplying new focuses for the articulation of interests and concerns. In particular, these issues are argued to be central to the emergence and identification of the 'new middle classes', a topic which will be explored at greater length in a later chapter .

The third aspect of the status concept which may be identified is its use to describe non-market-based claims to material entitlements or 'life chances'. Thus the term may be used to describe pre-industrial 'estates' in contrast to 'classes', or the traditional claims of a particular caste grouping. Weber described status situation, in contrast to the economically determined class situation, as 'every typical component of the life fate of men that is determined by a specific, positive or negative, social estimation of *honor*' (Weber in Gerth and Mills 1948: 187). Even in contemporary capitalist societies, the occupational order is socially, as well as economically, structured. An instance which has already been explored at some length is that of gender. Occupational segregation means that the 'life fates' associated with particular occupations have been crucially affected by the gender of the likely occupant. The occupational order is also shaped by explicit status claims. One example would be that of professionalism. Many professional groups (such as doctors, or lawyers) rest a part of their claim to material rewards on their undertaking *not* to exploit their skills to their full market advantage, and to practise 'institutionalized altruism' in respect of their clients (Crompton 1990a).

One of the most frequently employed uses of the concept of status as entitlement, however, has been in T. H. Marshall's development of the concept of *citizenship*.[4] As we shall see in a later chapter, Marshall has described the development of social citizenship – that is, the right of all 'citizens' to services such as education and benefits such as those provided by the welfare state – to be one of the most important developments to affect stratification systems in the twentieth century. The analysis of the interrelations between 'class' and 'citizenship', therefore, provides another potentially fruitful way forward for class and stratification analysis.

Large-scale, aggregate-level 'class analysis' in sociology, as in the work of Goldthorpe and Wright, has sought systematically to exclude considerations of 'status' from its investigations. In this book it is being suggested that an explicit recognition of the *inter-relationship* of class and status is also necessary. It is further being argued that a different methodological approach will also be required. Large data sets and sample surveys have had, and continue to have, a central place in empirical investigations of the 'class structure'. However, it has been argued that the investigation of the *processes* of class structuring – which will include the examination of aspects of status – requires an alternative methodology. Similarly, although large data sets may provide useful attitudinal data relating to topics such as class consciousness, the dynamics of the processes and organizations which shape this consciousness can only be explored using a methodology which views the social unit (the neighbourhood, the trade union, the workgroup, the political party) as a whole – that is, the *case study*.

Many recent empirical investigations of class processes which have employed the case-study method have been carried out by sociologists who have self-consciously embraced a 'realist' approach to their empirical work (Bagguley et al. 1989; Savage et al. 1992). However, the methodology of the case study is not specific to realism. Indeed, it may be argued that the case study still remains as the bedrock of empirical investigation in the social sciences, despite the fact that, as a research method, it has been variously dismissed as unscientific, capable only of generating, not testing, hypotheses, prone to bias and arbitrary interpretation, and so on. The methodological issues raised by these criticisms are complex. They will therefore be simply stated as follows. (a) The case-study approach should not be taken as synonymous only with qualitative methods, or ethnography. A case study may be quantitative, as was, for example, the early investigation of the 'Affluent Worker' by Goldthorpe et al. Case studies of particular occupations have also frequently incorporated extensive programmes of interviewing and the quantitative analysis of interview data – as, for example, in Newby's study of agricultural workers. (b) Case studies are in fact the *only* method whereby collective action may be explored in its context; they facilitate theoretical/logical thinking and thus *causal* explanations. Often, cases are judged on their 'typicality', but, as Mitchell (1983) has argued, they should be judged on the basis of the validity of their analysis, rather than their typicality. In any event, case studies are not immune to empirical evaluation. Besides the relatively orthodox strategy of replication, the theoretical reasoning developed in the context of a particular case study may be subjected to empirical scrutiny through a process of comparison, particularly cross-national comparisons (Pickvance 1992). These points are made in order to emphasize that to advocate the method of the case study should not be taken to imply a recourse to mere description, or to abandon any attempt at the rigorous investigation of the topics at issue.

In this chapter so far, we have argued that the limitations of employment aggregate class analysis serve to underline the argument that class analysis in its entirety should be seen as incorporating case studies of the processes of class formation, as well as the investigation of class effects. As we shall see, such an approach will reveal the complex sources of labour market structuring, and in particular, the role of social status. These issues will be further discussed in later chapters. Class analysis, however, has from its infancy also been associated with broader issues than either labour market structuring or its impact on individuals. That is, it has been intimately bound up with theories of society and broader social change, and it is to these topics that we now turn.

Recent social theory

As discussed in the Introduction to this chapter, debates relating to social theory have always had a significant impact on class analysis. During the 1980s and 1990s, many of these debates have centred on critiques of 'Modernity', rather than 'Industrial Society'. 'Modernity' describes a broad sweep of social change incorporating more than just 'Industrialism', or the development of capitalism. It develops a similar contrast with 'traditional' societies, but incorporates changes in ideas, and cultural and political change (including the emergence of the nation state) as well. It has been argued that the project of modernity began with the efforts of the Enlightenment thinkers 'to develop objective science, universal morality and law, and autonomous art according to their inner logic' (Habermas 1983). Thus modernity is concerned with the processes of rationalization, order, and the identification of the systems and structures which achieve this ordering. The development of capitalist industrialism and the modern world occurred together; indeed, the development of the social sciences – as represented by the works of Marx and Weber – might be regarded as integral to modernity as a project.

In contrast, 'post-structuralist' theorizing rejects the notion that there can be any constant social unity. Rather, order is seen as having been discursively *imposed.* Rational order (or rather, the creation of the disciplined self) is seen as having been a part of the Enlightenment project. Foucault (1977) argues that 'man' is not and cannot be the centre, the knowing subject, the proper study of the human sciences. Rather, it is discursive 'scientific' practices which constitute 'man'.[5] Thus the 'modern' subject is not a constant 'thing' (i.e. there is no 'essential', universal, human being), but rather, a discursive creation. 'Post-structuralist' theory has much influenced Laclau and Mouffe's 'Post-Marxist' critique of classical Marxism. Laclau and Mouffe (1985, 1987) have developed a critique of Marxism which emphasizes the discursively constructed nature of human society; 'discourse' replaces 'ideology' as a central concept in 'post-Marxism'.[6] Marxist theory and its development stands accused of 'essentialism' and 'dualism', and in arguments which echo those of 'New Times' theorists Laclau and Mouffe also challenge the primacy given to 'class' in classical Marxist theory: *'There are* interests, but these are precarious historical products which are always subjected to processes of dissolution and redefinition. What there are not, however, are *objective* interests, in the sense in which they are postulated in the "false consciousness" approach' (1987: 97). Thus the working class has no privileged role in the anti-capitalist struggle, and other radical anti-capitalist social movements such as environmental groups, not linked to any particular position in the social structure, will assume importance (1987: 104). In contrast to what they perceive as the essentialism and economic reductionism (or 'monism') of classical Marxism, Laclau and Mouffe suggest that oppositional struggles in fact only emerge when the democratic discourse becomes available, when ideas of liberty and equality become humanly *possible.* This occurred, they suggest, at the moment of the French Revolution, which began the 'democratic revolution'. The absolute power of 'the people' was asserted, thus introducing 'something truly new at the level of the social imaginary' (1985: 155). The *ancien régime*, which had rested upon a perception of society in which individuals appeared fixed in differential positions, and was justified by the logic of the divine will, at this point in history received its fatal blow.

Not surprisingly, there have been substantial responses to Laclau and Mouffe's 'post-Marxist' arguments from left theorists who have maintained that classes, and class action, remain central to Marxist political thought (Geras 1986, Wood 1986). Wood argues that Laclau and Mouffe's analysis of 'classical Marxism' rests upon a caricature which effectively reduces Marxist theory to an economically and technologically over-determined 'straw person'. 'Democratic discourse', she argues, is *constituted* by class conflict, rather than being its source, and there was a long history of class conflict *before* the French Revolution. In contrast to Laclau and Mouffe, Wood emphasizes the *social* (rather than 'discursive') origins of political movements.

Thus post-Marxism has an emphasis upon the constructed and contingent nature of interests (including class interests) which are brought into being by discourse rather than as a consequence of one's place in the economic order (as orthodox Marxists would argue). Structures are, so to speak, 'built into' individuals, much as a speaker 'knows' a range of grammar and syntactical rules 'which are not contained within the speech act, but are nevertheless necessary to either understand it or to produce it' (Giddens 1986: 61). Structure in this sense is an 'absent totality' (ibid.). Thus in post-structuralist analyses, 'class' is a function of narrative and language, rather than being 'produced' by economic circumstances or even cultural developments. For example, Joyce, writing of the nineteenth century in Britain, argues that: 'Class identities were, therefore, a product of arguments about meanings, arguments which were primarily political in character. Class does not seem to have been the collective cultural experience of new economic classes produced by the Industrial Revolution' (1995: 322).

'Postmodernism' is closely related to the post-structuralist critique of modernity in that it is characterized by a similar emphasis on plurality and diversity, and on the absence of any 'totalizing' societal force. It is a term currently in widespread use within the humanities and social sciences, but it is one which is exceptionally difficult to define – not least because its ramifications can be extended to incorporate practically every aspect of the human condition. In art and culture (understood as symbolic representations) postmodernism has been contrasted with the modernist aesthetic ideal, which, although laying stress on creativity and self-invention, was seen as exhausted, and institutionalized in the museum and the academy. In contrast, postmodernism in the arts is characterized by:

> the effacement of the boundary between art and everyday life; the collapse of the hierarchical distinction between high and mass/popular culture; a stylistic promiscuity favouring eclecticism and the mixing of codes; parody, pastiche, irony, playfulness and the celebration of the surface 'deathlessness' of culture; the decline of the originality/genius of the artistic producer; and the assumption that art can only be repetition. (Featherstone 1991: 7–8)

Thus broken pediments on skyscrapers, the artfully mixed and pastiched covers of magazines, and pop music phenomena such as punk rock and the 'rave' scene – are all manifestations of these cultural trends.

The shift from 'modernism' to 'postmodernism' in artistic production is seen as being accompanied by a corresponding shift from 'modernity' to 'postmodernity' in social thought. As Featherstone has noted, therefore, 'to speak of postmodernity is to suggest an epochal shift or break from modernity involving the emergence of a new social totality' (1991: 3). As Kumar hàs argued, the idea of postmodernity breaks down the dividing-lines between the different realms of society – political, economic, social and cultural. The different realms are collapsing into each other, but this pluralism:

> is not ordered and integrated according to any discernible principle. There is not, or at least no longer, any controlling and directing force to give it shape and meaning – neither in the economy, as Marxists had argued, nor in the polity, as liberals had thought, nor even, as conservatives had urged, in history and tradition. There is simply a more or less random, directionless flux across all sectors of society. The boundaries between them are dissolved, leading however not to a neoprimitivist wholeness but to a postmodern condition of fragmentation. (1995: 102–3)

However, as we shall see, some sociologists adopting the 'postmodern' label claim to have identified in *consumption* a new 'controlling and directing' force (Pakulski and Waters 1996b). We will return to these arguments in the next section of this chapter.

Some have argued that a shift to a new social totality is occurring because of the inherent weaknesses of the Enlightenment project. The calculation and rationality of social thought might have created substantial material advances – but it has also contributed to the horrors of Nazi death camps, and Stalin's Soviet Union. Others have located this shift in the increasingly frantic pace brought about by modernity itself. Harvey (1990) argues that in the modern world, the dimensions of space and time have been subject to the persistent pressure of capital circulation, accumulation and crisis, and that, in periods of uncertainty, the search for a solution inevitably involves a loss of confidence in rational, 'scientific' reasoning. He suggests that:

> The crisis of overaccumulation that began in the late 1960s and which came to a head in 1973 has generated exactly such a result. The experience of time and space has changed, the confidence in the association between scientific and moral judgements has collapsed, aesthetics has

triumphed over ethics as a prime focus of social and intellectual concern; images dominate narratives, ephemerality and fragmentation
take precedence over eternal truths and unified politics, and explanations have shifted from the realm of material and political-economic
groundings towards a consideration of autonomous cultural and political practices (1990: 327–8)

In short, the economic and political changes described in chapter 4
above have also been associated with profound *cultural* changes
which, some have argued, are reshaping the very nature of the
world. The demise of modernity, therefore, is also argued to signify
the end of the era of 'totalizing discourses', or 'meta-narratives'
(large-scale theoretical interpretations of purportedly universal
application) which seek to explain and control the human condition.

Theorists of postmodernity, therefore, emphasize the growing significance of cultural and consumption practices for our understandings of identities and behaviour in contemporary societies. This
emphasis conflicts with a 'class' model (loosely defined) of explanation, which would emphasize the significance of relations of production (rather than consumption), and economic, rather than cultural,
locations and processes. In the next chapter, we will examine more
closely some of the different arguments relating to the growing significance of consumption, including topics relating to consumption
sector cleavages, the blurring of 'production' and 'consumption'
identities in employment, and the 'cultural production' of classes –
particularly the middle classes. In the rest of this chapter, however,
we will examine the broader claims of some postmodernists, in particular, claims that a fundamental 'societal shift' is under way as we
approach the end of the second millennium.

Farewell to class societies?

An extraordinarily wide range of arguments have been engaged in
amongst those authors who have commented, in one way or
another, on future societal developments, and it is impossible to discuss all of them. Two themes, however, have been relatively constant: first, the trend towards increasing individualization; and
second, the increased emphasis given to culturalist, rather than
materialist, explanations.

In its simplest formulation, 'individualization' describes a situation in which individuals are relatively unconstrained by law, tradition or other social ties, and thus are 'free' to make choices and

develop as they wish. 'Individualization' may be seen to have been integral to the development of the Enlightenment project, which was concerned to liberate the individual from tradition and superstition in favour of rationality and science. As both Marx and Weber argued, the 'sovereign' individual, able freely to alienate (i.e. sell) his or her own labour, was necessary for the development of capitalist industrialism (see chapter 1). There is nothing new, therefore, about the development of individualization as such.

However, it has recently been argued that in 'late' or 'reflexive' modernity, there has been a 'categorical shift' (Beck 1992: 127) in the relationship between the individual and society. In brief, Beck argues that changes in both family and local communities – the increasing rate of family dissolution, the disintegration of older (particularly working-class) communities,[7] together with changes in the nature of work itself (discussed in chapter 3) has meant that individuals have increasingly become the source of, responsible for, their 'own' biography, that is, people are forced to *choose*. At the same time, the marketization and standardization of biographical 'resources' means that this choice is itself programmed:

> The individual is indeed removed from traditional commitments and support relationships, but exchanges them for the constraints of existence in the labour market and as a consumer. . . . The place of *traditional* ties and social forms (social class, nuclear family) is taken by *secondary* agencies and institutions, which stamp the biography of the individual and make that person dependent upon fashions, social policy, economic cycles and markets. (1992: 131).

In a parallel fashion, Giddens argues that the erosion of traditional ties and conventional social arrangements (e.g. in which an individuals social location operated as an indicator of their reliability as far as other individuals were concerned) has resulted in the emergence of the 'pure relationship', that is, a relationship independent of formal ties which is entered into out of choice and then 'reflexively organized, in an open fashion, and on a continuous basis' (1991: 91). The individual, increasingly, is responsible not only for this organization of interpersonal relations but also for the body; anorexia nervosa, for example, is described as 'a pathology of reflexive self-control' (1991: 105). It is not too difficult to see that increasing individualization, if indeed it is under way, would be contrary to the development of social classes, particularly the development of *collective* class *identities*. It is somewhat debatable, however, whether a relative absence or erosion of collective identity (even if it is occurring) indicates that a society is no longer class-divided.

As has been noted above, 'postmodernism' originally developed as a critique of culture and aesthetics, and this critique has been developed into the assertion that cultural consumption has itself become a (if not the) driving force in postmodern society. In the next chapter, we will be exploring a range of different arguments relating to the topic of consumption, but for the moment we may rest with Kumar's useful summary statement of the argument: 'In the late capitalist stage, culture itself becomes the prime determinant of social, economic, political and even psychological reality ... Culture has become "a product in its own right"; the process of cultural consumption is no longer merely an adjunct but the very essence of capitalist functioning' (1995: 115–16). This assertion of the primacy of culture and consumption, therefore, would seem to be in direct contradiction to the assumption that in *class* societies, the processes of economic production and the market serve to delineate interests, identities and action. If broadly materialist explanations are to be rejected, can it be argued that we are, any longer, living in class societies?

Although Lash and Urry (1994) still retain the use of the word 'class' to describe broad occupational categories, their discussion of current and future trends suggests that a profound societal transformation is, indeed, taking place. They describe a four-stage model of capitalist development: first, locally competitive liberal capitalism, which prevailed in the nineteenth century, followed by (in the twentieth century) 'organized' capitalism. 'Organized' capitalism was nationally based, and describes, in broad outline, the development of large bureaucratic firms, together with labour union organization and governmental strategies of economic management – that is, the set of societal arrangements that have been described as 'Fordist' (see chapter 4). 'Disorganized capitalism'[8] describes the 'post-Fordist' breakdown of 'Organized capitalism'. It is characterized by fragmented and flexible production systems, in which capitalism itself becomes global as 'the various subjects and objects of the capitalist political economy circulate not only along routes of greater and greater distance, but also ... at ever greater *velocity*' (1994: 2). Lash and Urry argue that out of this third stage there is developing a global 'economy of signs and space', characterized by an increasingly significant 'reflexive' human subjectivity, arising out of a process of de-traditionalization in which social agents are 'set free' in order to be self-monitoring and reflexive.

Flows – of people, of information, of ideas, of images, of technol-
ogies, of capital – rather than structures, dominate economies of
signs and space. These flows are evident in global capital markets,
controlled from head office sites in global cities, and globalized
popular culture, as well as in mass tourism and migration. Production, as well as the workers in it, has itself taken on a 'reflexive'
character, as information systems become increasingly central. The
worker, they argue, is increasingly no longer circumscribed by the
constraints of 'structure', but is responsible for its transformation
(1994: 122). The massive growth in both services and cultural production only serves to reinforce this reflexivity. In 'socio-economies'
it is culture, rather than economic position, that gives meaning to
social practices, and it is consciousness or reflexivity that determines
class (i.e. occupational) structure. Often, Lash and Urry's tone is a
positive one, for example describing the 'reintegration of conceptu-
alisation and execution' in the circumstances of information-rich,
reflexive, production systems. However, they also identify the simul-
taneous expansion of 'wild zones', such as the 'collapsing empires' of
state socialism, as well as the areas and localities into which are concentrated the very poorest or 'underclass', that is, those who have lost
out following the decline of unskilled jobs that pay a living wage
(these jobs *were* available during the Fordist/corporatist compromise).

Lash and Urry's argument is dense and complex, and a detailed
critique will not be developed here. However, before we consider
the broad implications of their arguments, we will review in brief a
very similar, and more explicit, set of claims that 'class is dead' in
'postmodern' societies. In a similar fashion to Lash and Urry, Pakulski and Waters (1996b; see also Waters 1996) periodize capitalist
development, but into three phases, rather than four. The term 'economic class' society they largely reserve for capitalist industrialism
in the eighteenth and nineteenth centuries (the competitive liberal
capitalism identified by Lash and Urry). During this phase, they
argue, interest groups were *economically* determined (bourgeoisie,
proletariat, etc.), and this was reflected in patterns of domination
and conflict. Culture was also class-divided. The next phase they
identify is the 'organized class' or 'corporatist' phase, which is paralleled by Lash and Urry's 'organized capitalist/Fordist' description.
'Classes' are politically organized, and 'the cultural realm ... unified
under the state umbrella ... It can thus be turned into an industri-
alised or mass culture' (Waters 1996: 73). The third (and currently
emerging) phase is that of 'status-conventionalism', in which stratification emerges from the sphere of culture and its consumption.

Pakulski and Waters employ a definition of 'class', and 'class society', which is both comprehensive and specific, and which is modelled on Marx and Engels' more economistic formulations. Class, they argue, describes the primary causal role of capital and labour market capacities in structuring material interests and social relationships; thus it should give rise to the most important social groupings in society; these groupings (classes) give rise to the most important and persisting bases for consciousness, identity and action outside the arena of economic production; and they are also the principal 'makers of history' (Pakulski and Waters 1996b: 10. It may be noted that on this definition, only very brief periods of history – if indeed, any at all – would correspond to the definition of an economic class society). Pakulski and Waters argue that emergent status conventionalism is under way because of the increase in individualism brought about by changes in the nature of employment, together with the declining capacity of the national state – the key actor in organized-class society – to control the economy. In part this is because of economic globalization, but it is also a result of increasing pressures on the state from different interest groups, articulated by 'identity politics'. In 'post-class', postmodern, status-conventional societies, occupation becomes a badge of status, together with other dimensions of status that have become 'value infused, symbolicized and reflexive ... Identity is ... not linked either to property or organizational position. Under conditions of advanced affluence, styles of consumption and commitment become socially salient as markers and delimiters' (Pakulski and Waters 1996b: 156). Thus, they argue, culture and consumption practices have emerged as significant causal forces in the 'multiple mosaic of status communities' (Waters 1996: 80) that characterize 'status-conventional' societies.

Above we have briefly reviewed two ambitious attempts to develop what are, in fact, new postmodern 'meta-narratives' which, the authors argue, will enable us to better grasp the rapid social changes and developments associated with 'late', 'reflexive', or 'post' modernity.[9] Both Lash and Urry, and Pakulski and Waters, argue that a 'societal shift' is under way in that *consumption* and its associated practices have become the driving forces of postmodern societies. Both emphasize that instability, fragmentation, individualization and social fluidity have become more prevalent in postmodern societies, in contrast with the collectively organized 'class' stabilities of the 'Fordist' era. Both, moreover, are explicit that 'economies of signs and space' or 'multiple mosaics of status communities' are characterized by conflicts and inequalities – Lash and Urry, in particular, devote considerable attention to the question of the 'underclass'.

Because both sets of arguments are extremely complex, it is not too difficult to make criticisms of various points of detail. Lash and Urry's discussion of the 'collective reflexivity' of Japanese production systems, for example, makes little mention of the great majority (around 80 per cent) of the Japanese labour force who are not employed by the major firms offering these conditions – and more generally, their description of changes in the nature of employment pay little attention to the explosion of routine, low-level, service work. As we have noted in the last chapter (p. 105), the use of the Alford index, which Pakulski and Waters use to describe the decline of 'class politics', has been widely criticized as not taking into account the significance of shifts in the occupational structure. More generally, the point may be made that the trends these authors emphasize are not particularly new but, rather, represent the continuous development of features which have always been present in different societies at different times. For example, the individual's 'working' on the body is hardly new – it may be suggested that the nineteenth-century woman lacing herself into her corset is closely paralleled by the 'reflexively modern' woman working out in the aerobics class, for example.

Debates about 'post-industrialism' are not new either (see Bell 1973). Sayer and Walker have argued at some length that the supposed economic and occupational shift to services has been much exaggerated. Many jobs labelled as 'services', they argue, are in fact productive activities: 'A legal brief or an environmental impact statement is simply intellectual craft applied to paper, as a chair is woodcraft applied to lumber' (1992: 63); similar arguments, they suggest, might be applied to many financial 'services', transport, and information services such as computer packages. They argue that the 'transition to the service economy' is in fact better conceptualized as a 'widening and deepening' of the social and technical divisions of labour, itself a part of the more general process of industrial evolution and capitalist development. Complex hierarchies have evolved, and the division of labour has become extended, as in, for example, pre-production design and marketing, resulting in the growth of 'indirect labour' in respect of the production process. Thus Sayer and Walker insist upon 'certain indelible continuities with the past, continuities which the theory of services denies' (1992: 57) – in short, they insist that *productive*, rather than consumption, activities are still most important in contemporary societies, and the concepts developed to analyse production remain the most significant explanatory tools.

The explanatory primacy of consumption, therefore, remains a contested topic (although perhaps we should say topics, because, as we shall see in the next chapter, there are many different facets to these discussions). We will be discussing a number of the very different issues raised by postmodern theorists in later sections of this book. However, there is a point of general criticism, concerning an important underlying assumption made by both Lash and Urry and Pakulski and Waters, that it is useful to raise at this stage. This is the assumption of what Waters describes as the 'perfectionalisation of the market'. To put the point in its full context: 'The force of detraditionalisation might be better expressed as the "perfectionalisation of the market" ' (1996: 82). To make the same argument in another way, one of the reasons why consumption achieves explanatory primacy is because consumers (with resources) are increasingly able to get what they want; one of the reasons why consumers are able to get what they want is that information has become increasingly available because all kinds of markets have been 'detraditionalized'. For example, Lash and Urry (1994: 286–8) describe the transformation of the financial markets of the City of London from a closely-packed square mile which used to operate on the basis of proximity and close personal ties into a deregulated, unconstrained, detraditionalized arena in which massive fortunes were made and lost during the 1980s.

'Detraditionalization' means that everything has become 'marketized', the postmodernists argue.[10] Niche marketing and fashion shapes the choice of the 'neo-tribe', 'reflexive consumer' and 'status communities', rather than the preferences shaped by place and traditional 'belonging'. Individual rewards are increasingly separated from the 'closed' arrangements of status traditions and organizational hierarchies, and Waters (1996: 83) argues that the cultural economy is becoming a measure of individual worth; this may be described as the marketizing of the personality. However, the extent to which markets have in fact been 'perfectionalized' (or indeed, may ever be so rendered) may be seriously questioned. Indeed, the systematic problematizing of market rationality has formed the bedrock of the sociological critique of economics. As Durkheim argued nearly a century ago: 'All that is in the contract is not contractual'; that is, contracts invariably incorporate *social* as well as economic or rational considerations (consider, for example, the labour contract). Markets cannot function in the absence of a parallel structure of social relationships. It is not simply that due regard has to be given to the cultural context of market relationships (for example, there are considerable cross-national variations in the extent to which they are expected to be accompanied by gift-giving), but rather, that the market itself is a social construct, that is embedded in constructs of social relations (Granovetter 1985). Moreover, economic relations are by no means coordinated entirely (or even largely) by markets, but also by custom, coercion, and democratic negotiation (Sayer and Walker 1992).

In short, to the extent that the thesis of detraditionalization rests upon the parallel thesis of the perfectionalization of the market, then there are considerable problems in making this case. Indeed, it is somewhat paradoxical that the economic success of many of the nation states whose emergence has been identified as central to the process of world-wide 'globalization' (including Japan, and the 'tiger economies' of South East Asia) is grounded in firms and organizations structured along both actual and quasi-family principles, and characterized by extensive recruitment (of key personnel) along these lines. Rather than the market having been perfectionalized, it may be suggested that there have in fact always been fluctuations in the extent to which market principles have been adopted as a mode of societal regulation; both *de jure* as well as *de facto*. The politics of the present era have indeed seen a shift towards the marketization of society but it is by no means complete, and as Polanyi has argued: 'To allow the market mechanism to be the sole director of the fate of human beings and their natural environment ... would result in the demolition of society' (1957: 73).

Discussion and conclusions

In this chapter, we have first developed our critique of employment aggregate class analysis, emphasizing both the difficulties of developing a truly comprehensive measure of 'class' within the employment structure, as well as the gaps in its coverage. In particular, it has been pointed out that neither of the major practitioners of the employment aggregate approach (Goldthorpe and Wright) has incorporated any empirical examination of the *processes* of class formation – for example, the accumulation of wealth, and/or the structuring of employment and labour markets – in their programmes of class analysis. Rather, their empirical investigations have focused upon the *effects* of class (as they have defined the concept), rather than its origins. It was suggested that the examination of class processes would require a rather different methodology, in particular, the case-study approach, and would also require the systematic incorporation and examination of a number of factors – in particular, social status – which Goldthorpe and Wright have (on methodological grounds) systematically excluded from their investigations.

In contrast, those authors who have focused their attention on whether or not a 'societal shift' (i.e. from a class society to something else) is under way *have* tended to examine in some detail the modes and processes of class formation. Thus they have argued that in the individualized postmodern present, processes of consumption, rather than production, both shape identities as well as providing the rationale for new social groupings. In this process, they suggest, older (class-based) institutions either decline or change their character.

We have already indicated a number of difficulties with these 'societal shift' arguments, and our critique will be developed in subsequent chapters. However, in conclusion to this chapter, it is important to emphasize again a very important point. This is that those sociologists engaged in the discussion of medium and long-term societal developments (this would include Giddens and Beck, as well as Lash and Urry and Pakulski and Waters) should be seen as being engaged in a very different type of sociological enterprise as compared to the comparative survey work of Goldthorpe and Wright (II). It is true that employment aggregate and societal shift debates *are* both elements of the discourse of 'class analysis' as a whole, but both their methods and major foci are very different. It is frankly confusing when firm distinctions are not drawn between these rather different aspects of the field. Unfortunately, these distinctions have not been maintained in recent discussions and debates (and this criticism, as we have seen in the last chapter, may be made of the defenders of 'class analysis' as well as the critics), which have, as a consequence, not clarified matters as much as they might have done.

A recent contribution (Lee and Turner 1996) illustrates this problem. Lee and Turner (following Holton 1996; see also Holton and Turner 1989) make a distinction between the 'strong' and 'weak' usage of class in sociology. It will be argued here that this distinction is in fact a misleading one. The notion of 'strong' versus 'weak' implies a continuum: that what is under discussion is 'more' or 'less' of the same phenomenon, capacity, or whatever. However, Lee and Turner's characterization does not describe a continuum, but what are, in fact, a set of contrasts. Furthermore, it may be argued that there are very important mis-allocations (of class analysts) within these contrasts.

The 'death of class', as described by Lee and Turner, concerns 'the theoretical and methodological issue of whether class is simply a metaphor for socio-political aspirations or really works as a concept and a tool for sociological research' (1996: 3). This implies that we have to make a choice between the different meanings of the class concept (described in chapter 1), whereas it has been stressed throughout this book that the most sensible way forward is to recognize the plurality of different approaches to and meanings of class, rather than choose between them. Lee and Turner identify 'strong' class theory with Marxism. 'Weak' class theories are described as merely asserting that there are 'empirically identifiable groupings of individuals who have certain analytically significant situations (such as their possession of property or highly paid skills) in common' (1996: 9–10). 'Weak' class theory is described as Weberian. 'Strong' class theory is described as representing a 'structural' sociological approach, 'weak' class theory as an 'action' approach, as follows:

'strong'	'weak'
Marx	Weber
structure	action

Lee and Turner suggest that class analysis is often characterized by explanatory failure, in which 'strong' approaches fall back on 'weaker' explanations in the light of contradictions. They repeat one of Lockwood's criticisms of the problem of action in Marxist class theory discussed in the last chapter – that contingent historical circumstances can always be identified in order to explain the failure of proletarian action to materialize. Wright is characterized as a leading example of 'strong' (Marxist) class theory, whereas Goldthorpe is a leading example of 'weak' (Weberian) class theory. However, it may be noted that on the basis of Lee and Turners' own description of 'weak' class usage, then Wright II would, in fact, be placed in this ('weak') category.

Contrary to Lee and Turner, it may be argued that Marx's and Weber's theoretical accounts of the significance of social classes, and class conflict, for the nature and development of industrial capitalist societies do not give 'stronger' or 'weaker' accounts of the same phenomenon, rather, they are *different* accounts (see Crompton and Gubbay 1977; also chapters 1 and 2 this volume). Both Marx and

Weber were concerned to develop theories which explained the nature and development of capitalist industrialism, and, as we have seen, there were fundamental differences between them. Weber rejected Marxist materialism, identifying alternative sources of societal structuring. Weber was an advocate of 'value-free' social science, Marx was a political activist. Marx considered class struggle inevitable, Weber thought it contingent. Thus Marxist ('strong') class theory cannot be described as 'falling back on' 'weak' Weberian class theory (e.g. in response to the failure of class action) as they are *alternative* theories.

Neither of these nineteenth/early twentieth-century sociologists actually engaged in large-scale, cross-nationally comparative, sample surveys. To the extent that Wright may be described as a Marxist (that is, Wright I), then clearly, he may be distinguished from Goldthorpe in respect of his theoretical orientations. Goldthorpe has made it clear that he does not consider his version of 'class analysis' to be guided by any particular theory, and, as we saw in the last chapter, the changes in his approach make it increasingly inappropriate to describe him as a 'Weberian'. Nevertheless, there are clear theoretical differences between Goldthorpe and Wright. In respect of their empirical work, however, we have seen that Wright's and Goldthorpe's positions have converged over the years. There are very many similarities and parallels between Erikson and Goldthorpe and Wright II, and these have been acknowledged by representatives of both 'sides'. Although, therefore, Goldthorpe and Wright might represent different theoretical traditions, in respect of their empirical work, there are many similarities.

In this chapter, it has been argued, therefore, that one major contrast which should be made within different approaches to class analysis is between the relatively narrow, 'independent variable' specialty of the employment aggregate approach on the one hand, and the more inclusive and wide-ranging 'societal shift'-type arguments on the other. From this perspective, Wright II and Goldthorpe are both in the *same* category of 'class analysts'. To the extent that relevant empirical arguments are developed, then there are and can be useful dialogues between practitioners of these rather different types of 'class analysis'. For example, in a subsequent chapter we shall see that 'employment aggregate' practitioners have provided relevant evidence relating to claims that have been made regarding the individual characteristics of the so-called 'underclass', and in the previous chapter, we have briefly reviewed the debate relating to class dealignment in voting behaviour.

To repeat, therefore, one of the concluding points of our previous chapter, holistic characterizations of the nature of contemporary societies, and the possible shifts in their essential characteristics, should be distinguished from empirical studies of the 'class structure' in which a classification of employment (i.e. class scheme) is used as an independent variable. The employment aggregate approach can be used to provide empirical evidence relating to specific propositions developed by theorists of society and social change, thus the two approaches are related to each other. However, abstract theoretical arguments concerning the 'death of class' are logically distinct from the question of whether employment classifications are useful social indicators, and it is likely that, even if this demise could be satisfactorily demonstrated to all concerned, they still would be.

In this chapter, we have noted deficiencies in the employment aggregate approach, as well as in the 'end of class' arguments. It has been suggested that many of the arguments contributing to the 'societal shift' debate are not particularly new. It has also been pointed out that the methodology of employment aggregate class analysis means that the systematic empirical investigation of the *processes* of class structuring has not been a feature of the research programme of either of the two main schools of employment aggregate class analysis. In the next chapters of this book, we will bring together these critical emphases. Although the fact of a fundamental 'societal shift' may be disputed, nevertheless, this does not mean that there have been no changes. There have, and these changes may be systematically explored via an empirical examination of the processes of class structuring.

Thus in the next chapter we will examine a range of different debates with a common theme – that is, the meaning and significance of consumption in relation to the different approaches to class analysis, and the processes of class formation (in respect of the latter, we will focus in particular on the middle classes). This discussion will necessarily incorporate a consideration of the relative significance of status in these processes, in the sense of consciousness communities and lifestyle categories. The following chapters will take up the topic of status in the third sense identified in this chapter – that is, status as a non-market-based claim to material entitlements or 'life chances'. Besides discussing the question of gender, one of our major topics will relate to the status of citizenship, and its relation to the development of the so-called 'underclass'.

Notes

1 This assertion should be modified, as it would be possible for sociologists to develop complex measures taking into account 'contextual effects', etc. (e.g. Szelenyi and Olvera 1996). These would, however, be too complex for general use and probably impossible to apply cross-nationally. An alternative, non-occupation-based, measure has also been suggested, particularly in debates relating to the growing significance of consumption, which will be discussed in the next chapter. However, it would be difficult to decide on useful consumption-based items – consider, for example, the transformation of the television from luxury item to basic necessity since the Second World War.

2 This is discussed in full in the first edition of this book (1993), pp. 95–6.

3 Marshall et al. do provide a suggestive mapping of the interaction of class and status (1988: 199). However, their substantive discussion is concerned to demonstrate the continuing salience of 'class' – as they define it.

4 It may be noted that T. H. Marshall's ideas on citizenship developed out of his earlier work on professionalism; see Crompton (1990a) for an account of this.

5 Those influenced by Foucault are prone to make frequent reference to the 'panopticon', a prison building constructed according to rational, scientific principles in which prisoners could be observed without their being able to see or communicate with others. The aim of the panopticon was to reform (i.e. reconstitute) the individual, in the absence of any 'extraneous' influences.

6 'The idea of a world organized through a stable ensemble of essential forms is the central presupposition in the philosophies of Plato and Aristotle. The basic illusion of metaphysical thought resides precisely in this unawareness of the historicity of being. It is only in the contemporary world, when technological change and the dislocating rhythm of capitalist transformation constantly alter the discursive sequences which construct the reality of objects, that the merely historical character of being becomes fully visible' (Laclau and Mouffe 1987: 97).

7 It may be noted that the disappearance of community is usually linked with the disappearance of *status* communities, that is localities in which everyone 'knew their place'.

8 The title of Lash and Urry's previous book (1987) is *The End of Organized Capitalism*, and refers to this period.

9 As we have seen, the theoretical impact of post-structuralism and postmodernism is reflected in the rejection of the idea that a single 'organizing principle' or 'meta-narrative' that explained societal organization might be identified. Thus it might be suggested that neither Lash and Urry nor Pakulski and Waters are 'postmodern' theorists. However, Pakulski and Waters have themselves embraced the description. Lash and Urry have rejected the 'postmodern' label, but, as Kumar (1995: 139–40) has argued in an illuminating critique, they may nevertheless be described as 'closet postmodernists'. Rather than continue with a semantic debate, therefore, we will simply describe these authors as 'postmodern'.

10 It should be noted that, in this respect, Lash and Urry enter more caveats than Pakulski and Waters. Furthermore, others (and, rather confusingly, Lash 1994) have suggested that detraditionalization incorporates more complex processes than marketization alone.

6 Lifestyle, Consumption Categories and Consciousness Communities

Introduction

To emphasize the pervasive links between stratification systems and varying patterns of consumption might appear to be nothing but a statement of the obvious. The consumption and display of scarce material and cultural goods has always, throughout the prehistory and history of human societies, been used as a marker of power and domination, whatever the sensual advantages and gratifications associated with the possession of and access to these scarce resources might also be (Veblen 1934). However, a common theme which links a number of somewhat diverse approaches focusing on consumption is the suggestion that, in the advanced industrial societies, the increase in economic productivity and the capacity for wealth creation which has taken place since the Second World War has reduced (relatively) the significance of the production and acquisition of basic material needs in the lives of families and individuals in general. Thus, with the rise in standards of living, it is argued that issues related to *consumption*, rather than production, are becoming more relevant; and that 'lifestyles', rather than 'classes' are playing an increasingly important part in shaping a whole range of attitudes and behaviours.

Thus there has been a recent and rapid increase in the level of sociological attention directed at consumption. Not surprisingly, these discussions have also been linked to the rapid flux of cultural change, which has accompanied the social and economic changes associated with the development of industrial economies in the late twentieth century. As we have seen in the last chapter, it has been argued that societies have moved from 'Fordism' to 'post Fordism'; from 'modernity' to 'postmodernity'. Issues relating to consumption are related to class theory and analysis in a number of ways (Crompton 1996b). First, there is a predominantly British debate located within the 'new urban sociology' relating to the significance or otherwise of 'consumption-sector cleavages'. This debate has been closely associated with issues relating to occupational class, and has taken up many of the themes, as well as the methodologies, associated with the employment aggregate approach to 'class analysis' (for example Dunleavy 1980; Saunders 1990b).

Secondly, increasing affluence (for the majority) has resulted in an increase in the attention being paid to consumerism, taste and consumer culture (Warde 1990). Theoretical developments in these areas have tended to make rather different assumptions about, and draw on rather different approaches to, issues relating to social class than those found within the debates relating to consumption-sector cleavages. They are characterized by an emphasis on the cultural and social, rather than the economic, construction of 'classes', and therefore a feature of all such accounts is their emphasis on the *active* construction of social differences. Indeed, full-blown 'culturalism' views culture as largely autonomous; thus class cultures are seen to *shape* class processes rather than being ideological reflections of them (Hall 1981), and, as we have seen in the last chapter, Pakulski and Waters (1996b) have argued that 'status-conventional' societies are stratified by consumption, rather than class, processes. The 'middle classes', in particular, have been the subject of much debate in this respect.

Third, there are the set of questions emerging out of the postmodernist emphasis on the supposed erosion of the boundaries between the 'separate realms' of society. We have already touched upon these issues in our discussion of Lash and Urry's account of the increasingly 'reflexive' character of cultural production. Recent developments in the conditions of work and employment in the cultural and service industries, it is argued, have led to an increased blurring of the distinction between 'work' (as employment) and other social spheres. One consequence of this, it may be argued, has been a fundamental change in the nature of the identities generated by the experience of 'work' itself. In particular, it is suggested, new management techniques have resulted in the kinds of conflictual 'class' identities, which once emerged as a consequence of employment experiences, becoming a thing of the past.

In this chapter, we will discuss each of these issues in turn. We will be returning again to the theoretical issues raised in chapter 2 – that is, the nature of the links between 'structure' and 'action', 'classes-in-themselves' and 'classes-for-themselves'; as well as giving some prominence to another topic which has always been important within stratification theory – the relative significance of the economic versus the cultural in the structuring and perpetuation of systems of social inequality. Thus we will be examining a number of important dimensions, cultural as well as economic, of the contemporary processes of employment and labour market structuring. In our brief examination of the cultural structuring of the contemporary middle classes, we will also consider the potential impact of the increasing number of women moving into 'middle-class' occupations.

Consumption-sector cleavages

Much of the debate surrounding the issue of consumption cleavages has focused on the (often polemical) work of Saunders (1986, 1990b). His arguments are also linked to the social consequences of the development of the entitlements of citizenship, which will be discussed in the next chapter. Saunders has argued that, with the advent of the 'welfare-state deal', new social divisions, arising out of the process of consumption, were emerging in 'welfarist' industrial societies (the 'welfare-state deal' describes the kinds of societal arrangements which, in previous chapters, have been variously described as 'Organized capitalist', 'corporatist', 'Fordist', etc.). The major axes of differentiation of such societies, Saunders argued, were increasingly *not* to be found in relations of production and/or the market, but between those who are able to satisfy their main consumption needs through personal ownership, on the one hand, and those who are forced to rely on collective provision through the state on the other.

Reliance on the state for the provision of consumption is a matter of degree rather than absolutes; public health and education, for example, are consumed more widely within the British population than transport, housing or reliance on state benefit for cash income.

Saunders argues that those reliant on state or socialized consumption suffer a disadvantage parallel to that experienced by the non-owners of productive capacity (1987: 312). Furthermore, a process of 'social restratification' is in process in that consumption cleavages are becoming more, not less, important. This 'breakdown of productivism' is already apparent in the phenomenon of 'class dealignment' in voting behaviour in Britain. As discussed in previous chapters, 'class alignment' in voting refers to the situation, which persisted for many years after the emergence of Labour as a mass political party, in which a majority of the occupationally identified working classes voted for the Labour Party. However, between the general elections of 1945 and 1983 the Labour share of the working-class vote fell from 62 per cent to 42 per cent (Sarlvik and Crewe 1983).[1]

Saunders's major empirical arena for the exploration of his arguments, however, has been in the area of housing. He argued that those in the population who are disadvantaged in the market, and thus forced into a reliance on state-provided (local-authority) housing have emerged as a peculiarly deprived 'underclass' in Britain. Thus when the Conservative government, elected in 1979, put into practice its policy of selling off local-authority-owned housing to tenants at substantial discounts, Saunders welcomed this as a move in the extension of the privatization of consumption, and thus the extension of real consumer power. His arguments are accompanied by others, drawing on biology and psychology, concerning the individualistic tendencies of the British. These, Saunders argues, are satisfied through the 'ontological security' engendered by a 'home of one's own'.

Marxist urban sociologists had argued, echoing earlier debates concerning 'false consciousness', that home ownership should not be seen as an expression of some kind of natural desire, but rather has been a means by which capitalists have manipulated and fragmented the working class, as well as fuelling a variant of 'commodity fetishism' which perpetuated their ideological domination. However, many non-Marxist experts in the field of social policy have also been highly critical of the neo-liberal strategies of the British government of the 1980s (including the privatization of local-authority housing), which have exacerbated the range of material inequalities in British society (Walker and Walker 1987).

These changes, it is argued, have important political effects. It is suggested that those who satisfy their consumption needs through private purchase will tend to align themselves with political parties which stress the importance of individual self-reliance, and the

market, rather than the state, provision of consumption requirements in fields such as housing, health, education and transport. As
we have seen, the resurgence of right politics and government has,
indeed, been associated with an emphasis on the need to roll back
state provision in these areas, and to reprivatize significant aspects
of civil society. Whether these changes have been structurally driven
by the 'fiscal crisis of the state' (that is, the fact that the costs of welfare-state expenditure simply outran the state's capacities to provide
them), or whether they are, rather, a consequence of the *political*
motivations of governments in power is an important question
which will not be pursued here (Hamnett 1989). For the moment,
however, we will focus on those arguments which have explored
Saunders's assertion that consumption should be regarded as an
independent dimension of social stratification.

The empirical procedures through which these arguments have
been addressed have been straightforward. The nature (that is,
whether public or private) and extent of access to the different
aspects of consumption – education, health care, transport and, most
importantly, housing – has been measured against occupational
class, and the strengths of the different associations evaluated. In a
review of this empirical evidence, Hamnett (1989) has concluded
that in all of these respects occupational class is still powerfully associated with variations in consumption, and that although occupational class cannot be held to *determine* patterns of consumption at
the individual level, at the aggregate level, occupational class
remains the primary determinant of consumption patterns.[2] A further stage of the argument concerns the relative strength of the association between occupational class, on the one hand, and
consumption-sector measures, on the other, to attitudinal indicators
such as voting behaviour and political preferences (Dunleavy 1980).
This kind of evidence assumed particular relevance in the debates
which surrounded the Conservative government's policy of selling
(at a discount) local-authority (that is, public-sector) housing to sit-
ting tenants. The 'right to buy', it was argued, caused a change in
political allegiance, as those who had purchased their council houses
switched their votes from Labour to Conservative as their housing
status was transformed.

As with the association between occupational class and patterns
of consumption, the empirical evidence relating to the association
between housing tenure and political preference, and occupational
class and political preference, suggests that the strongest association
remains that with occupational class – despite the fact that the 'right

to buy' does appear to have changed a number of individual instances of voting behaviour (Saunders 1990b). It is important to stress, however, that the continuing strength of the association between occupational class and a range of behavioural and attitudinal factors does not mean that nothing has changed. The transformations of the occupational structure, as well as the massive changes in the distributions of housing tenure and other patterns of consumption in Britain which have taken place since the end of the Second World War, have had a considerable impact on the overall pattern of stratification. It is the *association* between the different factors which has remained relatively constant, rather than their form or composition. What the consumption-sector debate has demonstrated, however, is that, for the reasons which have been extensively rehearsed in previous chapters of this book, occupational or employment class (in all its variety) still remains as a very powerful indicator of the structure of material advantage and disadvantage, and associated attitudes, in contemporary societies.

Much of the dialogue relating to consumption-sector cleavages, therefore, has been conducted within the employment aggregate framework of 'class analysis'. As we have seen, this approach attempts to bring together, through the use of employment-derived 'classes', theoretical debates relating to 'social class' with empirical analyses of material inequalities and attitudes or 'class consciousness'. Using a suitable class scheme, a 'class structure', composed of employment aggregates, is located within the employment structure. The relationship between this structure and various factors corresponding to attitudes, consciousness or action can then be explored. The linkages between structure and consciousness may be regarded as contingent, but, to the extent that they are demonstrated, this may be taken as evidence to support the continuing validity of this approach to 'class analysis'. 'Consumption sector' has been suggested as an alternative to 'occupational class' (that is, a 'consumption scheme' has been argued to be more closely associated with particular factors, such as voting, than a 'class scheme'), but in fact the empirical evidence suggests that the strongest associations of different aspects of behaviour and attitudes are still those with occupational class. There does not seem to be any firm evidence that 'consumption categories', as identified by the dominant source of consumption provision (state or private) are actually in the process of developing into 'consciousness communities'. Thus causality is imputed to occupational class rather than consumption sector (which, amongst other things, enables 'class analysts' of all political persuasions who have engaged in these debates to argue for the continuing relevance of class despite the changes associated with contemporary industrialism).[3]

Finally, it should be noted that Saunders's arguments concerning the significance of 'housing classes' have in any case been overtaken by events (Savage and Warde 1993). The collapse of the housing market in the early 1990s has resulted in many mortgaged home owners experiencing negative equity rather than 'ontological security', and many who bought public housing under the 'right to buy' have experienced considerable financial difficulties. These developments have added further complexities to the association between housing tenure and social and political identities and behaviour.

Culture, class and occupation

Debates relating to consumerism and taste proceed from a rather different set of assumptions relating to 'class analysis'. Saunders has largely engaged with the 'employment aggregate' approach which, as we have seen, takes the occupational structure as its starting point. However, the investigation of 'lifestyle' assumes from the beginning that social (and occupational) reality is actively constructed. Those concerned with the sociology of consumerism have also used investigative strategies rather different from those developed within the occupational employment class approach to class analysis, and have drawn on anthropological, as well as sociological, approaches.

Nevertheless, occupational class has been widely utilized as an element in discussions relating to the culture of consumption. The components of different lifestyles have been systematically related to employment-derived aggregates or classes; 'taste maps' have been identified which correspond to 'occupational maps' (Bourdieu 1986; Douglas and Isherwood 1980). That the consumption of goods correlates broadly with social standing, and that occupation provides a reasonable indication of this social standing, are both generalizations which would be widely accepted. The way in which consumption has been used to indicate or claim rank or special status has been a source of endless human fascination, and the inspiration for countless novels, artistic works, media representation and other forms of cultural expression. For example, at the time of writing there is appearing on television a situation comedy in which the main storyline is provided by the central character's relentless efforts to display the 'correct' consumption behaviour ('Keeping up Appearances');[4] and classic drama has also used this theme (for example Molière's *Bourgeois Gentilhomme*). However, although the association of consumption and rank is a perpetually fascinating aspect of human behaviour, the mapping of taste by itself remains a largely descriptive exercise – although it is one which is endlessly repeated.

The sociological interest in the relationship of taste to stratification systems, however, goes beyond the mere demonstration of their association, to explore the ways in which taste may be seen to be a resource which is deployed by groups within the stratification system in order to establish or enhance their location within the social order. In the next section we will examine the work of Bourdieu, who has developed these insights in his analysis of the significance of 'cultural capital'. First, however, we will briefly examine some of the methodological implications of the cultural exploration of occupational differentiation, with particular reference to the contrasts between this approach and aggregate-level explorations of the occupational-class structure.

The empirical demonstration, at the aggregate level, of the association between occupational classes and patterns of advantage and disadvantage, political attitudes and so on has been firmly established – it has been demonstrated by, amongst other things, the outcome of the consumption-sector cleavages debate in urban sociology which has been briefly reviewed above. However, the analysis of occupational aggregates has not been directly concerned with the empirical examination of the actual forces which are transforming the occupational structure. As we have stressed in previous chapters, employment aggregate class analysis has been mainly concerned with the examination of the *outcomes* of occupational differentiation, rather than the processes of occupational differentiation. Wright does give a theoretical (but not an empirical) account of the process of occupational structuring in Marxist terms. Goldthorpe's theoretical account of the generation of his class scheme is less specific, but nevertheless he is explicit that the occupational aggregates he identifies 'represent the past product and current expression of inequalities in social power and advantage' (1983: 467). However, as Savage et al. have argued: 'It is very difficult to integrate a theory of class based on a synchronic examination of class positions into an account of diachronic historical change ... it tends to lead to a mode of class analysis in which the structure of class positions is taken as given and is not itself subject to inquiry' (1992: 227).

Thus whereas empirical research within the employment aggregate approach has attempted to discern, within the occupational structure as a whole, the *outcomes* of processes of class structuring (or class formation), the investigation of the relationship between class and culture, or 'lifestyle', has a major focus on the exploration of class *processes.*[5] In this approach, therefore, occupations are not taken, albeit implicitly, as 'givens', but are regarded as the outcomes of contestation, struggle and conflict – and the direct investigation of these struggles is the major focus of empirical work. In short, the very fluidity of the occupational structure is itself an object of investigation. This has led to a significant difference in emphasis as far as the theoretical arguments concerning 'structure' and 'action' in respect of class analysis are concerned. Whereas both Goldthorpe and Wright regard 'structure' and 'action' as analytically separable, the work of authors such as Bourdieu (and Savage et al. 1992) is associated with an ontology which assumes the 'intrinsically double' nature of social reality and thus, as in Giddens's account of 'structuration', holds together 'structure' and 'action' in their empirical accounts of class processes (or formation).

Social class and the work of Pierre Bourdieu

Bourdieu's (1986, 1987) work has been the subject of increasing attention in Anglo-American sociology. His conceptualization of social class is extremely general, going beyond both Marx and Weber, who both defined class in respect of the economy – notwithstanding their very real theoretical differences. Bourdieu has been influenced by both Marx's and Weber's theoretical work. However, as Brubaker has argued, 'The conceptual space within which Bourdieu defines class is not that of production, but that of social relations in general. Class divisions are defined not by differing relations to the means of production, but by differing conditions of existence, differing systems of dispositions produced by differential conditioning, and differing endowments of power or capital' (1985: 761). Thus Bourdieu identifies four different 'forms of capital' – economic, cultural, social and symbolic – which together empower (or otherwise) agents in their struggle for position within 'social space'. As a consequence of these different empowerments, individual classes come to develop and occupy a similar habitus: 'understood as a system of dispositions shared by all individuals who are products of the same conditionings' (Brubaker 1985: 762). This description bears a superficial resemblance to the conventional sociological strategy of 'class analysis' described earlier – that is, 'class-producing' factors are first identified, then linked with attitudes and predispositions or 'consciousness'. However, whereas the approach of authors such as Lockwood, Dahrendorf, Goldthorpe and Wright locates the class structure, in a relatively *concrete* fashion, within the occupational (or employment) structure, Bourdieu's emphasis on the diverse and socially constructed nature of 'classes' leads him to describe class boundaries as like 'a flame whose edges are in constant movement, oscillating around a line or surface' (1987: 13).

Although, therefore, Bourdieu employs aggregate occupational categories in his vast ethnographic study of the French class structure (1986), he does not consider these categories to constitute 'classes', even though he recognizes that occupation is generally a 'good and economical' indicator of position in social space, and provides information on occupational effects such as the nature of work, the occupational milieu, and 'its cultural and organizational specificities' (1986: 4). Nevertheless, the classes so identified are not 'real, objectively constituted groups' (p. 4). The commonalities of their location, their similar conditions of existence and conditioning, might indeed result in similarities of attitude and practices. However, Bourdieu argues that:

> contrary to what Marxist theory [he is here making specific reference to Wright's attempt to construct a Marxist occupational class scheme] assumes, the movement from probability to reality, from theoretical class to practical class, is never given: even though they are supported by the sense of one's 'place' and by the affinity of habitus, the principles of vision and division of the social world at work in the construction of theoretical classes have to compete, *in reality*, with other principles, ethnic, racial or national, and more concretely still, with principles imposed by the ordinary experience of occupational, communal and local divisions and rivalries. (1987: 7)

In *Distinction* Bourdieu uses the class concept, therefore, as a generic name for social groups distinguished by their conditions of existence and their corresponding dispositions (Brubaker has described the aggregates identified by Bourdieu as 'status groups'). The conditions of existence identified by Bourdieu include economic capital, which describes the level of material resources – income, property and so on – that may be possessed by an individual or a group, as well as cultural capital, which is largely acquired through education, and describes the intangible 'knowing' which, amongst other things, can both secure and perpetuate access to economic capital. Thus his approach leads to an exploration of the *processes* of social differentiation which goes beyond the mere mapping of tastes. The exploration of these processes requires the interpretation of the aggregate-level association between occupational groups and patterns of consumption, as well as the development of cultural case studies which have also focused upon the uncovering of causal links.

Bourdieu's work, therefore, is primarily concerned with the active processes of class structuring, or class formation. Thus his major focus has been on *change*, as new groups emerge out of the struggle for position within social space. In some contrast, much of the discussion relating to occupational and employment-based class schemes has been concerned with whether newly emerging occupations and jobs can be fitted into *existing* occupational classifications (Wright, for example, has explicitly identified this as one of the major foci of his research). This focus within Bourdieu's work on the emergence of the new is no doubt one of the factors which has resulted in the widespread application of his insights to the analysis of the 'new middle class', which will be discussed in the next section.

The 'new middle classes'

As we have seen in previous chapters, shifts in the occupational structure (deindustrialization, technological change, the growth of the service economy) have resulted in an increase in those kinds of occupations which have always been categorized as 'middle-class' – particularly administrative, professional and managerial occupations – as well as the expansion of new occupations such as computer experts and psychotherapists. Thus the term 'middle class' encompasses a wide variety of occupational groupings. It might include quite low-level service employees – such as, for example, workers in the 'hospitality industry' – as well as the new service professionals – social workers, librarians, physiotherapists – associated with the growth and development of the welfare state.

This diversity of 'middle-class' occupations has been cited in arguments to the effect that the 'middle class' cannot be usefully regarded as a single entity, but is a multitude of fractions with (often) conflicting interests – between men and women, between public service and private-sector employees (Duke and Edgell 1987, Savage et al. 1992). Such arguments would appear to be contradicted by the assertion, particularly by Goldthorpe (1980; 1987) that the 'service' class is in fact securing and consolidating its advantaged position, and is thus a source of societal stability. In fact, it is possible for both sets of arguments to be correct. As we shall see, there is much fragmentation and instability between the different groupings that go to make up the 'middle classes'. Nevertheless, it is also the case that the relatively privileged are in a better position both to defend their own interests, and to pass them on to their descendants. Thus it is not surprising that a nominally defined grouping of the relatively privileged – such as Goldthorpe's 'service class' – should prove, in aggregate, more efficient at passing on their occupational status to their children than the less privileged are at actually *improving* the occupational status of their offspring, as Goldthorpe's studies of social mobility have demonstrated. It is also not particularly unusual for the better-off to wish to defend the status quo (we will be returning to these issues in the final chapter of this book).

The way in which different theorists have approached the topic of the new middle class(es) has reflected the occupational diversity within these groupings. Marxists (and those influenced by Marx's work such as Abercrombie and Urry 1983) have distinguished between the routine, deskilled, non-manual workers and the upper levels of management; these higher levels would be located by Wright in the bourgeoisie, by Abercrombie and Urry in the 'service class'. Wright's distinction between 'skill' and 'organizational' assets corresponds to the established sociological distinction between 'managers' and 'professionals', and this has been taken up by Savage et al. (1992; see also Butler and Savage 1996). The categories of Weberian class analysis have distinguished between 'service', 'subaltern service' and 'intermediate' locations in the occupational structure (Goldthorpe 1980; 1987). A common feature of these established frameworks of class analysis, whether Marxist or Weberian, is that employment, production and/or market relationships are regarded as crucial to the placement of the 'class'. Thus implicitly the class placement of these newly emerging groups is decided with reference to conventional, *economically* derived criteria of class location.

However, as we have seen in the last chapter, 'postmodern' theorists have argued that in the present era it is increasingly cultural, rather than economic, factors which determine societal structuring. There has, it is argued, been a 'general liberation of stratification from social-structural milieux so that it becomes precisely cultural rather than social, focusing on life style rather than life chances, on consumption rather than production, and on values rather than interests. The emerging pattern of stratification will be fluid and shifting as commitments, tastes, and fashions change' (Waters 1996: 80). Thus within the sociology of consumption, there have developed arguments to the effect that the growth of these 'new middle-class' occupational categories is not a response to the changing requirements of the economy. Rather, their rise to prominence should be seen as an outcome of the wider cultural changes which have created demands for the satisfaction of new needs. Those whose occupations are concerned with the satisfaction of these needs are also viewed as having taken an *active* role in both the identification of the needs and the manner in which they are met.[6]

Many of these commentaries have drawn upon the empirical work of Bourdieu (Featherstone 1987, Lash and Urry 1987, Wynne 1990; Savage et al. 1992). Within the dominant class, Bourdieu draws a basic distinction between the bourgeoisie – high on economic capital, relatively low on cultural capital – and the intellectuals – high on cultural capital, relatively low on economic capital. Tastes within these groupings differ; whereas the intellectuals have a preference for aesthetic modernism, bourgeois taste tends towards the baroque and flamboyant. The younger elements within the bourgeoisie, however, tend to be high on both economic and cultural capital – the bourgeoisie in France having retained their children's positions by, amongst other things, the strategic use of the *Grandes Ecoles* and the US business schools. Thus the new bourgeoisie, writes Bourdieu:

> is the initiator of the ethical retooling required by the new economy from which it draws its power and profits, whose functioning depends as much on the production of needs and consumers as on the production of goods. The new logic of the economy rejects the aesthetic ethic of production and accumulation, based on abstinence, sobriety, saving and calculation, in favour of a hedonistic morality of consumption, based on credit, spending and enjoyment. (1986: 310)

There is in this argument of Bourdieu's a clear parallel with those developed by Bell in *The Cultural Contradictions of Capitalism* (1976). Bell argued that contemporary American society comprises of three distinct realms – the economic, the political and the cultural – each of which is governed by a different 'axial principle'. The culture of modernism sought to substitute for religion or morality an aesthetic justification for life, but in sharp contrast to this postmodernism has completely substituted the *instinctual*. Thus impulse and pleasure alone are considered as real and life-affirming. As a consequence, American capitalism has lost its traditional legitimacy, which was based on a system of reward rooted in the Protestant sanctification of work, and 'the hedonism as a way of life promoted by the marketing system of business, constitutes the cultural contradiction of capitalism' (Bell 1976: 84).

However, whereas the logic of Bell's arguments suggests the need for some kind of moral renewal, Bourdieu's analysis is more concerned with the way in which different groups struggle for position within the changing social space – a space which they are simultaneously creating. Bourdieu suggests that in their struggles to establish their dominance, the new bourgeoisie finds a natural ally, both economically and politically, in the 'new petite [petty] bourgeoisie'. This group 'recognizes in the new bourgeoisie the embodiment of its human ideal' – the 'dynamic' executive – and 'collaborates enthusiastically in imposing the new ethical norms (especially as regards consumption) and the corresponding needs' (1986: 366). Thus the new petty bourgeoisie is represented in occupations involving presentation and representation, and in all institutions providing symbolic goods and services, cultural production and organization. Such occupations would include sales, marketing, advertising, public relations, fashion, interior design, as well as journalists and other media employees, craftspersons etc. Occupations concerned with bodily and emotional regulation would also be included – vocational guidance, youth and play leaders, sports and exercise experts, and quasi-medical professions such as dietitians, psychotherapists, marriage guidance counsellors and physiotherapists (1986: 359). These 'indeterminate' positions, argues Bourdieu, are attractive to those individuals endowed with a strong cultural capital (that is, superior family background) imperfectly converted into educational capital, or rising individuals who have not obtained completely the educational capital needed for the top positions, and lack the cultural and social capital required to make this final leap. Thus the new petty bourgeoisie is split between the *déclassé* and the upwardly mobile.

These 'need merchants', 'new cultural intermediaries', as Bourdieu describes them, act as a transmission belt to pull into the race for consumption and competition those from whom it means to distinguish itself (1986: 365). In a similar vein, Lash and Urry (1987) draw upon the insights of Baudrillard to argue that in contemporary consumer capitalism we no longer consume products, but *signs*, thus the 'new petite bourgeoisie' (for Lash and Urry part of the lower echelons of the 'service class') have developed as 'sign-producers', to some extent displacing the 'commodity-producers' of 'organized' capitalism. Such groups and individuals are using their cultural capital to establish new systems of classification which actively *create* the jobs to suit their ambitions. Featherstone (1991) emphasizes the rapid inflation in consumer tastes, as dominant tastes (or 'positional goods') are brought within the reach of an ever-widening circle of consumers. Foreign holidays, cheap champagne, designer sports-wear – all these goods lose their relative cultural value as they become more accessible, and in the 'leap-frogging social race to maintain recognisable distinctions', the cultural producers, the 'spe-cialists in symbolic production', come into their own (1991: 89).

Bourdieu has drawn a distinction between the *déclassé* and the upwardly mobile within the new petty bourgeoisie. Featherstone emphasizes the difference – which may be a source of conflict – between the 'economic' and the 'cultural' producers, differentiated by their relative possession of economic and cultural capital. Both of these groups may be upwardly mobile but, whereas the 'culturally' upwardly mobile have achieved such mobility through formal edu-cational routes followed by entry into professional occupations, the 'economically' mobile may lack such qualifications, having 'made the grade' through work-life mobility, usually in the private sector. Wynne (1990) has described the differentiation of the lifestyles of these two groups, which broadly reflect the kinds of differences of taste which Bourdieu identified between the bourgeoisie and the intellectuals. The 'economic' petty bourgeois are described by Wynne as the 'drinkers', characterized by a leisure style which besides regular convivial drinking includes family holidays taken in hotel packages, eating out at steakhouses, entertainment prefer-ences for musical comedy and large spectacle, and a preference for comfort and tradition in home furnishing. In contrast, the 'cultural' 'sporters' are more preoccupied with style, rather than comfort, to holiday in a *gîte* or make other personal arrangements, to join hobby clubs and voluntary associations, and to patronize avant garde the-atre and classical music concerts. Thus through their very different lifestyles, the economic and the cultural petty bourgeois are con-structing and affirming their social position.

Work by Savage et al. (1992) has developed further this mapping of cultural (consumption) tastes on to different sections of the mid-dle class. Public-sector professionals (whose tastes closely resemble those of the 'sporters' identified by Wynne) are revealed, by market research surveys, to have an 'ascetic' lifestyle which is characterized by sport and healthy living, a relatively low consumption of alcohol, combined with 'high-cultural' activities such as plays, classical music and contemporary dance. This group is high on cultural, but low on economic, capital. A further group identified by Savage et al.

correspond broadly to the 'drinkers' identified by Wynne. Managers and government bureaucrats, on the other hand, are characterized by 'undistinctive' patterns of consumption, having average or below average consumption scores on high culture and exercise alike, and showing a preference for a cleaned-up version of the 'heritage' or 'countryside' tradition in their consumption patterns. As Savage et al. note, this 'undistinctive' group are not identified within Bourdieu's framework, perhaps because of the anti-intellectualism which has characterized managerial groupings in Britain, in some contrast to France.

The third group of middle-class consumers identified by Savage et al. are the 'postmoderns'. This postmodern lifestyle is characterized by an absence of a single organizing principle in respect of consumption: 'high extravagance goes along with a culture of the body: appreciation of high cultural forms of art such as opera and classical music exists cheek by jowl with an interest in disco dancing or stock car racing' (1992: 108). These patterns may be broadly associated with the 'hedonism' identified (and lamented) by Bell, as well as with the 'new petite bourgeoisie' described by Bourdieu. However, Savage et al. emphasize that these consumption patterns are found not just amongst the newer occupations centred upon the cultivation of the body and the emotions, but amongst professionally educated private-sector workers more generally: 'barristers, accountants and surveyors partake in the post-modern lifestyle as much as sex therapists or advertising agents' (1992: 128). Cultural assets have been commodified, and practices considered to have an 'auratic' (or 'special') quality by previous generations – opera, skiing holidays, historic housing (albeit a luxury conversion or newly built in a traditional style) – are now accessible to those who have the money to pay for them. In non-sociological language, this is 'yuppie' culture.

The cultural fragmentation within the middle class, therefore, reflects the economic and spatial fragmentation within these groupings which had already been identified by those working within more orthodox frameworks of 'class analysis' (Savage et al. 1988, 1992, Crompton 1992). What those writers who have emphasized the significance of the development of 'postmodernism' and associated lifestyles argue, however, is that (a) culture should be regarded as an *independent* variable in the construction and consolidation of class position or 'habitus', and that (b) the hyperinflation of symbols associated with the growth of consumer capitalism has, relatively, increased the significance of culture in the processes of class structuring. A major consequence of these changes is the development within the middle occupational stratum of a 'cultural mass' of symbol producers. These changes have also had political consequences which are succinctly summarized by Harvey:

> The politics of the cultural mass are . . . important, since they are in the business of defining the symbolic order through the production of images for everyone. The more it turns in upon itself, or the more it sides with this or that dominant class in society, the more the prevailing sense of the symbolic and moral order tends to shift . . . the cultural mass drew heavily upon the working-class movement for its cultural identity in the 1960s, but the attack upon, and decline of, the latter from the early 1970s onwards cut loose the cultural mass, which then shaped its own identity around its own concerns with money power, individualism, entrepreneurialism, and the like. (1990: 348)

These arguments are highly suggestive, but they raise important questions relating to both causality and the permanance or otherwise of their impact. Have cultural changes actually *caused* the neoliberal turn to 'marketization' – of which the commodification of culture may be regarded as one aspect – which has taken place over the last decade? Or might it be that a political emphasis upon the overwhelming legitimacy of 'market forces' has created a cultural anomie, a situation exceptionally favourable to the challenging and commodification of normative cultural judgements of all kinds? Savage et al.'s arguments suggest the latter interpretation. They argue that the significance of bureaucratic structures to middle-class careers is declining as firms increasingly use market mechanisms, rather than managerial hierarchies, to structure their activities, externalizing aspects of production, drawing on the labour of specialists, and so on (the so-called 'flexible firm'). They also argue that in Britain, the role of the state in both legitimating cultural assets and providing direct employment to large numbers of professional workers has changed to one of underwriting market provision. These twin factors, they suggest, have changed the basis of the legitimation of cultural assets: 'Increasingly cultural assets can be legitimised through their role in defining and perpetuating consumer cultures associated with private commodity production. Those receptive to the post-modern lifestyle increasingly look to the market to legitimate and reward their cultural assets' (1992: 215). However, what the market giveth, it also taketh away. Viewed from the standpoint of the recessions of the 1990s, the 1980s yuppie culture of 'postmodernist' consumption may appear more as the transient activities of the *nouveaux riches* than as a manifestation of a deep-seated cultural change.

The middle classes, therefore, have been seen as becoming increasingly fragmented, and as a consequence even more unlikely to develop any kind of conscious *collective* social (or 'class') identity. However, it may be suggested that to the extent that the middle classes *have* manifested forms of collective organization, this has usually been in order to protect their individual interests – as in, for example, the activities of professional groups (Freidson 1986). In recent years, employment insecurity amongst the middle classes has intensified – even though, as we shall see in chapter 8, they have actually improved their earnings situation relative to the lowest-paid. Much anxiety, nevertheless, centres on the bureaucratic career, as organizations downsize, 'delayer', and the ethos of the 'lean corporation' is promulgated (Womack et al. 1990). Industries which once were the locus of the classic (male) bureaucratic career, such as retail banking, have been transformed. The clearing banks[7] once provided a stable route for the reasonably qualified (GCSE level) school leaver to progress from clerical to managerial level, and this state of affairs persisted into the 1980s (Crompton and Jones 1984). Today, however, these organizations have been transformed. Recruitment has been stratified according to educational level and, realistically, only those recruited to managerial trainee grades (requiring relatively high levels of pre-entry qualification) will get promoted. The old structure of hierarchical grades has been transformed, and job mobility is now as likely to be sideways (in order to enhance an individual's 'skill portfolio') as upwards (Crompton 1989a, Halford and Savage 1995). As banks face a worsening financial climate, there have, increasingly, been redundancies associated with organizational restructuring.

In general, job insecurity would seem to be increasing – the frequency with which people change jobs shows a definite upward trend (Gregg and Wadsworth 1995) – and working hours for those in work have got longer. It is suggested that this reflects a culture of 'presentism', that is, the need to demonstrate a level of organizational commitment which both justifies continuing employment and indicates suitability for promotion. Increased competition and job mobility, both internal and external, is likely to lead to increasing individuation (as described by Beck 1992). It may be suggested that older generations of the middle classes had a collective interest in preserving the stable hierarchies which were important mechanisms in preserving their individual advantages. Indeed, the level of collective representation in the clearing banks – the 'aristocracy' of clerks – was in fact quite high, although it was not accompanied by any radical ideology (Lockwood 1958; Blackburn 1967). Contemporary organizational change and development, however, has reduced even further the likelihood that the expanding middle classes might be a source of radicalism – despite the hopes of left-leaning social scientists of the 1960s and 1970s (Crompton 1979; Gouldner 1979; Walker 1979).

The middle classes and the gender question

The process of the formation of traditional managerial and professional occupations signified the emergence of the modern, non-entrepreneurial, bourgeoisie. It was accompanied by the exclusion of women from the better-paid jobs, and from access to professional training and employment, together with their confinement to the 'domestic sphere' (Davidoff and Hall 1987). Thus in relation to the professional and managerial middle classes, women figured largely as either subaltern, 'semi-professional' employees (e.g. nurses and other ancillary professions servicing the male-dominated medical profession), or as the wives of professional and managerial men, providing the domestic supports which made it possible for their husbands to carry out jobs in the 'public' sphere (Crompton 1986). Thus the middle classes were male-dominated, particularly in their upper reaches.

Today, the situation is changing. As women have increased the level of their labour force participation, so they have also improved the level and extent of their academic and professional qualifications. Over the last ten years, women in all countries have been steadily increasing their representation in professional and managerial occupations, as is indicated in table 2. Despite the differences between individual countries, table 2 suggests that it is, nevertheless, possible to make some broad generalizations as to the patterning of women's entry into professional and managerial occupations. First, the increase of women in such occupations is, in general, greater than the increase in their representation in the labour force as a whole. Second, the increase of women in professional and managerial occupations is not evenly distributed, and is moulded to existing patterns of gender segregation. Thus the level of increase of women in some heavily feminized professions such as teaching is relatively low, suggesting that in some countries these occupations might be nearing female saturation. However, the increase in the proportion of women in some professions where they are very under-represented,

Table 2 Women in employment, 1980s and 1990s

	United States		Britain		France	
	% increase women (1983–1995)	% women 1995	% Increase women (1981–1991)	% women 1991	% Increase women (1982–1990)	% women 1990
Women in total labour force	2.4	46.1	5.0	44.0	2.5	42.0
Teachers	3.8	74.7	5.6	68.8	2.4[b]	56.6[b]
Engineers	2.6	8.4	4.0	6.6	5.1	11.0
Public servants[a]	11.3	49.8	20.0	52.0	4.3	44.2
Financial managers	11.7	50.3	11.4	21.0	8.6	37.8
Marketing and sales managers[a]	14.1	35.7	16.5	28.9	21.8	44.0
Law professionals	10.4	26.2	12.5	27.5	8.0	33.0
Doctors	8.6	24.4	6.5	30.6	8.6	34.9

[a] Occupational groupings may not be exactly comparable.
[b] Secondary school teachers only.
Sources: Statistical Abstract of the United States 1996; HMSO, Census Tables, 1981, 1991; Institut National de la Statistique et des Etudes Economiques, Recensements de la population 1991.

such as engineering, is also low, suggesting the likelihood of the continuing under-representation of women in these occupations. Well above average rates of increase in the numbers and proportions of women are to be found in 'people-focused' management jobs such as public service, marketing and finance (indeed, an important element in the organizational transformation of banking, as briefly described above, has been the increased recruitment of women to managerial positions).[8] Above average rates of increase are also found in the classic professions of medicine and the law.

Thus the increase of women in higher-level occupations has been heavily concentrated in the service-type aspects of management and the professions – as Esping-Andersen has argued, the 'post-Fordist' service economies are increasingly dominated by women's employment. Case-study evidence (Devine 1992, Evetts 1994, Halford and Savage 1995, Crompton and Le Feuvre 1996) suggests that women tend to cluster in positions in which (a) it is possible to work flexibly and thus combine employment with family life, and/or (b) consolidate their positions through the exercise of individual skills, rather than organizational office-holding. These studies also demonstrate that women are still subject to masculine exclusionary practices in some better-paid and higher-level occupations, such as surgery within medicine. All of these factors make it likely that the entry of women into professional and managerial occupations will have relatively less impact (at the level of 'lived experience') than might have been anticipated, and that men will continue to dominate the higher levels of the occupational structure.

This non-random movement of women into the higher levels of the occupational structure should not simply be taken as evidence of the persistence of occupational segregation by sex – important though this fact is. Rather, it also provides further empirical evidence in support of the argument that the occupational order is, in essence, socially, as well as economically, structured. It is also important to recognize that gender is an important dimension in the cultural restructuring of the middle classes.

However, the increase of women in higher-level occupations will be reflected in a corresponding increase of substantial dual-earner households. At the aggregate level, this will be reflected in an increase in the extent of social and economic polarization. We will be returning to this important topic in subsequent chapters. In the next section of this chapter, however, we will examine the third consumption-related argument which is held to be eroding stratification systems in the 'postmodernist' era. This is the blurring of the distinction between 'work' as employment and other social spheres – in particular, that of consumption and thus, of the producer/consumer distinction.

From 'abstract labour' to 'customer care'

The growth of the service sector, and service work more generally, reflects not only a change in the structure of class places but also a change in the kind of work undertaken by many individuals who might be considered objectively 'working-class' in occupational terms. For, increasingly, the qualities demanded of many workers rest not simply on labour or even technical skills, but *social* skills. That is, skills of welcoming, selling, soothing and so on (as has often been noted, these have conventionally been regarded as particularly 'feminine' qualities, and women, of course, predominate in service employment). These demands for social skills, it may be suggested, have affected the *content* of the employment relationship, if not its form. Thus low-level service employees receive training in 'customer care', and there has been an increasing focus on personnel strategies such as 'Total Quality Management'. Managers in all sectors of the economy are now encouraged, not simply to produce maximum output from their employees via rational accounting techniques, Taylorist systems of work organization and so on, but also to build a *commitment* to the organization at all levels of employment (Peters and Waterman 1982). Such prescriptions go beyond established strategies of socially responsible control such as paternalism, or 'human relations' (Mayo 1975), and the 'needs' of the worker are seen as incorporating not just the satisfaction of material needs, and satisfying social relations, but nothing less than the realization of the full human being. Employers and their representatives, therefore, are increasingly calling upon the services of a new breed of experts concerned with the management of the body and the emotions – counsellors, assertiveness trainers and so on. As we have noted above, this trend has led to a proliferation of 'new middle-class' occupations.

New strategies of labour management, however, are attempting to transform not only the nature of the employment relationship but also the way in which work itself is carried out. As we have seen in the previous chapter, Pakulski and Waters have argued that 'managerial and labouring functions are becoming reintegrated . . . Industry is becoming "culturalised" ' (Waters 1996: 82), and Lash and Urry argue that in 'socio-economies' production is becoming increasingly 'reflexive', as the worker is, increasingly, no longer circumscribed by the constraints of the 'structure' of work but is responsible for its transformation – particularly in the new and expanding industries such as leisure and the media. It may be suggested that there are two, subtly different, points being argued here. On the one hand there are arguments, such as those of Du Gay (1993), which suggest that in employment sectors such as retailing, the involvement of the personality of the worker (i.e. retail employee) in the employment process effectively blurs the distinction between 'producer' and 'consumer', leading to a subsequent blurring of identities and breaking down of boundaries. This argument, it may be suggested, draws upon an established tradition of sociology and anthropology which has always emphasized the extension and incorporation of social relationships and economic categories (Davis 1985). On the other hand, there are arguments which focus more directly upon new managerial techniques and their consequences for workplace relations (and ultimately, 'class'-based identities).

'Total Quality Management', for example, incorporates service (consumer)-type relations into the core of organizational structuring. Firms compete via their services to customers; teams within firms compete via their services to other teams as the service relationship becomes generalized throughout the process of production itself. In such systems, much emphasis is placed upon the 'empowerment' of the workforce. The quality of customer service provided by the organization has emerged as a major strategy whereby modern organizations compete with each other in their struggles to ensure profitability. Ensuring that employees provide this high-quality personal treatment to customers, it is argued, cannot be achieved through either increasing direct managerial control of employees, or standardizing service provision via bureaucratic rules. Thus the key to success lies in changing the attitudes and orientations of employees: 'Internalisation of quality norms is a prescription of the quality management literature, which emphasizes the development of a culture of quality among all organizational members' (Rosenthal et al. 1997: 482). One of the ways in which this internalization is achieved is through workforce 'empowerment', in which the employee is given more discretion and responsibility – for example, a salesperson is allowed to decide whether a customer should be given a refund without having to consult management.

Clearly, these trends, if they are occuring, are very different from the processes of 'deskilling' and work routinization analysed by Braverman as being an inevitable feature of the development of 'monopoly capitalism' (see chapter 2, p. 39), and might be cited as evidence for Lash and Urry's arguments about the increasing 'reflexivity' of modern production. However, the rather rosy picture of Total Quality Management and workforce empowerment painted by some management theorists has been challenged by others. Workforce 'empowerment' has been accompanied by an increased monitoring of individual performance, and individualized, performance-related pay schemes are on the increase (Millward et al. 1992). Frenkel et al.

(1995: 774) have described this as 'info-normative' control, that is 'control based on data objectification (performance standards) and employee accommodation or commitment to performance standards'. Thus it is argued that contemporary management techniques are in fact a combination of increased control and surveillance, work intensification, and the manipulation of meaning via ideology or discourse (Willmott 1993).

Are new management techniques, therefore, an indication of a fundamental shift in production in postmodern, postindustrial, advanced service economies, which is generating an increasingly 'reflexive' labour force? Or are they just an ideological sham, a further twist in the apparatus of management (capitalist) control? As with many of these 'either/or' questions that are posed during debates in 'class analysis', there is empirical evidence for both 'sides' of the argument (contrast Rosenthal et al. 1997 with Sewell and Wilkinson 1992). It is also important to remember that there are extensive areas of employment, and employment relations, where these new managerial techniques are not particularly relevant, particularly in the 'McDonaldized' reaches of the service sector (Ritzer 1996). However, a national survey (Gallie 1996; Gallie and White 1993) found that 62 per cent of people who had been in the same occupation for five years reported that the skill level of their job had increased. People who worked in jobs which were concerned primarily with people were the most likely to report job satisfaction, and 'the higher the level of social skills required by the job, the greater people's satisfaction with their work' (Gallie and White 1993: 60). Thus it would seem that the shift to service jobs *has* been associated with an increase in job satisfaction, although levels of stress in work have risen alongside skill increases.

Workforce 'empowerment' and skill enhancement, however, run in parallel with other aspects of service work which undermine individuality. Leidner's (1993) evidence from case studies of McDonald's restaurants and insurance sales shows that whereas routinized service interactions often helped the workers to do their jobs, and boosted their confidence, at the same time the standardization of personal interaction in work was seen as compromising norms of individual 'authenticity' which were highly valued in society as a whole. This particular dimension of service work, it may be argued, exists in some conflict with the emphasis on increasing 'individuation' in 'reflexive modernity'. Individuals, it is clear, may be extensively manipulated as well as 'empowered'. There are apparently many elements of continuity, as well as change, in the experience of work as employment. Nevertheless, it is not difficult to see that increasingly individualized management techniques, in combination with an emphasis upon normative change as far as the workforce is concerned, are likely to work against potential forms of workplace-based collective action.

Summary and conclusions

This chapter has explored various dimensions of the sociology of consumption which have been developed with reference to the analysis of social stratification. It was shown that the debates relating to 'consumption-sector cleavages', first introduced by Saunders and Dunleavy, have operated within a terrain which was largely marked out by the orthodox sociological tradition of occupational-class analysis represented by authors such as Goldthorpe and deriving from the work of Bendix, Lipset, Dahrendorf and Lockwood, whereby theories of social class are used to locate occupational 'classes', in relational terms, within the structure of employment. As the defenders of this position have not been slow to point out, in statistical terms, occupational class remains the most important single variable associated with patterns of consumption and consumption-related attitudes (Goldthorpe and Marshall 1992).

In contrast, the debates relating to consumerism have not been cast within the framework of orthodox employment-aggregate class analysis. This is not particularly surprising. As has been argued in chapter 4 above, one feature of the development of employment-aggregate class analysis was that its practitioners, neo-Marxist and neo-Weberian alike, were at some pains to distinguish their development of 'theoretical' class schemes from the occupational rankings and prestige schemes which characterized earlier empirical approaches – such as Warner's – to the study of social stratification. An unanticipated consequence of this drawing of a (legitimate) analytical distinction between 'class' and 'status', however, is that the systematic investigation of the role of culture (understood as status or prestige) in class structuring has developed independently of the analysis of 'social class' as economically defined.

As we have seen in chapter 2, the classic theories of Marx and Weber identified 'classes' as groups within the social structure emerging from the dominant patterns of production, distribution and exchange. The relationship to the dominant mode of production assumed most significance for Marx; the workings of the capitalist market were more significant for Weber. Social scientists have developed these insights in order to distinguish, within the structure of employment, occupational (or employment) aggregates with particular characteristics deriving from the economic processes which Marx and Weber identified. However, the extent to which this sociological venture has proved successful has always been contested.

In the first place, the analytical split between structure and action, upon which attempts to identify a 'class structure' rest, has been contested by developments in social theory. The indivisibility of structure and action, that is, the intrinsically double nature of social reality, has been emphasized by authors such as Giddens and Bourdieu:

> Human agency and structure ... are logically implicated with one another ... Understood as rules and resources implicated in the 'form' of collectivities of social systems, reproduced across space and time, structure is the very medium of the 'human' element of agency ... agency is the medium of structure, which individuals routinely reproduce in the course of their activities. All social life has a recursive quality to it, derived from the fact that actors reproduce the conditions of their social existence by means of the very activities that ... constitute that existence. (Giddens 1987: 220–1)[9]

There is in any case a persisting tradition within 'class analysis' which has forcefully denied the possibility of such a separation. A major representative of this approach within social history is E. P. Thompson, whose work has had a considerable influence on other social scientists. The development of humanistic Marxism in the Gramscian tradition similarly held to the impossibility of the analytical movement, in a mechanistic fashion, from economic 'base' to ideological 'superstructure'. Within sociology more generally, the empirical analysis of social class has always incorporated the systematic linking, through case-study research, of social imagery and economic class position.

Another major challenge to the possibility of the precise empirical identification of an economic 'class structure' within the structure of employment has come from those authors who have argued for the indivisibility of the 'economic' from the social or cultural within the stratification order. Arguments against the economic reductionism or determinism which has sometimes characterized 'class analysis' have emphasized the continuing significance of the *status* order in the location and structuring of occupations – where status is understood as the persistence of 'custom and practice' (Wootton 1955) as

well as the projection of group attributes on to occupational roles –
as is evidenced, for example, by the historical devaluation of
'women's work'.

However, because of the sharp distinction which has been drawn
between (economic) 'class' and (cultural) 'status' in stratification
theory and research, the contemporary investigation of status and
'lifestyle' has proceeded along rather different channels from those
dominant in 'class analysis'. Many of these investigations have from
the beginning assumed the intrinsically double nature of the social
world, and have focused upon the investigation of the processes by
which groups attain, establish and retain their positions within the
social order. In these struggles, both economic and cultural factors
(or 'economic capital' and 'cultural capital') are seen as important.
In contrast to employment aggregate class analysis, therefore, the
'cultural' and the 'economic' have not been separated. The sociology of consumption has additionally argued that taste, culture and
lifestyle are, with the development of 'postmodernity', becoming
more significant in class structuring – particularly in respect of elements of the 'new middle class'.

Yet one need not necessarily adhere to the view that there has
been an epochal shift in the direction of 'postmodernity' in order to
recognize that the increasing attention that has been paid to the
analysis of 'lifestyles' has provided us with a number of important
insights into contemporary social changes.[10] The analysis of the
processes of occupational structuring (or class formation) is as
important to stratification theory and research as is the investigation
of their outcomes through the analysis of occupational or employment-based aggregates. The claim that cultural or 'lifestyle' factors
have become more significant in this structuring should also be
taken seriously. The expansion of the service economy is itself an
indication of the increase in the resources devoted to consumption
activities, and time-budget studies demonstrate the increase in
leisure time (Gershuny and Jones 1987). Cultural practices, often
centred on consumption, have always loomed large in the constitution of social class groupings. As Scott has argued: 'The business
class (in Britain) as a whole is characterized by a high degree of
social cohesion, the main supports of this cohesion being its system
of kinship and educational experience' (1982: 158). Scott has therefore emphasized the significance of *status* in the consolidation and
perpetuation of the upper class: 'The hierarchy of status ... is ... an
important element in the legitimation of power structures, and the
dynamics of status group relations are ... integral elements in class

reproduction and in the formation of power blocs' (1991: 5). The features which he identifies in his discussion of status processes – education, leisure patterns and so on – closely correspond to the 'cultural capital' which Bourdieu has similarly identified as being of crucial significance to class formation.

However, as we have seen in the last chapter, 'postmodern' theorists have gone beyond the mere recognition of the significance of 'culture' in the structuring of stratification and inequality to argue that increasing 'individuation' in contemporary societies means that it is the manner in which the individual *constructs* himself/herself – that is, consumes – that is now central to stratification systems, rather than the individual's position in an economic order. Consumption practices, it is asserted, have even penetrated into the world of work itself, and the boundaries between producers and consumers have been broken down. This argument is difficult to sustain. It is true that employees have always worked for more than just money alone, as has been demonstrated by a long tradition of industrial sociology. Nevertheless, contemporary management techniques and strategies clearly reflect attempts at employee control, as well as empowerment, and it is frankly optimistic to assert that managerial and worker functions have been integrated, and/or that workers are no longer constrained by management controls. There is also the (rather obvious) point that access to material resources is necessary to sustain consumption in the first place. Indeed, it may also be argued that economic position – and even more importantly, *exclusion* from economic participation – has been of considerable significance in the shaping of a major feature of contemporary stratification systems, particularly with reference to the so-called underclass. As we shall see in the next chapter, it is not cultural, but largely economic, factors which determine the circumstances of individuals in the poorest circumstances. Thus the increasing significance of consumption and lifestyle in late twentieth-century capitalism should not be allowed to obscure the fact that the economic factors identified by the nineteenth- and early twentieth-century theorists of social class still play a major part – indeed, *the* major role – in the structuring and persistence of systems of social inequality.

Notes

1   A part of the decline in the working-class element in the Labour vote is to be explained by the long-term decline in the 'working class' within the employed population. The extent to which class dealignment is also a consequence of vote-changing within the working class is a matter of some controversy. See Marshall et al. (1988, ch. 9).

2   Hamnett (1989: 227) states that: 'we can reject the view that variations in housing tenure, educational attainment and health conditions are primarily a product of culture rather than class'. His use of the concept of 'culture', however, is rather odd given that none of the statistical evidence he reviews provides a measure of 'culture'.

3   As we have seen in previous chapters, those engaging in the consumption sector debates within urban sociology have not always been aware of, or sensitive to, the theoretical differences between different occupational-class schemes.

4   BBC Television. These efforts are constantly frustrated by the behaviour of her decidedly working-class relatives.

5   Aggregate-level indicators, it must be stressed, also give insights into the ways in which occupational aggregates seek to maintain and reproduce their position within the system of stratification – e.g. in their consumption of different kinds of education.

6   It might be noted – and this is a very important point – that middle-class groupings such as managers and professionals have always had an enhanced capacity to determine the needs which they supply.

7   So-called because they 'cleared' all cheques at the end of every day. They included Barclays, Lloyds, the Midland and Natwest.

8   In recent decades, much employment in the financial sector has been re-focused on sales. See Halford and Savage (1995).

9   This stance may be criticized, however. It may be argued that a position of analytical dualism is to be preferred – that is, distinguishing the 'parts' from the 'people' in order to examine their interaction, but recognizing that neither of them can exist without the other (Archer 1996; see also Layder 1994). Structuration theory incorporates a 'decentering of the subject' in which human beings become people through drawing on structural properties to generate social practices. Thus structure only becomes 'real' when instantiated by agency. However, at the level of the social, institutions have a reality which is experienced as such by individuals, and it is important to continue to recognize this.

10 For example, the application of these insights to the analysis of inner-city regeneration or 'gentrification' (Zukin 1988).

7 Citizenship, Entitlements and the 'Underclass'

Introduction

In chapter 5, we examined a range of different uses of the 'status' concept. It was emphasized that 'prestige' is only one dimension of the concept, which has also been used to describe patterns of consumption or 'lifestyles', as well as claims to entitlements which do not rest upon power in property or the market. In chapter 6, we have focused mainly on the topics of prestige, consumption and 'lifestyle'. In this chapter, we will explore the interaction of class and status in respect of status claims – particularly those developed in respect of the different dimensions of 'citizenship', and the consequences of exclusion from this status.

Class power and status power represent different claims to material resources, and Weber suggested that they existed in a cyclical relationship: 'When the bases of the acquisition and distribution of goods are relatively stable, stratification by status is favoured ... Epochs and countries in which the naked class situation is of predominant significance are regularly the periods of technical and economic transformations' (Gerth and Mills 1948: 193–4). Recent contributors to debates on class and stratification have reworked these insights. As we have seen in chapter 5, Pakulski and Waters (1996) have argued that increasing individualization means that we have moved beyond 'class' to 'status conventional' societies stratified largely by consumption (that is, they have focused largely on the prestige and 'lifestyle' dimensions of the status concept). Scott (1996), in contrast, has remained close to Weber's analysis, emphasizing that 'status' should be seen as a continuing independent dimension of stratification, rather than as having replaced 'class'.

Our discussion of 'status' in this chapter will focus largely on status entitlements and their consolidation. Even in circumstances in which access to property and the market – that is, class situations – are the major determinants of material circumstances, non-market and non-property factors – that is, the social and moral claims associated with status – are nevertheless of persisting significance. Traditional evaluations associated with gender, race and age all affect levels of remuneration in contemporary societies, for example. In this chapter, we shall see that class-based organizations (trade unions) have actively pursued status claims – most particularly, in respect of the development of social citizenship. The pursuit of status equalization by disadvantaged groups such as women and ethnic minorities has also had a substantial impact on the stratification order.

In the first chapter of this book, we emphasized the fictional nature of the 'pure' capitalist market society. A 'market society' is an ideal type, rather than a description of any actually existing societal form. In reality, no society exists or persists in the absence of some kind of regulation, and the market is by itself insufficient as a regulator of capitalist industrialism (Polanyi 1957, Hutton 1995). In a capitalist market society, sources of regulation which afford some protection for the individual may be found in aspects of pre-capitalist or 'traditional' societies which have persisted into the modern age – we may mention, for example, structures of family or kinship obligations or, more contentiously, Hirsch's (1977) identification of the 'moral legacy' of religious doctrine. There are also contemporaneously forged institutions which have been developed in order to check the free play of market forces. These would include, for example, trade unions and occupational associations, but foremost amongst these institutions is the modern form of the status of citizenship.

'Citizenship' is a term which denotes full and participating membership of a nation state, that is, it does not necessarily incorporate all persons resident within a given territory. In the ancient world of the Greek city states, for example, the term was reserved for free adult males alone; women, slaves (including debt slaves), foreigners and the young were excluded from participation in the *polis*. This exclusion of some long-term or permanent residents still persists in the modern world. In Germany, for example, even the German-born children of *Gastarbeiter* ('guest workers') are not, in law, full 'citizens'. We should also remember that in a number of advanced Western industrial societies women have for much of the twentieth century been denied full civil and political rights – in France, for example, women were not enfranchised until after the Second World War.

Citizenship implies both rights and duties: rights against the arbitrary exercise of state power, as well as duties in respect of the state's activities. Thus the citizen has the right to hold private property, the state has the right to levy taxes. As far as stratification analysis is concerned, a crucial aspect of citizenship is that it cannot be marketed; it is not a commodity but rather denotes a particular aspect of the social *status* of the individual or group. Sociological analyses of the concept have been dominated by T. H. Marshall's 'Citizenship and social class' (1963), an account which Lockwood has described as 'the only work of post-war British sociology which ... bears comparison with, and stands in a direct line of succession to those classical texts which mark the origins of modern sociology' (1974: 363).

T. H. Marshall and the development of the concept of citizenship

Marshall's brief text derives from lectures delivered in 1949, published in 1950. His major thesis is that the basic equalities which in contemporary Western industrialized democracies are shared by all 'citizens' serve to both reduce and make legitimate the persisting inequalities of (capitalist) social class. In an oft-quoted phrase, he asserts that 'in the twentieth century citizenship and the capitalist class system have been at war' with each other (1963: 87). Marshall identifies three elements of modern citizenship: civil, political and social. Civil citizenship describes those rights necessary for individual freedom – 'liberty of the person, freedom of speech, thought and faith, the right to own property and to conclude valid contracts, and the right to justice'. Political citizenship refers to the right to participate in the exercise of political power, which in contemporary societies corresponds to universal suffrage, without such restrictions as property qualifications, and the right to hold political office. These two aspects correspond, broadly, to the liberal ideal of citizenship. To these basic rights of the individual Marshall added a third dimension, social citizenship, which he described as 'the whole range from the right to a modicum of economic welfare and security to the right to share to the full in the social heritage and to live the life of a civilized being according to the standards prevailing in the society' (p. 74). These rights, he argued, are associated with the development of the institutions of the modern welfare state.

Marshall developed his arguments through an analysis of recent British history. Chronologically, civil rights in England began to be established in the seventeenth century and were largely accomplished by the eighteenth century, during which equality before the law was established and the last elements of servile status were abolished, leaving individuals free to enter employment, to make contracts, to change employers, and so on. Political rights were progressively attained by increasing numbers of the population during the nineteenth century, although full political citizenship for adults, including women, was not achieved until the twentieth. The major achievement of the twentieth century, however, lay in the development of the welfare state and the growth of social citizenship. Another important development spanning the nineteenth and twentieth centuries was the growth and legal recognition of trade unionism, which Marshall describes as a 'secondary system of industrial citizenship parallel with and supplementary to the system of political citizenship' (p. 98).

The major contribution of citizenship to class abatement lies in its social dimension. The incorporation of social rights into the status of citizenship creates a universal right to real income which is not proportional to the market value of the claimant. The rights of social citizenship incorporate 'no longer merely an attempt to abate the obvious nuisance of destitution in the lowest ranks of society. It is no longer content to raise the floor level in the basement of the social edifice, leaving the superstructure as it was. It has begun to remodel the whole building, and it might even end by converting a skyscraper into a bungalow' (pp. 100–1). In short, the rights of social citizenship make a significant contribution to 'the modern drive towards social equality' (p. 73).

Marshall's analysis of citizenship has been tremendously influential. However, Marx (1843) had already expressed his objections to the real value of modern democratic, or bourgeois, citizenship (that is, individual freedom, universal suffrage, and equality before the law). Of what significance are these individual rights, he argued, in class-divided societies in which individuals do not have the *practical* ability to exercise them? Political equality can accommodate itself all too easily to structural inequalities in the distribution of wealth and power, and yet these systematically undermine any formal equality in rights. Indeed, he argued that these 'bourgeois freedoms' were both necessary to the development of capitalist society and served to perpetuate it. By declaring distinctions based on birth, rank, education and occupation to be 'non-political', the state effectively sanctions these inequalities. In a similar vein, left critics of Marshall's thesis argued that the development of the welfare state had signified, not class abatement or amelioration but, rather, the necessary strategies of the capitalist state in response to the changing requirements of the capitalist mode of production – an interpretation supported by structuralist Marxism's identification of education and welfare systems as 'ideological state apparatuses'. In this view, for example, educational provision (for Marshall a central component of social citizenship) would be viewed not as an element of class abatement but, rather, as a channel through which capitalism acquires the kinds of employees it requires (Bowles and Gintis 1976).

In some contrast to these left critics, others saw in Marshall's arguments a more positive and indeed optimistic account of the integration of the working class into capitalist society through the development of citizenship and the subsequent decline of class and class conflict (Bendix 1964). Such interpretations had a strong parallel with the 'optimistic' liberal perspective on the development of industrial societies which has been described in previous chapters; for example, in the assertion that with industrialism there would develop a society in which individual attainments would more or less match individual abilities. The equal status of citizenship, it was suggested, would make a significant contribution to this equalization of opportunities.

Recent discussions of Marshall have highlighted the ambiguities, and some of the deficiencies, of his original account. Before we proceed to an examination of these arguments, however, it would be useful to attempt to resolve, in brief, the differences in the current political uses of the concept. On the political right, there is a considerable emphasis upon the *duties* of the citizen, through the notion of 'active citizenship'. 'Active citizenship', through such schemes as neighbourhood watch, voluntary social service, and so on, might also be seen as a part of the right's strategy of moving away from the state's provision of welfare services, which were seen by Marshall to be central elements of 'social citizenship'. The 1991 Conservative 'citizen's charter' also sought to further empower the individual in

respect of large, public-service bureaucracies – for example, in insti-
tuting a system of payment to passengers to compensate them for
the late arrival of trains.

Recent debates in social democratic politics have also argued that
the question of individual freedom is central to socialist, as well as to
right-wing politics. We may recall, for example, the 'New Times'
criticism of socialism's over-identification with 'productivism' and
'classism'; this has been linked, by authors such as Laclau and
Mouffe, with the necessity for socialism to have a strong commitment to the deepening and expansion of individual freedoms (1985:
176ff). A recent commentary states this case succinctly: 'It is liberty
rather than equality that socialists now turn to with enthusiasm, with
personal freedom given greater prominence in most left agendas . . .
than the redistribution of wealth' (Andrews 1991: 12). Recent events
in Eastern Europe, it might appear, serve to strengthen these kinds
of argument, as the ideology of centrally planned, redistributive
state socialism has been rejected via popular protests in which
demands for individual liberty are prominent.

However, an emphasis on individual rights has been bound
together with the necessity for state intervention in the concept of
'stakeholding' (Kelly et al. 1997). 'Stakeholding' argues not for
redistributive equality, but rather for equality of opportunity; that is,
all 'stakeholders' (citizens) should be guaranteed a minimum
endowment of capabilities and opportunities (training, education,
job opportunities etc.). Thus *inclusion* in society, rather than
absolute equality, is the key concept. At the same time, it is argued
that the market by itself is not sufficient to provide opportunities,
and thus a wide range of institutions – employment organizations
and financial and political systems – will have to be reformed in
order that the majority might be included. It might be suggested,
therefore, that proponents of 'stakeholding' are laying a major
emphasis upon the necessity, for the individual, to achieve the *practical* capacity to achieve citizenship rights through skills, education
and job opportunities.

We will return to these broad issues in our concluding chapter,
but to return to the debates initiated by Marshall's work: a number
of critical themes have emerged even amongst commentaries that
have been basically favourable to his analysis. These are, first, that
Marshall's account was somewhat ethnocentric and, second, that it
provided an over-optimistic, evolutionist model of the development
of citizenship. The first point of criticism must surely be accepted, as
Marshall's discussion focused only on the English case. Both Mann

(1987) and Turner (1986, 1990) have contributed comparative socio-historical analyses of the development of civil rights, political rights and welfare entitlements in different nation states. These accounts are also critical of the evolutionism implicit in Marshall's scheme, as they suggest that in particular national circumstances the development of rights may not follow the trajectory suggested by Marshall – in late nineteenth- and early twentieth-century Germany, for example, civil and social citizenship advanced faster than political. Such historical discussions are important for our comprehension of the general character of citizenship, but of more immediate concern to our present discussion is the relationship of citizenship to stratification systems.

As we have seen, Marshall argued that citizenship and the class system were at war with each other. Marshall did not go to great lengths to spell out his conceptualization of 'class', but it is reasonable to assume that he was describing the structure of market-related inequalities characteristic of capitalism, as well as the social differentiations associated with them (Barbalet 1988). Thus citizenship not only blunts the edge of market inequalities by 'creating a universal right to real income which is not proportionate to the market value of the claimant' (T. H. Marshall 1963: 100), but also promotes an awareness of the common situation of all 'citizens' which overrides, or at least reduces, the consciousness of social differences. Thus the identification of citizenship by Marshall, Lockwood argues, provides the 'clearest and most cogent' answer to the question which was raised by Durkheim: 'namely, what is the basis of the "organic solidarity" of modern societies?' (1974: 365). Lockwood argues that citizenship has emerged as a central element in the *modern* status order, in contrast to the status order of the feudal era which capitalism eventually dissolved, and which was based upon legally sanctioned *inequalities*, rather than the common rights of all 'citizens'.

Dahrendorf (1988) has developed Marshall's arguments in his description of the conflict between 'provisions' (economic growth and material plenty) and 'entitlements' (citizenship rights) as 'the modern social conflict'. This conflict has arisen and persists, Dahrendorf argues, because a certain degree of inequality is required to stimulate economic growth. However, the claims of 'provisions parties' are consistently challenged by 'entitlements parties', not least because the process of the development of 'citizenship' is far from complete: 'In the world at large ... barriers of privilege remain the key issue. Citizens have not arrived, they have merely gained a new vantage point in the struggle for more life chances' (1988: 47).

Dahrendorf's discussion serves to highlight another aspect of the relationship between class and citizenship which has gained considerably in emphasis since Marshall's initial formulation. To describe class and citizenship as 'at war' with each other suggests conflict, but the suggestion that this leads to class abatement suggests also the long-term reduction of class conflict. This was certainly the interpretation put on Marshall's work by some of the earlier commentators making use of Marshall's framework (Halmos 1970). More recent commentaries, however, have tended to stress the inevitability of the persistence of conflict. Indeed, it is clear that Marshall himself saw that 'the basic conflict between social rights and market value has not yet been resolved'. This argument has been extended, however, by those who have stressed not only the continuing nature of the conflictual relationship between citizenship and class, but also the *origins* of citizenship in class conflict (Giddens 1982b).

Giddens argues that Marshall failed to emphasize that citizenship rights have not come about through some natural process of evolution – even though this process may have been stimulated by such massive shocks to the system as, for example, war, as Marshall recognized – but only through the process of *struggle*: 'In my view it is more valid to say that class conflict has been a *medium of the extension of citizenship rights* than to say that the extension of citizenship rights has blunted class divisions' (Giddens 1982b: 174; emphasis in original). The right to vote had to be fought for, and the extension of social citizenship may be seen as the outcome of the political aspirations of the enfranchised working class. Similarly, the rights of workers to organize in trade union activity are not best conceptualized as the more or less inevitable extension of civil citizenship – as 'economic civil rights' or 'industrial citizenship', as Marshall described them – but had to be fought over and were bitterly contested by the ruling class. Indeed, the institution of trade union rights was (and is) interpreted by liberal ideology as being in basic conflict with the individual rights of civil citizenship. The erosion of trade union rights which was a feature of Conservative government policy in Britain was often carried out under the banner of the sacrosanct nature of individual freedoms – as in, for example, the right not to belong to a union and the abolition of the 'closed shop'. Recent historical developments such as these reforms of trade union legislation, as well as policies directed at the dismantling and 'marketization' of the institutions of the welfare state, have also led authors such as Giddens to emphasize, in some contrast to Marshall, the essentially fragile and contested nature of modern citizenship. In our brief examination above of 'right' and 'left' political perspectives on the nature of citizenship, and the rights and duties associated with it, we can indeed see that 'social' citizenship is not to be regarded as a stable or permanent outcome of the development of modern industrial societies.

Authors such as Giddens (1982b) and Mann (1987), therefore, have emphasized the role of class conflict in the development of citizenship – whether citizenship is viewed as the outcome of working-class struggle or ruling-class strategy. Turner (1986), however, although similarly regarding the development of citizenship as the outcome of struggle and conflict, has emphasized above all the significance of *non-class* social movements in its genesis. As we have seen in our previous discussions, 'social movement' is a somewhat imprecise descriptive term which has increasingly been used to identify forms of collective organization which self-consciously seek to change or defend some feature of a society, which possess a distinct ideology, but which are not tied to any specific class or locale (as are, for example, class-based political parties or nationalist movements). Offe (1985b) has identified 'new social movements' as highly significant in the context of the 'new politics', and as being concerned with issues such as ecology and the built environment, peace and human rights – particularly feminism (although there are those who might balk at the identification of feminism as 'new').

Much of Turner's argument relating to the inadequacy of 'class' as an explanatory variable in the description of the evolution of citizenship stems from his observation that the ethnocentric nature of Marshall's original formulation renders it inappropriate for the analysis of the development of citizenship in modern societies which lack a feudal past, or where the final transition from the past had been violently achieved by dramatic events such as defeat in war. As well as class conflict, therefore, Turner emphasizes the significance of war and migration to the development of citizenship. Migration is of significance both in the case of migrant societies such as those of the United States and Australasia, and where rural-urban migration has a role in breaking traditional ties and obligations within the nation state. War not only has the impact of speeding up indigenous processes of the development of citizenship (for example, it is widely acknowledged that in Britain the extension of the franchise to women was justified with reference to their participation in the war effort during the First World War), but also may result in the imposition of democratic institutions, including citizenship, on defeated societies, as was the case in Japan after the Second World War.

These arguments of Turner's may be seen as simply extending Marshall's original account of citizenship's historical origins to incorporate the historical realities of cross-national variations, but he presses his case for the significance of non-class social movements in the development of citizenship beyond this. Indeed Turner criticizes class-based interpretations of the expansion of citizenship (such as those of Giddens and Mann) as reductionist, and argues instead that 'the notion of social movement provides us with a valid approach when understanding the nature of citizenship within recent capitalist history ... Social movements which aim to change society in the name of a generalised belief inevitably raise questions about the nature of participation in society and thus are inevitably movements about the rights of citizenship' (1986: 89, 92). This conclusion has been contested by Barbalet (1988). However, it may be suggested that debates about whether 'classes' or 'social movements' are more (or less) important to the growth of citizenship are not particularly helpful, as, in reality, *both* have contributed significantly to its development – indeed, Turner himself would seem to take up this position (Turner 1988).

Marshall identified three aspects of modern citizenship: civil, political and social. Both the kinds of rights associated with these different dimensions, as well as their interrelationship, have, as we have seen, been extensively debated (Barbalet 1988). Leaving aside these complex issues, however, it is not particularly contentious to draw an important distinction between, on the one hand, civil and political citizenship, and, on the other, social citizenship. Civil and political citizenship obviously involve rights, but their institution does not *directly* involve or address distributive issues. Indirectly, of course, as the Marxist critique has argued with some force, these rights might be held to legitimize distributive (or class) inequalities by defining them as 'non-political'.

In contrast, social citizenship *is* directly concerned with distributive issues, in its guarantee of certain rights to material benefits that are associated with the status of 'citizen'. This is, after all, why Marshall and those who have followed his arguments have described citizenship and the class system as being 'at war' with each other. The significance of class conflict and struggle – whether actual or anticipated – in achieving the material gains associated with social citizenship cannot be disputed. It should also be recognized that besides the advancement of the status of citizenship, class-based distributive conflict has also been frequently associated with other status claims – as in, for example, trade union claims for a 'fair wage', or in seeking to perpetuate 'traditional' pay relativities such as those between the skilled and the unskilled (Marshall et al. 1988, Wootton 1955). The 'institutionalized altruism' of professional groupings may also be cited as an example of a status claim which has material consequences (Crompton 1990a). Thus status claims have always been widely utilized in arguments concerning the distribution and legitimation of market inequalities, and one of the most important in modern societies is related to social citizenship. In this important sense, therefore, class-based groupings – understood as groups organized in relation to their position in the social division of labour – have shaped, and continue to affect, the definition of social citizenship.[1]

Social citizenship, therefore, attempts to mitigate the inequalities associated with the unequal distribution of private property and market rewards in class societies. In contrast, the institutions of civil and political citizenship served to ameliorate the *status* inequalities associated with traditional, pre-industrial societies. Indeed, it is paradoxical that the status claims of class-based organizations in market societies have actually contributed to the perpetuation of some of the traditional material inequalities associated with status – of which one of the most obvious is the systematic exclusion of women from access to the better-paid and more prestigious occupations by trade unions and professional organizations. As we shall see in our subsequent discussion, many of the 'rights' of social citizenship may be seen to consist in large part of social insurances which relate to the (male) citizen as an *employee,* rather than accruing to all citizens irrespective of whether they are male or female, black or white. Nonetheless, although it may be argued that the initial conceptualization of liberal bourgeois citizenship excluded many 'traditionally' defined as of inferior status – such as women – it has proved ultimately powerless to resist the claims for civil and political rights articulated by feminists and others. The written (and unwritten) constitutions of the major industrial nations remain formally committed to ideologies of universalism, and, although it is true that such ideologies have frequently given way to expediency, it is a sociological fact that such ideologies exist and have frequently been used in arguments against the perpetuation of institutions which discriminate against particular groups. Turner is correct to emphasize that claims on behalf of these groups have often been pressed most powerfully not by classes, but by social movements.

Women and citizenship

We have seen that the main thrust of the socialist/Marxist critique of the real significance of civil and political citizenship is that these individual rights have little impact upon, and may underpin and legitimize, structures of material inequalities. Feminists have developed their critique of citizenship even further, arguing that it is not only the case that individual civil and political rights have had little effect on the material position of women, but also that 'citizenship' itself has been from earliest origins a *gendered* concept; and moreover one that has systematically excluded women.

In a powerful critique, Pateman (1988, 1989; see also Phillips 1990) demonstrates that the original social contract, as described in the writings of political theorists such as Locke and Rousseau, from the first excluded women as 'citizens'. Women were viewed as creatures of passion rather than rationality, lacking the capacities required to participate as citizens and indeed as capable of bringing considerable disorder into the public sphere. The rights of men over women were seen to be natural rather than political; the contract theorists rejected the legitimacy of paternal rights, but absorbed and simultaneously transformed conjugal, masculine patriarchal right. Thus men's domination of women within marriage was universally accepted. The 'fraternal social contract' therefore 'constitutes patriarchal civil society and the modern, ascriptive rule of men over women' (Pateman 1989: 43). Citizenship is fundamentally *gendered*, and although a supposedly gender-neutral category incorporates essentially masculine attributes and characteristics such as participation in warfare, long-term adult participation in economic life (employment), and so on. The concept of citizenship abstracted from the differences between men and women and, as a consequence, one sex (men) became the norm.[2]

The material benefits of social citizenship, therefore, have had very different consequences for men and women. We have seen that social citizenship has been regarded as contributing to 'class abatement' because, amongst other things, the institutions of the welfare state include rights to real income which do not depend on the market value of the claimant. Thus the development of social citizenship has been seen as a response to a major dilemma of liberal democracy – the fact that the free play of the market will include losers as well as winners. Unemployment benefits, old-age pensions etc., may be viewed as rights to which citizen-employees who are not particularly successful in the competitive struggles of the market are entitled – but what of those who are regarded as incapable of full market participation? As a consequence, feminists have argued, women have been incorporated into the welfare state not as workers or citizens, but as dependants and welfare providers – more particularly, as wives and mothers. Thus welfare policies have often served to reproduce the patriarchal structures of family life.

For example, in Britain, the Beveridge Report (1942), which laid the foundations of the postwar welfare state, assumed that 'during marriage most women will not be gainfully employed'; married women were thus regarded as their husband's dependants, and exempted from unemployment and sickness benefit schemes. As Beveridge argued: 'The attitude of the housewife to gainful employment outside the home is not and should not be the same as that of the single woman. She has other duties ... In the next thirty years housewives as mothers have vital work to do in ensuring the adequate continuance of the British Race and of British Ideals in the world' (cited in Wilson, 1977: 151–2). In the United States, a sharp separation is drawn between 'social security', where benefits are paid to those who have 'earned' them during working lifetimes (the 'deserving poor'), and 'welfare', or public handouts to the (undeserving) poor – many of whom will be unsupported mothers (Pateman 1989: 187).

The exclusion of women from civil and political citizenship, and the reproduction of patriarchal institutions via social citizenship, has from the first been resisted by feminists. As Mary Astell was asking at the end of the seventeenth century: 'If all Men are born free, how is it that all Women are born Slaves?' Thus from the eighteenth century onwards liberal feminists have been engaged in struggles to achieve the status of citizens for women. Characteristically, this struggle has taken the form of arguing that women are in no sense 'naturally' inferior, but have capacities equal to those of men, and should not, therefore, be debarred from full citizenship. However, as Pateman has argued, this liberal feminist strategy carries with it an apparently insoluble dilemma: if citizenship itself is defined in masculine terms, how can women become partners to a *fraternal* social contract?[3]

One consequence is that women seeking equality have often been constrained to behave as surrogate men, commonly by remaining childless. Historically, the 'career woman' has been assumed to have a career rather than a family, a condition which was imposed on many women in England by marriage bars (for women only) which persisted in many areas of bureaucratic employment until the late

1950s. The conflict between 'equality' (with men) and 'difference' (as women) is one which defies a neat theoretical and practical resolution within contemporary feminism (feminist authors including Cockburn (1991) have stressed the importance of working within *both* frameworks. See also Marshall (1994). This contradiction is reflected in the history of the feminist movement in Britain and the United States. Once the struggle for women's suffrage had been achieved, the feminist movement in both countries diverged between liberal 'equal-rights' and 'welfare feminist' activities. Welfare feminism supported protective legislation for women in employment, for example, whereas this was opposed by equal-rights feminists who argued that such legislation would hamper the struggle of women for equal opportunities in employment (Banks 1981).

There are no ready answers available to these difficult questions, although Cockburn has suggested that it is in practice possible to transcend the contradiction of 'equality *vs.* difference': 'Men tell us "women cannot claim to be equal if they are different from men. You have to choose." We now have a reply. If we say so, as women, we can be both the same as you *and* different from you ... What we are seeking is not in fact *equality*, but *equivalence*' (1991: 10). Thus although it may be conceded that the gendered nature of citizenship status renders its achievement problematic for women, this should not be allowed to obscure the fact that women's struggle for citizenship status has brought with it many benefits. What Walby (1990) has described as 'first-wave' feminism in Britain extended from 1850 to 1930. During this period, women acquired the right to vote, to control their own property, to enter universities and professions, and to live independently of their husbands; that is, they achieved most of the elements of civil and political citizenship. Left critics of the hollow nature of civil and political equality have rightly stressed their compatibility with material inequalities; for women, the situation is compounded by the fact that, even when civil and political equality has been formally achieved, they have had to contend with both material and sexual inequalities – particularly in respect of employment.

Social citizenship, as we have seen, has been directly concerned with the reduction of material inequalities. The role of the class struggle in developing the institutions of social citizenship has been considered above. T. H. Marshall described 'the basic civil right' in the economic field as 'the right to work' (1963: 77); Giddens and others have emphasized the political significance of 'industrial citizenship' (that is, the recognition of trade unions and the institutions of collective bargaining) in extending the boundaries of social citizenship. However, women have not, until recently, spent most of their adult lives as full-time employees, and indeed have often been denied 'the right to work' by the very institutions which existed to defend these rights on behalf of adult males. Thus whilst it is true that worker's organizations have struggled to establish rights to welfare, these frequently assumed the form of work-related social insurances such as unemployment benefits and pension rights. What is less often emphasized, moreover, is the role of women, as feminists, in the struggle to establish welfare rights not related to employment. The concerns of women with children and the family has resulted in a long history of specifically female concern with the establishment and development of welfare and human-service institutions – some directed at women themselves, others at the promotion of material supports for family life. Women such as Octavia Hill, Florence Nightingale, Marie Stopes, Eleanor Rathbone and many others have all made significant contributions to developments in health, housing and welfare legislation which established what Marshall described as social citizenship. In Britain, welfare feminists worked closely with the Labour Party, and Banks has argued that 'to a large extent we may see the welfare state in Britain as a product of an alliance between welfare feminism and the Labour Party' (1981: 174).

As the critiques of Pateman and others have demonstrated, therefore, although the development of the welfare state has brought with it many material advantages for women, its institutions were originally developed in a manner designed to reproduce the patriarchal model of the 'male breadwinner', leaving the major domestic responsibilities to women.[4] Thus women are still the major providers of welfare – as low-paid workers in the public sphere and as unpaid workers in the private (Finch and Groves 1983). The reproduction of such patriarchal institutions became a major target against which the arguments of 'second-wave' feminism were developed.

As a number of recent historical discussions have stressed, feminism as a social movement has a long history (Banks 1981; Walby 1990). Nevertheless, it is possible to identify two exceptional waves of feminist activity: the first extending from the middle of the nineteenth century to the interwar period, the second from the 1960s until the present day.[5] Like the first wave, which had developed in association with the anti-slavery movement, the second also occurred at the same time as attempts to extend the boundaries of civil, political and social citizenship for racially excluded groups. In the civil rights movements and the associated growth of left politics during the 1960s, however, women once again found themselves relegated to typing, making the coffee, and providing moral support. Second-wave feminism, therefore, moved swiftly from a concern with equal rights towards a critique of the fundamentally 'gendered' nature of modern society, reflected not only in the separation between 'public' (male) and 'private' (female) spheres of activity, but also within the public sphere itself – as demonstrated, for example, in the extent of segregation by sex within employment. Thus during the 1960s and 1970s there were important legislative gains related to equal pay and opportunities in Europe and North America, and during the 1980s a significant shift beyond this in the direction of equal value.

Equal opportunities relate to both equality of access and the absence of direct and indirect discrimination in employment (the latter would include, for example, the requirement to be geographically mobile in order to achieve promotion, a requirement which would work against the circumstances of many women): equal-value legislation, however, is potentially much more radical in its impact. The principle of equal pay for work of equal value brings with it the necessity to re-evaluate the principles which have traditionally underpinned the relative ranking of occupations and the material rewards associated with them – and a major factor which has contributed to this ranking is, of course, that sex-typed 'women's' occupations will be ranked lower than men's. In the welfare sphere itself, feminists have pressed for the material recognition of women's unpaid contributions – for example, for the right to payments for women caring for elderly dependants – as well as for the reform of the benefits system away from a structure which reproduced patriarchal family relations; these have, however, not been sufficient to prevent the feminization of poverty. Second-wave feminism, in an echo of the purity campaigns of the first wave, has also directed attention towards violence against women and their exploitation in sexual relations. Divorce and abortion law reform, together with the recognition of and protection from domestic violence, have been important elements in the struggles of women to achieve control over their own bodies. One outcome of these pressures has been that, in court decisions in Scotland and England, the legal possibility of rape within marriage has been established, thus overturning the man's right of physical access, with or without her consent, to his wife's sexual services.

With considerable over-simplification, therefore, a major focus of the struggles of second-wave feminism might be viewed as the attempt to establish and extend the rights of civil and social citizenship on behalf of women. In so doing, as feminist theorists have argued, customary definitions of what constitutes civil society have been challenged, as has the relative ordering of work and occupations held by 'citizens' (Eisenstein 1981; Pateman 1988, 1989). Walby (1990) has described the transition from the nineteenth- to the twentieth-century status of women as one from 'private' to 'public' patriarchy. However, it is possible for state policies to be developed that do not simply reproduce patriarchal institutions, but rather actively seek to reform them. For example, Hernes (1987) has described Scandinavian welfare states as 'woman-friendly', as actively developing policies which level patriarchal inequalities. Such policies would include the state's taking on the responsibility for work which has traditionally been carried out by women – in particular, caring work of all kinds (childcare, eldercare, etc.). As a consequence of these policies, Scandinavian countries such as Sweden and Denmark are characterized by very high levels of employment amongst women, together with a narrowing of the wage gap. In Sweden, for example, women's average earnings are 90 per cent of men's.

In the language of social stratification, it is true that women do not constitute a 'status group' (Lockwood 1986). Nevertheless, more or less concerted actions by feminists have, over the last one and a half centuries, served to enhance the relative status of women, both nationally and internationally. The gradual achievement of the different elements of citizenship by women has had an impact on the location of women within the stratification system, both individually and collectively. More women are entering higher-level professions and occupations, as we have seen, and in the arena of party politics all of the major parties in Britain are acutely aware of the political significance of their stance on gender. In the 'New Labour' government elected in 1997, 101 of the Labour MPs were women. It is important not to be complacent – Dahrendorf's comments to the effect that full citizenship has not yet arrived for the majority apply with particular force in the case of women – but it is equally important to recognize the changes that have taken place, and their implications for the structure of social stratification in advanced industrial societies.

Race and citizenship

There are a number of difficulties associated with the use of the term 'race' in sociology. The category was not included in the initial formulation of general theories of social inequality by nineteenth-century social theorists, and the nature of the conflict, exploitation and oppression which have been associated with and justified by 'racial' distinctions has made social theorists less, rather than more, likely to accept that they are rooted in any 'biological' difference. Investigations commissioned by organizations such as UNESCO have concluded that the human species had a single origin, and that although human groups could be classified on the basis of physical indices such as hair and skin type, such classifications had to recognize that there were considerable physical overlaps between one group and another.

One response to the rejection of the biological foundation of 'racial' distinctions has been to emphasize the significance of *ethnicity*, rather than race. This approach focuses upon the cultural differentiation of various ethnic groups; but, as Rex has argued, such an emphasis on 'difference' has a tendency to leave out of account the extent of the *inequalities*, rooted in oppression, coercion and exploitation, between ethnic groups. Rex, therefore, prefers to use the term 'race relations' to describe situations of particularly severe conflict and oppression in which it is not possible for an individual to leave the subordinate group, and which are justified by the dominant group in terms of some kind of deterministic theory – situations, in short, in which race and ethnicity are 'role signs' (Banton 1967) which lead to the assignment of positions in the overall system of exploitation (Rex 1986, 1987).

There is not the space here to go into the details of the history of European domination since the sixteenth century, which included booty capitalism, slavery, colonial exploitation and economic oppression and which has resulted in the widespread identification of blackness as a negative role sign. The harsh material realities of racism are not being denied; nevertheless, the fact remains that the systematic material inequalities and ascriptive distinctions which are associated with the physical marker of 'race' have come into conflict with the universalistic values of 'citizenship'.

In the British context, citizenship has acquired a particular significance in respect of race. The first generation of 'new Commonwealth' (that is, West Indian and Asian) immigrants who arrived during the 1940s and 1950s faced few legal restrictions; under the British Nationality Act 1948 they were allowed to enter Britain freely, to find work, to settle and to bring in their families. However, the increase in immigration during subsequent years led to growing social unease and to political agitation for controls. Thus the preferential status of Commonwealth immigrants in Britain has been whittled away by a succession of restrictive measures, culminating in the Immigration Act 1971, which restricted the right of abode to 'patrials', or persons having parents or grandparents who lived in Britain (a barely disguised measure to protect the rights of entry of whites from the 'old Commonwealth' of Australasia, South Africa and Canada); reinforced the conditionality of entry on having obtained employment; and reduced entitlements to bring in families. The recent history of immigration controls in Britain, therefore, has made the right to British nationality, and thus citizenship, a significant issue in the politics of race relations in Britain. It should be made clear, therefore, that the discussion of 'citizenship' that follows is largely concerned with blacks whose nationality is not in question – that is, black citizens of Britain and the United States.

Marshall's analysis of the development of citizenship rights has been widely employed in discussions of the unequal situation of blacks. This is not surprising, given that there is systematic empirical evidence that in Britain and America, by comparison with the white population, blacks have lower-level jobs, live in poorer-quality housing, are more likely to be unemployed and thus more likely to be benefit dependent.[6] Although blacks may be citizens, therefore, the conclusion is inescapable that there exist systematic structural obstacles to the realization of their full citizenship rights. In the case of the United States, the origins of the black population in the institution of slavery is obviously a fact of considerable significance. The argument has often been made that in the case of the Northern States, successive waves of immigration from Europe, together with the open frontier to the West, facilitated individual mobility to an extent which restricted the growth of large-scale, overt class conflict during the nineteenth and early twentieth centuries. However, black migration from the American South has not been followed by any substantial immigrant flows from Europe, and the blacks have remained a ghettoized population at the bottom of the social hierarchy.[7] In 1965, Parsons described American Negroes as the 'prototypically disadvantaged category' within American society, and argued that their inclusion within American society depended for its success on the 'much more effective institutionalization of Marshall's social component of citizenship' (Parsons 1965: 736). Blacks had already organized in pursuit of citizenship through the Civil Rights movement of the 1960s, and even before this, the rulings of the Supreme Court had forced some desegregation in education and employment. Since the Civil Rights campaigns, however, Affirmative Action and Positive Discrimination – which have taken the form, for example, of black quotas in college education, special programmes for blacks, etc., may be seen as direct and interventionist attempts to 'effectively institutionalize the social component of citizenship'. The fact that these actions have met with only limited success should not be allowed to undermine their significance.

The situation in Britain is rather different. The black community has its origins in immigration rather than slavery – although the relevant point should be made that the black West Indian population is itself of slave origin, and the British were the major colonists in Africa and Asia. Rex (Rex 1986; Rex and Tomlinson 1979) has argued that black immigrants in Britain are at a disadvantage because as recent entrants (and for a number of other reasons) they have been excluded from the British working class and thus the 'welfare-state deal'; like Parsons, therefore, Rex sees the material situation of the black community as stemming from blacks' lack of access to social citizenship, despite their formal possession of civil and political rights.

Rex (1986: 66) describes the 'welfare-state deal' as follows:

1 That workers shall have the freedom to engage in collective bargaining over their wages and conditions.

2 That the government shall take the responsibility for planning the economy in such a way that nearly full-employment is achieved.

3 That the best way of achieving this is through a mixed economy, so that both total free enterprise and total collective ownership are ruled out.

4 That workers in times of unemployment, ill-health and retirement will be entitled to a basic income paid for on the basis of compulsory insurance contributions by employers and workers.

5 That all people will be entitled to a basic standard of health, housing, education and other personal social services, the cost of which will be borne partly by general taxation.

Like Giddens, Rex regards the benefits of social citizenship as having been fought for and achieved through a process of class struggle. His account also incorporates the existence of Keynesian strategies in respect of the regulation of the national economy, as well as the Marshallian concept of social citizenship. As such, it assumes a particular mode of incorporation of the indigenous male working class which, it has been argued, has served to reproduce patriarchal structures in respect of the family and welfare institutions (Jensen et al. 1988). Nevertheless, Rex's analysis remains of value as it serves to illustrate the manner in which blacks have been excluded from the benefits of social citizenship in Britain during the immediate postwar period. Blacks were not at all prominent – as members or officials – in the trade union movement in Britain during the period when the unions had their greatest level of access to government – that is the 1950s to the 1970s. This relative lack of union protection, in combination with the extensive segmentation of the labour market, rendered the black population most vulnerable to unemployment. Access to local-authority housing (the major form of lower-class housing provision in the postwar period) depended upon length of residence; thus the immigrant population was at a serious disadvantage. The educational system is both highly competitive and residentially stratified, and minority children were as a consequence placed overwhelmingly in the worst sections of the worst schools. The 'authorities' in respect of the black population are drawn largely from the indigenous white population; racial harassment on the part of groups such as the police has contributed further to the marginalization of the immigrant community. For all of these reasons, therefore, Rex argues that the immigrant population (and its children) has been excluded from the 'welfare-state deal' struggled for by the British working class, and thus also from the benefits of social citizenship. As a consequence, Rex suggests that minorities of immigrant origin may be described as an 'underclass', 'who instead of forming an inert and despairing social residue, organize and act in their own "underclass" interest often relating themselves to colonial class positions' (Rex and Tomlinson 1979: 328).

Rex is careful to emphasize that the 'underclass' description does not apply to all blacks. An (increasing) minority have achieved both economic and social success, and Rex anticipates that, as the size of the relatively advantaged group within the immigrant community increases, so a process of assimilation will occur. His use of the term 'underclass', it should be stressed, differs from its more usual use to describe groups who have failed altogether to become economically self-supporting – as, for example, in Myrdal's (1962) description of the situation of the blacks in the United States. As we shall see, this use of the term has become highly contentious, particularly in the light of right-wing arguments to the effect that, far from ameliorating class conflict, the effect of the development of social citizenship and the welfare-state deal has been to *create* an 'underclass' in advanced industrial societies.

Social citizenship and the 'underclass'

Marshall's discussion emphasized that the concept of social citizenship encompassed not only welfare rights and entitlements as such, but also the equipping of all 'citizens' for full participation in society. Thus Marshall's discussion paid particular attention to education, which has always been seen as a key factor as far as equality of opportunity is concerned. As we have seen above in our consideration of 'stakeholding', recent discussions have stressed the necessity for the inclusion of the individual via a minimum endowment of capabilities and opportunities, for which the state has a major responsibility. It is somewhat paradoxical, therefore, that recent discussions of the 'underclass' have argued that individuals have been excluded from the societal mainstream *because* of the granting of the welfare rights of social citizenship.

Besides examining an important stratification phenomenon which has received considerable attention over the last decade, our discussion of the 'underclass' debate will also be used to make an important methodological point concerning the utility of different approaches to 'class analysis'. We have emphasized in this book that different approaches to 'class analysis' have their strengths and weaknesses, and that it is not particularly useful to try to establish which is 'better' or 'worse', 'right' or 'wrong'. We have shown that arguments about whether or not a major 'societal shift' to a 'non-class' society is under way need to be distinguished from the 'employment aggregate' approach to class analysis with which they have often engaged (e.g. Lee and Turner 1996). By its very nature, the 'employment aggregate' approach tends to emphasize stability, rather than change; thus an apparent conflict between these two approaches is hardly surprising.[8] We have drawn a further (methodological) distinction between the primary focus of 'employment aggregate' approach on the empirical *consequences* of class (i.e. employment) position, in contrast to other approaches which have examined the *processes* of class formation. These latter studies have tended to use a case-study approach, and have also included an explicit recognition of the many-stranded reality of the processes generating a group such as those in poverty. Our examination of the 'underclass' debate will bring together these rather different methodological approaches to 'class analysis'. Thus studies of the processes of excluded group formation have utilized the case-study approach, whilst the examination of wider questions relating to the culture and morality of the supposed 'underclass' (i.e. the *consequences* of location in the 'underclass) have also used the employment aggregate approach.

It is beyond dispute that social and economic polarization is on the increase, particularly in societies, such as the US and the UK, where there has been a deliberate turn to the market, together with the removal of social protections. In Britain, the Rowntree Report (1995) demonstrated that the income share of the poorest fifth of households fell from 10 per cent in 1978 to 7 per cent in 1990, whereas the income share of the richest 10 per cent rose from 36 per cent to 42 per cent. If the level of poverty is taken as that of income support, then in 1989 20 per cent of the British population lived in poverty, as compared to 14 per cent in 1979 (Devine 1997: 234). There are a number of different factors contributing to this increase in inequality (we will be returning to this discussion in our concluding chapter) but, besides the absolute rise in unemployment, one important reason has been the widening gap in wage rates between the poorest and the highest paid.

However, neo-liberals have argued that the welfare benefits available to the poorest members of society have also played an important part in increasing inequality via their role in the creation of an 'underclass'. In chapter 1, we have discussed in brief the neo-liberal argument that attempts to achieve equality of outcome through, for example, programmes of affirmative action for disadvantaged groups might undermine legal or formal equalities (see above, p. 6). In a similar vein, libertarian critics of welfare-state provision have argued that the *compulsory* redistribution of income should be kept at a minimum, and that individuals should be free to determine the nature and extent of their own welfare provision. These arguments do not imply that those without resources should be left to starve, but they do indicate the targeting (that is, means-testing) of the benefits which are available in any 'minimalist' system of provision (Peacock 1991). As Plant (1991) has argued, neo-liberals have stressed the value of negative liberty – that is, the absence of intentional coercion – as against positive liberty – that is, the actual possession of powers, resources and capacities to act. A further twist to these arguments is developed by those who suggest that collective provisions have actually had the effect of undermining individual capacities. Thus state provision for the economically disadvantaged is argued, by some right-wing theorists, to be making an active contribution to the problem it is trying to solve, through the creation of 'welfare dependency' and thus the development of an underclass.

We have already encountered variants of these arguments in previous chapters. Saunders, for example, has identified the 'major fault line' in countries like Britain as being between 'a majority of people who can service their key consumption requirements through the market and a minority who remain reliant on an increasingly inadequate and alienative form of direct state provision' (1987: ch. 3). This split, he argues, is affecting 'the material life chances and cultural identities' of the people involved – that is, they are increasingly disempowered in respect of the ('normal') majority who can service their needs through the market. In a similar vein, Murray has written of the 'Great Society' welfare reforms in the United States in the 1960s that 'The first effect of the new rules [i.e. increases in welfare] was to make it more profitable for the poor to behave in the short term in ways that were destructive in the long term. Their second effect was to ... subsidize irretrievable mistakes. We tried to provide more for the poor and produced more poor instead' (1984: 9). It should be recognized that the 'underclass' is a highly contentious concept. Some have argued that the term has been developed not in order to describe an objective phenomenon or set of social relationships but, rather, as a stigmatizing label which effectively 'blames the victims' for their misfortunes. Thus Dean has argued that ' "Underclass" is a symbolic term with no single meaning, but a great many applications ... It represents, not a useful concept, but a potent symbol' (1991: 35).

In fact, the notion of an underclass has a long history, although the same label has not always been used. Marx, for example, described the 'lumpenproletariat' of the nineteenth century in terms which closely resemble twentieth-century accounts of the underclass. In the most general terms, the concept describes those in persistent poverty, who are not able, for whatever reason, to gain a living within the dominant processes of production, distribution and exchange. In one sense, it might be suggested that the existence of such an underclass is in fact normal in a competitive capitalist society, which will inevitably produce losers as well as winners. As we have seen, social citizenship has been regarded as a kind of legitimate compensation for these losers, hence its role in 'class abatement'. Perhaps because the underclass is defined with respect to its *lack* of direct structural relationship to the dominant processes of production and exchange, there has been a constant tendency to conceptualize it with respect to its supposed characteristics, rather than in respect to its relationship to other classes. These characteristics have usually been negative. It is, therefore, in the explanation of poverty – or why some people are losers whilst others are not, whether the causes of poverty are primarily structural or primarily cultural – that the 'underclass' concept assumes its contentious aspect.

A frequent explanation of individual inequality is that some people are simply more talented, and ambitious, than others; they deserve, therefore, to succeed. It is perfectly possible to hold to this meritocratic view, however, without designating the less talented and less ambitious as 'worse' – as in the phrase: 'There's always got to be a bottom brick.' Bottom bricks may be bottom bricks, but they are essentially the same bricks as the top ones. It is but a short step, however, from recognizing talent and ambition in the more success-ful to the argument that the more fortunate are in fact better, and therefore *morally* superior to the losers. Nineteenth-century debates on poverty linked such arguments to wider economic questions; charity was seen not only as destroying incentives amongst the poor but as jeopardizing the nature of the capitalist enterprise itself: 'Hunger must be permitted to do its work so that labourers are com-pelled to exert themselves. Otherwise they will reduce their efforts and destroy their only safeguard against starvation' (quoted in Bendix 1964: 58) – and not only the labourers, but the enterprise as a whole, will suffer. To these arguments Malthus added his theory of population: the poor have a natural tendency to increase their num-bers beyond that sustainable by the available food supply; this improvidence results from ignorance and a lack of moral restraint. Nothing less than a new set of moral values, therefore, will serve to improve the lot of those in poverty.

We may see, therefore, that arguments which hold the poor to be, in varying degrees, responsible for their own plight have a long his-tory, as have arguments to the effect that charity (or welfare) simply stops the poor from helping themselves. It is not surprising, there-fore, that such arguments have resurfaced with the increasing influ-ence of 'New Right' perspectives on welfare – although the intention of these brief remarks has been to suggest that they are not, in fact, so 'new'. Murray (1984) has argued that the 'Great Soci-ety' welfare reforms have created an 'underclass' in the United States. Murray identifies the underclass amongst particular groups of the poor – unmarried single mothers, labour-force drop-outs (the unemployed), and those engaged in criminal activities – and attempts to demonstrate that all of these activities have been positively encouraged by welfare reforms.

Murray argues, for example, that changes in the benefits systems associated with Aid to Families with Dependent Children (AFDC) in the US have made unmarried parenthood, without employment, a more attractive option for *both* parents. He also argues that the decline in rates of arrest has increased the possibility of getting away with criminal activity, and thus its economic attractions. Welfare reforms have taken away the incentive to work. Thus for those in the black ghetto (in the United States, these arguments have focused almost entirely on the problems of poverty amongst urban blacks) there has been, with these changes in incentives, a change in attitude. The black 'underclass' is demoralized, the capacity for self-help in the community has been cumulatively undermined by the policies of well-meaning white liberals. Although Murray has developed his empirical arguments largely in the US context, he also argues that such an 'underclass' is developing in Britain, and for similar reasons: 'Britain has a growing population of working-aged, healthy people who live in a different world from other Britons, who are raising their children to live in it, and whose values are now contaminating the life of entire neighbourhoods.' There are two steps, therefore, in Murray's explanation (he has recently re-stated these arguments – Murray 1990: 4; 1994): first, well-meaning reforms exacerbate the problem they are trying to solve, that is, poverty. Then, the poor develop a moral stance which effectively removes the will to effort and further deepens the cycle of poverty.

Much of Murray's case, therefore, lay in his attempts to demonstrate the individual moral and cultural inferiority of the least well-off members of society. It is not accidental that his later work *The Bell Curve* (Herrnstein and Murray 1994), argued that low intelligence was the principal cause of poverty.[9] His empirical evidence has been widely contested. Wilson argues that, if Murray's thesis was correct, trends in black joblessness and family dissolution should have gone into reverse when the real value of welfare programmes (to the recipients) declined sharply during the 1970s; in fact, they continued to increase. Similarly, the number of single-parent families grew during the same period, when the value of AFDC benefits was going down.[10]

More generally, Murray's arguments have been systematically criticized by those who have emphasized the political and structural reasons for the increase in persistent poverty, and other 'social pathologies' such as single parenthood, in the black ghettos of the US Northwest (Wilson 1987, 1993). These accounts, therefore, have focused upon the *processes* which have generated increasing social and economic polarization. Wilson argues that in the US the loss of manufacturing employment during the economic restructuring which followed upon the crisis of the 1970s had a particularly significant impact upon the inner city. Rising unemployment had been accompanied by a fall in the real value of wages, and thus an increase in poverty. The pattern of migration flows kept the age structure of the ghetto disproportionately young (and therefore more likely to have children), and the real decline in employment opportunities meant that young black women were confronting a shrinking pool of marriageable – that is, employed – men. The very success of Equal Opportunity and Affirmative Action programmes created an increasing black middle class who, given the long-term decline of overt discriminatory practices, have moved out of the ghetto – leaving those behind as the 'truly disadvantaged'. Thus vital elements of the black infrastructure, once provided by black professionals, have been removed, and with them the role models for the next generation.

Wilson, therefore, is not concerned to deny the increase in crime, poverty, single parenthood and so on which has occurred in the urban ghettos of America. He is, however, concerned to emphasize the macro-structural factors which have brought about such changes, and his analysis suggests that only macro-structural changes can alter the situation. The problems of the truly disadvantaged, he argues, require *non-racial* solutions. Macroeconomic policies are needed to promote growth and tight labour markets, and there should be increased resources devoted to education and training, in combination with universalist child support programmes and access to child care. In short, Wilson advocates the integration of social policy and economic policy.

An important feature of Wilson's argument is its emphasis upon the *spatial* dimension of the concentration of poverty. The spatial concentration of poverty, he suggests, means social isolation from the societal mainstream, exacerbated by factors such as poor and expensive public transport.[11] Wilson accepts that the combination of poverty, weak labour-force attachment and isolation from other groups of different class and/or racial backgrounds may lead to the more ready adoption of ghetto-specific practices such as 'overt emphasis on sexuality, idleness, and public drinking' (1993: 5). However, he is careful to draw a distinction between these associations and 'culture of poverty' arguments, which had suggested that the way in which the poor adapt to poverty (fatalism, the acceptance of anti-social behaviour, and so on) are transmitted between the generations, locking the poor into a 'poverty cycle' (Lewis 1959). As Wilson points out, cultural practices alone cannot be held to account for 'unemployment, underemployment, low income, a persistent shortage of cash, and crowded living conditions' (1993: 4). In a similar vein, Merton's analysis of the conflict between societal or cultural goals and the institutionalized means through which they could be achieved has already provided a framework through which 'deviant' responses might be understood. Thus, when the goal of economic success is dominant but the individual lacks the means through which to achieve it, 'innovation' (illegal activity) is a possible response. This argument, of course, is perfectly compatible with Murray's underlying logic. However, as Merton emphasized: 'These categories [such as 'innovation'] refer to role behavior in specific types of situations, not to personality. They are types of more or less enduring response, not types of personality organization' (Merton 1965: 140).

A similar position has also been forcefully argued by British critics of Murray, who have emphasized the similarities between Murray's arguments and previous theories which have stressed the significance of the 'culture of poverty' in contributing to 'cycles of disadvantage' (Walker 1990). Empirical work in Britain on 'cycles of disadvantage' had failed to demonstrate its malign and enduring effect: 'At least half of the children born into a disadvantaged home do not repeat the pattern of disadvantage in the next generation. Over half of all forms of disadvantage arise anew each generation' (Rutter and Madge 1976).

The spatial dimension of poverty has also been emphasized in British research. Morris's research on Hartlepool (1994, 1995) demonstrates how a town once dominated by heavy industry (construction, shipbuilding, engineering and steel) had, by the 1990s, become an area in which male unemployment stood at 20 per cent. Morris's study included the long-term unemployed as well as those with very fragmented employment histories – both of these categories having been incorporated into definitions of the 'underclass'. However, Morris found there were substantial differences between the long-term unemployed and the insecurely employed. The latter were more likely to be skilled (although not apprenticed) workers, whereas the long-term unemployed were overwhelmingly unskilled. This, argues Morris, should be seen as the *source* of their vulnerability, rather than corresponding to their 'class' position. However, differences in skill did not differentiate between insecurely employed men and those who were securely employed. Insecurely employed men were no less likely to be skilled but they were likely to be younger. Unlike the long-term unemployed, they had access to networks of contacts but these contacts were themselves likely to lead to insecure jobs. Like Wilson, therefore, Morris's work points to the significance of social contacts – or their absence. Her work demonstrates the complexity of circumstances amongst the very poorest households, and she suggests that the 'underclass' concept is in any case not sufficient as a description of contemporary poverty: 'the notion of the underclass is an oversimplification, contaminated by its use as a tool of political rhetoric, which has been too readily applied to complex social phenomena' (1995: 74).

Recent discussions within the 'underclass' debate, therefore, have tended to stress the need to move away from the 'structure versus culture' (or individual morality) debates. They have, therefore, focused upon a careful unpacking of the various social processes which have generated extremes of poverty. Not surprisingly, much of this discussion and research has been grounded in case-study research, through which these dimensions have been identified. However, arguments (such as those of Murray) that the lot of the very poor (or 'underclass') lies in their individual characteristics including low intelligence, inferior morals, and/or disinclination to work may also be usefully examined via the methodology of the large-scale sample survey, characteristic of the 'employment aggregate' approach and its variants. Gallie and Vogler's analysis of the Social Change and Economic Life Initiative data (1993) found that the unemployed were actually *more* likely to say that they would continue in employment even if there was no financial necessity than were the employed (77 vs. 66 per cent). That is, they appeared to be more 'committed' to the idea of work. Marshall et al. (1996), using survey data gathered in both Britain and the US, found that individuals living in poverty were *not* significantly more likely to express 'fatalistic' attitudes (supposedly an important element of the underclass 'culture of poverty') than those who were better off. This kind of evidence, therefore, demonstrates that the behavioural *consequences* of a supposed 'underclass' location are not, in fact, as would be predicted by Murray and 'culture of poverty' arguments.

The evidence presented in the 'underclass' debate, therefore, provides us with a useful example of the way in which different methodological approaches, which are characteristic of different approaches to 'class analysis', may be brought to bear on the same topic. Both the case-study investigation of social processes and survey evidence of the consequences of poverty and unemployment for individual attitudes have made important contributions to the empirical refutation of Murray's arguments. This fact helps us to appreciate an important point relating to the need to use a variety of methodologies in order to investigate complex phenomena. Morris has recently been very critical of the employment-aggregate approach, arguing that in her exploration of the social changes that have accompanied the shifts in employment in Britain (including the 'underclass' debate): 'It has been something of a puzzle for me that social class, the concept which most overtly and directly addresses issues of structured inequality, has seemed of little relevance to this work' (1996: 184). She criticizes the employment aggregate approach for its inability to accommodate the growing numbers of long-term unemployed, the fact that it is static, providing no indication of an individual's career, and for failing to give any indication of household circumstances – all features which she found to be central in her own investigations of the 'underclass'. These kinds of criticism would seem to be particularly appropriate when employment-aggregate practitioners such as Marshall et al. assert that as the non-employed have similar attitudes to the employed, they can be treated as 'displaced class actors'. Thus 'there is little to be gained by incorporating into the research programme of class analysis those individuals without employment' (1997: 93).

However, both of these apparently contradictory positions have some substance. As Morris argues, the employment-aggregate approach (most particularly, the categories of the Goldthorpe class scheme), is and are inadequate as far as an exploration of the *processes* of 'underclass' formation are concerned. Marshall et al. are not interested in these processes (i.e. the investigation of these processes lies outside the scope of their 'research programme' of class analysis as they see it); rather, their interest lies solely in particular features of the *consequences* of social location. Yet again, we are witnessing the apparent failure of the practitioners of different approaches to 'class analysis' to recognize the different, but complementary, nature of each other's positions.

To return to broader sociological themes: it is not particularly helpful to attempt to deny the capacity for autonomous action amongst those in poverty. It is important, however, that this capacity is not linked automatically to arguments like Murray's to the effect that it is the *peculiar* nature of the poor's capacity for action – in particular, their lack of moral values stemming from a 'culture of poverty' – which explains their material circumstances. Murray would argue (as would other right-wing sociologists such as Saunders) that they wish to *restore* the capacity for action to a population which has been deprived of it by the excesses of bureaucratic state welfare. As Murray has argued:

> Government cannot identify the worthy, but it can protect a society in which the worthy can identify themselves. I am proposing triage of a sort, triage by self-selection. In triage on the battlefield, the doctor makes the decision – this one gets treatment, that one waits, the other one is made comfortable while waiting to die. In our social triage, the decision is left up to the patient. The patient always has a right to say 'I can do X' and get a chance to prove it. Society always has a right to hold him to that pledge. The patient always has the right to fail. Society always has the right to let him. (1984: 234)

'The right to fail', however, has a chilling echo in the nineteenth-century arguments of Thomas Malthus:

> A man who is born into a world already possessed, if he cannot get subsistence from his parents on whom he has a just demand, and if the society does not want his labour, has no claim of right to the smallest portion of food, and, in fact, has no business to be where he is. At Nature's mighty feast there is no vacant cover for him. She tells him to be gone, and will quickly execute her own orders. (Malthus cited in Bendix 1964: 65)

Conclusion

Despite the many inadequacies that may be discovered in Marshall's original account of the growth and development of citizenship in modern industrial societies, his threefold distinction between civil, political and social citizenship has proved invaluable in understanding developments in social stratification since the nineteenth century. The universalistic ideologies of liberal democracy made it possible (and still make it possible) for those excluded to argue that the barriers to their status as citizens should be removed. Citizenship, however, has very often only been achieved through struggle, rather than granted as a right. Industrial citizenship (that is, collective bargaining rights) as well as the rights of social citizenship (particularly welfare rights) may be regarded as being in conflict with the interests associated with the dominant capitalist order.

It is legitimate, therefore, to view many of the citizenship gains of the population at large as the outcome of actual or anticipated class conflict. Despite Marx's predictions, class conflict in Western industrial societies has largely concerned itself with gaining some kind of protection from the ravages of the market for the subordinate classes, as well as (or perhaps, rather than) the revolutionary transformation of society itself. Paradoxically, therefore, class struggles have been significant in achieving significant *status* gains on behalf of subordinate classes – and amongst the most important of these has been the status of citizenship.

Initially, however, citizenship gains were largely achieved on behalf of a white, male working class. The rights of social citizenship, in particular, were modelled on patriarchal family structures. Parallel with working-class struggles, therefore, there have also been struggles on behalf of excluded groups such as women and blacks, initiated by non-class social movements. It is not being suggested that exclusion from, and gradual entry into, the status of citizenship is a sufficient explanation of the location of women and blacks within the stratification order; nevertheless, these processes are crucial to any understanding of their contemporary situation. In the modern era, new social movements are seeking to extend further the boundaries of citizenship to include animals and children, as well as more general concerns with the environment lived in by all 'citizens'.

As we have seen, much of the contemporary political debate over 'citizenship' is concerned with negative liberties rather than positive liberties, with an emphasis on personal freedoms rather than the redistributive issues. Any stress on the importance of personal freedoms, however, should not be allowed to override the simple fact perceived by an earlier generation of commentators (including Marx, and Marshall himself) that personal freedoms do not count for much in a situation characterized by gross material inequalities. It is paradoxical, therefore, that the rights of social citizenship are now under sustained attack by those, such as Murray, claiming to be motivated by the need to preserve personal freedoms.[12] These arguments, it cannot be stressed too often, repeat those in widespread use before not only social, but civil and political citizenship rights had been gained: 'The slave must be compelled to work; but the freeman should be left to his own judgement and discretion' (Rev. Townsend cited in Bendix 1964: 58).

Once gained, citizenship rights are universal; thus the erosion of citizenship affects more than just the working class. It is in this sense that the arguments of those who have argued that 'class' has become less significant in contemporary politics might be conceded. The rollback of social citizenship affects all of those who have gained from its implementation, or who might hope to benefit from its extension. The defence of citizenship, therefore, cuts across the boundaries of social class.

Notes

1   Indeed, it might be argued that Conservative government actions during the miners' strike in Britain (1984) included the erosion of aspects of civil citizenship concerned with freedom of movement, the right to protest, etc.

2   The 1789 declaration in France of 'the Rights of Man and Citizen' did not include women, and the Code Napoléon served further to establish the subordinate legal status of women in France.

3   Pateman argues that, to create a properly democratic society, it is necessary to 'deconstruct and reassemble our understanding of the body politic ... The most profound and complex problem for political theory and practice is how the two bodies of humankind and feminine and masculine individuality can be fully incorporated into political life. How can the present of patriarchal domination, opposition and duality be transformed into a future of autonomous, democratic differentiation?' (1989: 53). Pateman does not give an answer to this question, and it certainly lies outside this author's capacities.

4   It should be noted that the 'male breadwinner' model is particularly appropriate to the British case. In other European countries such as France, where women have historically been involved to a greater extent in paid employment, maternity legislation, family allowances etc. have been developed on the assumption that women, even mothers with children, would remain in full-time employment. See Jensen (1986); Crompton et al. (1990).

5   This generalization is broadly correct for Britain and the US; there are, however, European variations, paticularly in the timing and extent of first-wave feminism. See Evans (1987).

6   It should be noted that there are considerable differences, by ethnic group, *within* the black community in respect of these social indicators (see Brown 1984). These reflect important differences in family structures, regional variations, as well as the timing of successive waves of immigration.

7   A theoretical debate which has been of considerable relevance to the US case has concerned whether the situation of Southern blacks should be explored using the concept of 'caste' or 'class'; see Dollard (1957) and Cox (1959).

8   In the British debate in particular, two factors have contributed to this emphasis on stability. First, longitudinal studies of the 'class structure' have to assume that the occupational groupings they identify keep to their relative position(s) over time, otherwise comparisons are impossible. Second, the 'Nuffield programme' has emphasized the stability of *relative* opportunities, rather than the increase in *absolute* opportunities as far as mobility, educational opportunities etc. are concerned. This topic will be discussed at some length in our final chapter.

9   Herrnstein and Murray also argue that levels of intelligence differ amongst different ethnic groups. For a discussion and critique, see Devine (1997: 230ff).

10 Recent policies in the US have cut such benefits even further.
11 Lash and Urry (1994) also emphasize the growing problem of 'wild spaces' in 'reflexive modernity'.
12 A theoretical rejection of these arguments is developed in Plant (1991).

8 Retrospect and Prospect

Introduction

In this final chapter, we will be returning to some of the concerns relating to the understanding and explanation of social and material inequalities which we raised at the beginning of this book. More generally, we will also be suggesting that the most fruitful way ahead in 'class analysis' within sociology lies in the recognition of plurality and difference, rather than forcing a choice from amongst competing positions, or attempting to devise a completely new or revised theoretical approach.

In chapter 1 we emphasized the range of different meanings of the class concept. These included 'class' as prestige, status or style; 'class' as describing structured economic and social inequality; and 'class' as a label for actual or potential social and/or economic actors. If 'class' means different things to different people and in different contexts, then it follows that there can be no 'correct' meaning of the term. Our review of the field of class and stratification analysis has incorporated a wide range of approaches, reflecting the complexity of the concept itself. With considerable over-simplification, these different sociological approaches may be described under four major headings:

1   The study of the *processes* of the emergence and perpetuation of advantaged and disadvantaged groups or 'classes' within society. These studies are characteristically case studies – that is, they have a focus on a particular group, or set of occupations – and use a variety of research methods and data-collection techniques. Such studies

invariably reveal the complexities of group formation, and in particular the interpenetration of the 'economic' with the social or cultural. Thus they have focused not only on 'class' factors – that is, economic power as reflected in production and market relationships – but also on ascriptive (status) factors associated with gender, race and age, as well as cultural and normative assumptions, and the influence of contextual factors such as locality and community. To borrow an analogy from Wright (1997: 2), this is an approach to 'class analysis' as a 'dependent variable' enterprise, in which a particular 'class' is that which has to be understood and explained. A number of very influential studies of class processes in Britain include research on the affluent worker of the 1960s (Goldthorpe et al. 1969), Lockwood on clerks (1958) and Newby on agricultural workers (1977). Contemporary studies of class processes would include Morris on the 'underclass' (chapter 7), and Savage et al. on the middle classes (chapter 6). Such studies will often incorporate all of the different meanings of 'class' which we have identified – prestige and lifestyles, unequal rewards, and potential for action – in their investigations of the group(s) in question.

2 Second, there is the study of the *consequences* of class location. In this book, the major example of this approach which has been examined is the study of employment aggregates, in which employment is used as a proxy for class. Wright (1997: 3) has described this approach to class analysis as an 'independent variable' specialty, in which 'class' is the constant factor and its contribution to other factors – health, educational opportunities, social mobility etc. – is that which has to be explained. Thus in this approach it is important to isolate 'class' from other stratifying phenomena – gender, status, race, and so on. Much of this kind of work in Britain has followed through the 'political arithmetic' tradition (Halsey 1988), and thus there has been a major focus on patterns of social and economic inequality. There has also been a continuing interest in class action, as indicated by voting behaviour (see for example Heath et al. 1994). However, the way in which employment aggregates vote (or express their voting preferences) cannot be said to represent the study of classes *in* action as such.

Both of these approaches have a primary focus on 'class', although what is being investigated is somewhat different in each case. Both are associated with a tradition of empirical investigation. The third major theme we identify, however, is largely theoretical, and is considerably broader in its scope.

3 This is the discussion of the significance of 'class', and class

processes, for macro theories of societal change and development. As discussed in chapter 5, developments in both post-structuralist and postmodernist theory have argued (in the case of post-structuralism) for a radically transformed understanding of the 'class' concept, as well as (in the case of postmodernism) for the death of 'class' itself. Post-structuralism argues that 'classes' are a consequence of the changing flux of ideas rather than economic processes, and are therefore discursive, rather than economic, constructs. Postmodernism seeks to replace the classic theories of modernism. Postmodernists argue that as the concept of class (such as, for example, in the work of Marx and Weber) was developed in order to analyse 'modern' societies, then it has become increasingly irrelevant as far as the analysis of 'postmodern', 'late modern', or 'reflexively modern' societies are concerned. With increasing *individuation*, 'class', it is argued, is an anachronism. Thus these discussions have often tended to focus on the meaning of class (or its absence) as a source of individual identity. As we have seen (in chapter 5), contemporary identities are seen by these authors as being primarily shaped by cultural (that is, status or consumption), rather than economic, factors.

4 A fourth strand of debate focuses largely on the actor and relates to the investigation of the development of class and status cultures and identities. Given the recent 'cultural turn' in sociology, this approach has many overlaps with poststructuralism and postmodernism. However, as a tradition of social enquiry, it pre-dates these recent theoretical developments. For example, Willis's *Learning to Labour* takes much of its theoretical framework from the Marxist debates of the 1970s. During the 1950s and 1960s, anthropologically influenced sociology examined the difference between the 'roughs' and 'respectables' within the British working class (Klein 1965). In the 1930s, as we have seen in chapter 6, Warner investigated the class (status) cultures of 'Middletown', and Bourdieu has mapped class cultures in France in the 1970s. It may be suggested that the postmodernist turn has recently overtaken this *oeuvre*, as is described by the author of a recent study of working-class women:

> I watched 'class' analysis disappear from feminism and cultural studies as it [class] became increasingly more of an issue for the friends I had grown up with, the people I live(d) with and the women of this research. I felt caught in two worlds: one which theorized increased movement, access and playfulness and another which was regulated, circumscribed, denied ... As the differences between the two worlds widened (when fashions in postmodernism peaked) I used this book to try and make connections ... to make class matter. (Skeggs 1997: 15)

Much historical work has also had a primary focus upon the question of class identities and the shaping of class cultures (Joyce 1995). This was also a central concern of E. P. Thompson's *Making of the English Working Class.*

This short summary has emphasized that, within the different domains of 'class analysis', 'class' has had, and continues to have, a number of different meanings. Thus, although the various approaches to class analysis have many linkages with each other, we nevertheless have to be aware that one person's 'employment aggregate' is another's 'cultural community'; that is, that the same term – 'class' – may describe different phenomena depending on the theoretical perspective of the investigator.

This plurality of approaches and definition has been a substantial source of academic debate. Frequently, however, these debates have taken the form of what we have described as 'pseudo-debates', that is, debates in which the supposed protagonists have in fact radically different understandings of the concept of 'class'. Rather than continue to engage in these kinds of debate, it has been argued in this book that there can be no single, correct, definition of the term, but that rather, different versions focus on different aspects of the complex whole. However, it should immediately be emphasized that to advocate the need to accept plurality in class analysis should not be interpreted as a collapse into either relativism, or post-modern randomness. Debates may take place *within* these different domains, for example (e.g. when it is argued that Goldthorpe's class scheme is superior to the Alford index as far as the analysis of changes in voting behaviour is concerned – see p. 105). It is also justifiable to use evidence drawn from one strand to challenge the assumptions of another. For example, we have pointed to the persistence of (class-) structured social and material inequality in order to criticize post-modern theories of 'societal shift' (and we will be developing this argument further). To argue for the persistence of this aspect of 'class', however, does not necessarily mean that all elements of post-modern arguments relating to 'class' may therefore be rejected. For example, the shift to services and changes in the nature of 'work' as employment has had an impact on the kinds of identity likely to be associated with 'work', in that 'work' at the end of the twentieth century is relatively less likely to be associated with collective, conflictual identities than it once was.

A number of consequences follow from an explicit recognition of the plurality of themes and approaches. First, we should recognize that no single approach to 'class analysis' can incorporate all of the different elements of debate to be found within the area of class and stratification. It follows that all of these approaches will be partial in some respects. This suggests that attempts to achieve a synthesis of the different approaches, and/or develop a 'new approach' which would achieve the same objective (complete coverage of the field), are unlikely to be very successful. If plurality is to be accepted, then contradictions have to be tolerated. This point is emphasized by Bradley (1996), who suggests, following Berman, that rather than thinking in terms of 'either/or' (e.g. *either* a Marxist *or* a Weberian theory; *either* social stability *or* social fluidity and change), we should think in terms of 'both/and'. However, it may be suggested that Bradley does not completely follow through her own recommendations. She seeks to 'pull together classical or modernist approaches to understanding inequalities with the newer perspectives inspired by postmodernism and post-structuralism' (1996: 3). Her attempt at synthesis, and/or providing a 'better version' (p. 204) of modernist theory, contains many valuable insights. Nevertheless, ultimately it emerges as a series of descriptive statements relating to the interaction of class, gender, race and age, rather than a new theory as such. It is indisputable that the inequalities associated with class, gender, race and age *are* related to each other. However, rather than attempting to integrate 'modern' and 'postmodern' accounts of these phenomena, it is preferable to recognize that the theories in question not only give different versions of the same reality but also focus on different *aspects* of the whole. Thus 'class analysis' has to be seen as addressing a series of different *topics*, as well as reflecting a variety of theoretical perspectives.

If a synthesis of different approaches is not achievable, neither is it justifiable to argue that a single approach to 'class analysis' is to be preferred to all others. This tendency has unfortunately been a feature of the 'Nuffield' programme and those associated with it. For example, Marshall (1997: 2) has asserted that: 'Increasingly ... the sociological debate has featured the class categories devised by John Goldthorpe and his colleagues'. Marshall concedes the existence of other approaches to class analysis, but these are disparagingly rejected (as 'data-free', 'programmatic and rhetorical', etc.). He concludes that the employment aggregate approach is 'that version [of class analysis] which has proved most illuminating during these past two decades, and shows greatest promise for further sociological understanding' (1997: 27). However, as we have seen in the last chapter, Morris did not find this approach particularly helpful in her empirical studies of the 'underclass', and, as has been argued more generally, the employment aggregate approach is rather inadequate as far as the study of class processes and labour markets, and the generation of class identities, is concerned.

It would be unfortunate, therefore, if 'class analysis' were to be confined to the Nuffield programme (as Marshall seems to be suggesting), not because this programme is itself 'wrong', but because it represents only a part of the picture. Although its precise meaning may vary, 'class' remains a concept which links, however imperfectly, social structure with social action, and which can be used as an organizing concept for the investigation of a wide range of issues associated with social inequality and social differentiation. It is simply too important to get obscured by debates amongst sociologists. In the next sections of this chapter, therefore, we will first examine the topic of social mobility and the related question of the link between educational level and occupational achievement. The evidence will not only demonstrate both continuity and change in the 'class' structure, but will also enable us to examine conflicting explanations of inequality. Next, we will examine the important question of social and economic polarization. This will demonstrate that, although there remain significant (class) continuities in the constitution of inequalities, there have also been morphological shifts in their structuring. The understanding of these shifts does not require radically new concepts or theories, but they do have to be recognized.

Social mobility

Social mobility research measures the mobility of individuals between occupations and/or occupational origins, both between generations and over the lifecycle. An interest in social mobility extends across the political spectrum.[1] Evidence of high rates of social mobility may be used to argue that the society in question is characterized by achievement rather than ascription, that individuals reap their rewards according to their personal qualities, rather than on the basis of 'unfair' advantages such as inherited wealth, or personal connections – in short that a true meritocracy is in operation. Besides the powerful legitimation of structures of occupational inequality which such arguments bestow, social mobility also acts as an important 'safety valve' in advanced industrial societies:

Mobility provides an escape route for large numbers of the most able and ambitious members of the underclass, thereby easing some of the tensions generated by inequality. Elevation into the middle classes represents a *personal* solution to the problems of low status, and as such tends to weaken collectivist efforts to improve the lot of the underclass as a whole. It has often been suggested that upward mobility undermines the political base of the underclass most seriously by siphoning off the men best fitted for leadership. (Parkin 1972: 50)

This argument has been pithily – if unsociologically – expressed in the well-known ditty, sung to the tune of the socialist anthem 'The Red Flag': 'The working class can kiss my arse; I've got the foreman's job at last.' In a rather more serious vein, Marx wrote that: 'The more a ruling class is able to assimilate the foremost minds of a ruled class, the more stable and dangerous becomes its rule' (1974: 601).

In the United States, the study of social mobility has assumed particular significance because of its apparent association with what have been regarded as significant 'core values' of American society – that is, the belief that individual hard work, application and effort will eventually bring their rewards; that, regardless of social background or family connections, inherited wealth or aristocratic title, it is indeed possible for the suitably talented individual to rise from a log cabin to the White House (Devine 1997). The widespread popularity of such classic liberal ideas relating to individual opportunity was not, of course, confined to the United States, as nineteenth-century books such as Samuel Smiles's *Self-Help* (1859) indicate.

The extent of social mobility, therefore, has been widely used as a measure of the 'openness' of industrial societies, and high mobility rates seen as an indication that the liberal promise of equality of opportunity has indeed been achieved. Blau and Duncan's (1967) statistical investigation of a sample of nearly 21,000 men aged 20 to 64 (drawn in 1962) in the United States appeared to confirm that, even if this happy state had not yet arrived, the US was well on the way to it. Blau and Duncan used techniques of path analysis in order to explore (amongst a variety of other empirical associations) the relationship between social origins, education and career beginnings on subsequent career success. They concluded that, although social origins did indeed have an influence, educational background and training, and early work experience, had a more pronounced effect on chances of success (1967: 402).[2] They also demonstrated that rates of social mobility in the United States were high, and argued

that this was a consequence of the 'advanced level of industrialization and education'; other industrial countries would, in due course,
catch up (p. 433).

Thus, for Blau and Duncan, there can be little doubt that increasing social mobility is inevitable, as well as a Good Thing. The underlying optimism of their perspective is very evident:

> a fundamental trend towards expanding universalism characterizes
> industrial society. Objective criteria of evaluation that are universally
> accepted increasingly pervade all spheres of life and displace particu-
> laristic standards of diverse ingroups [and] intuitive judgments ... The
> growing emphasis on rationality and efficiency inherent in this spread
> of universalism finds expression in rapid technological progress and
> increasing division of labor and differentiation generally ... The strong
> interdependence among men and groups engendered by the extensive
> division of labor becomes the source of their organic solidarity, to use
> Durkheim's term, inasmuch as social differentiation weakens the par-
> ticularistic ingroup values that unite men. (1967: 429)

Blau and Duncan's work has been subject to extensive criticism. It
was suggested that, far from being a source of integration, extensive
social mobility might actually be a destabilizing element in industrial
societies. Lipset and Bendix (1959) argued that through the process
of mobility people lose their previous attachments to social collectivities which had contributed to their sense of self-worth and psychological stability, and the resulting 'status inconsistency' might be
a source of social disruption. As the above extract from their work
makes clear, however, Blau and Duncan's conclusions gave substantial support to the 'industrial society' thesis concerning the
inevitability of increasing social stability, equality of opportunity,
and societal convergence. These kinds of argument, as we have seen
(chapters 2 and 3), were strongly contested by those who emphasized continuing conflict and the persistence of *class* inequalities.

Blau and Duncan's model of mobility takes the occupational
structure to be a finely graded hierarchy, into which individuals are
sorted according to their (individual) attributes. However, as critics
such as Crowder (1974) have pointed out, a substantial degree of the
variance in status attainment is not explained by the Blau–Duncan
model, and indeed the wide distribution of income *within* educational attainment categories suggests that the relationship between
income and education is not linear. Crowder argued that the large
residual paths of the model are not to be explained, as Blau and
Duncan had suggested, by 'pure luck', but rather, are the outcome

of systematic *structural* constraints which shape not only the occupational system but also processes of allocation within it. These structural constraints include the institutions of political power and private property, and material and ideological constraints which specify the extent of control and the 'appropriate' behaviour associated with particular positions. In short, 'class' inequalities.

These arguments are echoed by Goldthorpe who, as we have seen, favours not a graded hierarchy of occupations (or status scale) but his theoretical class scheme. The use of such a scheme attempts to incorporate explicitly the kinds of structural constraints absent from the Blau–Duncan model. Goldthorpe claims that his scheme encompasses the dynamics of class relations; it is *relational*, rather than gradational.[3] Recent advances in statistical techniques, in particular, log-linear modelling, have made it possible to employ non-linear class schemes such as Goldthorpe's in social mobility research. In contrast, Blau and Duncan's statistical techniques (path analysis) presupposed a hierarchical (that is, gradational) ordering of the underlying categories (income, education, occupational status).

Log-linear models also offer a solution to other technical problems which have historically beset research in social mobility. Social mobility investigations record movement within an occupational structure at two (or more) points in time – but the structure itself is not stable. As industrial societies have developed, so there have occurred massive changes in the structure of occupations (and thus the 'class' structure), first from agricultural to industrial occupations, then, during the course of the twentieth century, from predominantly 'manual' to 'non-manual' occupations (chapter 4). For example, in Great Britain, non-manual workers increased from 18.7 per cent of the occupied population in 1911 to 52.3 per cent in 1981, with a corresponding decline in the proportion of manual workers (Price and Bain 1988: 164). Thus in any standard mobility tabulation comparing fathers' occupations with sons' occupations, the marginal totals will vary, reflecting the difference in the occupational structure at different times. In a simple 2×2 table comparing manual with non-manual, for example, there will be more manual fathers and, conversely, more non-manual sons. To put the point another way, given long-term changes in the occupational structure, a certain amount of 'upward' mobility is 'built in' or 'forced', given the under-supply of non-manual sons.

In Glass's study of social mobility after the Second World War (1954) this problem had been resolved by drawing a distinction between 'structural' and 'exchange' mobility.[4] The differences between the marginal totals in the mobility table are used to provide a measure of 'structural' mobility brought about through occupational changes. The further extent of mobility revealed in the table was described as 'exchange' mobility – that is, mobility net of structural effects.

There are a number of statistical problems associated with Glass's approach (Goldthorpe 1980; 1987: 74–5, Heath 1981). In consequence, approaches to the study of inequalities of opportunity have been developed which distinguish between 'absolute' and 'relative' mobility *rates*. 'Absolute' mobility describes the total mobility revealed in a mobility table, which would include the mobility brought about by changes in the occupational structure (or occupational 'upgrading' over time). 'Relative' mobility chances are calculated by comparing, for people from different occupational backgrounds, their chances of entering different 'classes'. This is described as a measure of 'social fluidity'; that is, as a measure of 'whether or not changes in the structure of objective mobility opportunities over time are being equally reflected in the mobility experience of individuals of all origins alike' (Goldthorpe 1980; 1987: 75). These chances are computed using odds ratios. These demonstrate the chance ('odds') of a service-class son being recruited to the service class, rather than to the working class, with the odds on a working-class son being recruited to the service class rather than the working class.[5]

Glass's (1954) research appeared to demonstrate that Britain was not a particularly 'open' society, in that long-range mobility (that is, from bottom to top, or from top to bottom) was relatively rare, and there was a high degree of self-recruitment to the 'elite' positions in British society. What mobility there was tended to be only short-range; that is, to positions more or less adjacent in the occupational hierarchy, from manual worker to supervisor, or clerk to lower-level manager. In particular, if mobility did occur across the boundary between manual and non-manual occupations (seen by many as representing the fundamental line of cleavage within the class structure), then this was highly likely to be only between adjacent classes – for example, from skilled manual to lower-level non-manual – within what has been described as the 'buffer-zone' of the class structure overall (Glass 1954; see also Westergaard and Resler 1975, Goldthorpe 1980; 1987).

Goldthorpe's 1972–4 enquiry into social mobility revealed a rather different picture. It suggested that a considerable amount of *long-range* mobility had in fact occurred – for example, 28.5 per cent of those in class I in the 1972 survey were from class VI and VII backgrounds (Goldthorpe 1980; 1987: 45). The sheer extent of mobility which had taken place also served to undermine the 'buffer-zone' hypothesis. The extent of mobility revealed by the Oxford survey might, of course, have been anticipated, given the long-term changes in the occupational structure which have led to an inexorable expansion of the middle and upper 'classes'. As a consequence, the extent of upward mobility in the population is far in excess of downward mobility.

However, Goldthorpe argues that these results did *not* demonstrate that Britain had become a more 'open' society. This (apparently) contradictory assertion can be demonstrated by evidence using the distinction between absolute and relative rates of social mobility, employing the techniques of odds ratios as described above. The analysis of relative mobility chances, or patterns of social fluidity, within the Oxford sample demonstrated that, despite high rates of absolute social mobility, there were marked, and persistent, differences in the *relative* chances of men of different social backgrounds moving into higher-level occupations. Put simply, the data revealed a 'disparity ratio' of 1 : 2 : 4 for the chances of access to classes I and II for men from 'Service', 'Intermediate', and 'Working' classes (1980; 1987: 50). Thus Goldthorpe concludes:

> the pattern of relative mobility chances . . . associated with the British class structure . . . embodies inequalities that are of a quite striking kind: in particular, those that emerge if one compares the chances of men whose fathers held higher-level service-class positions being themselves found in such positions rather than in working-class ones with the corresponding chances of men of working-class origins. Where inequalities in class chances of this magnitude are displayed – of the order . . . of over 30 : 1 – then, we believe, the presumption must be that to a substantial extent they do reflect inequalities of opportunity that are rooted in the class structure. (1987: 328)

Goldthorpe's class scheme, together with the associated emphasis on *relative* mobility rates has been developed in international comparisons of social mobility.[6] Comparative work allows for the testing of the 'industrial society' thesis of universally increasing openness and opportunity, which had been advanced in Blau and Duncan's work. However, different countries industrialize at different rates, and the process of industrialization does not always result in a uniform occupational outcome.[7] Such differences between the units of comparison have rendered cross-national comparisons highly problematic. Thus Featherman, Jones and Hauser (FJH) (1975) have advanced a modified version of the thesis of universalism. Absolute mobility rates may vary between different societies because of factors such as differences in the occupational structure, the size of the agricultural sector, and so on, but nevertheless the underlying 'mobility regime' – that is, *relative* mobility rates – would show a basic similarity in all societies with market economies and nuclear family systems. This has become known as the thesis of 'constant social fluidity'. Using a version of Goldthorpe's class scheme, the international group of researchers associated with the CASMIN project (Comparative Analysis of Social Mobility in Industrial Societies) has carried out a series of comparisons of relative social mobility. Their results have largely confirmed the FJH hypothesis in that basic patterns of relative mobility chances proved to be similar between different countries (Erikson and Goldthorpe 1993).

What are the *consequences* of social mobility for stratification systems? One important feature of advanced industrial societies which the finding of constant social fluidity does demonstrate is that, despite legislative efforts (such as educational reform etc.) to achieve greater 'openness' and equality of opportunity, this has not, as yet, been completely achieved. Although overall rates of upward mobility have risen, the different *relative* rates of class mobility prospects have proved remarkably resistant to change. All of the emphasis in the work of Goldthorpe and his colleagues, therefore, has been on the *stability* of relative chances, rather than on the changes in the occupational structure which have increased *absolute* levels of opportunity, and this has been the source of much criticism (e.g. Scott and Morris 1996).

Goldthorpe has also been accused of 'political bias' in the presentation of his data in respect of the British case. Saunders (1990a) has argued that Goldthorpe, as well as other 'left-wing' sociologists who have followed a broadly similar strategy in their analysis of contemporary British mobility patterns (in particular, Marshall and his colleagues at the University of Essex (1988)) have been excessively concerned with relativities, rather than absolutes in respect of social mobility. In contrast, Saunders emphasizes the significance of the *absolute* increases in mobility rates which have been brought about by economic expansion since the Second World War, and changes in the occupational structure. He also argues that presumptions as to the lack of 'openness' in British society are founded upon the unwarranted assumption that the different talents, aptitudes and abilities which shape 'life chances' *are* randomly distributed within society:

> Goldthorpe and many other contemporary sociologists effectively end up denying that ... natural inequalities can have any importance in influencing people's destinies. If, for example, the working class accounts for half of the population, then for Goldthorpe and for the Essex researchers we should expect half of all doctors, managers and top civil servants to have originated in the working class. If we find, as Goldthorpe did, that only one quarter of such groups are from working-class origins, then according to this reasoning we are justified in assuming that the 'shortfall' is entirely due to social barriers and that British society is therefore just as class-ridden and unjust as its critics have always maintained. In the idealised world of John Goldthorpe and other 'left' sociologists, people's destinies should be randomly determined because talents are randomly distributed. British society is thus found wanting because people of working-class origins are not in the majority in all the top jobs. This argument is ludicrous, yet in modern sociology it is all too rarely questioned. (Saunders 1990a: 83)

Saunders states a clear political preference for the neo-liberal argument, developed by economists such as Hayek, that a relative lack of regulation, together with its associated inequalities, within the capitalist marketplace is more dynamic than its 'regulated' alternatives and thus of more material benefit to the population as a whole. Goldthorpe has stated an equally clear preference for a degree of market regulation or 'corporatism' (Goldthorpe 1984a). There are theoretical arguments, and empirical evidence, which would be supportive of either perspective, but ultimately, judgements as to the superiority – or otherwise – of the alternatives on offer are unavoidably political.

Saunders's arguments also incorporate the neo-liberal assumption that an absence of regulation will allow the 'best' to achieve the most. That is, the greater the level of competition, the more likely it is that a true meritocracy will be achieved. That the greatest share of the available rewards do go to the 'best' or 'functionally most important' is, as we have seen, in chapter 1, a central argument of 'functionalist' theories of stratification. The functional theory of stratification has argued that social inequality is an 'unconsciously evolved device' whereby the most important positions are filled by the most qualified persons. If occupational class is taken to be an indicator of the importance of a position, and education is taken as an indicator of level of qualification, then functional theory would anticipate that those who achieve superior class positions will have higher levels of qualifications and, moreover, that education will be *more* important than class origins in getting higher-level jobs (as we have seen, this was, indeed, Blau and Duncan's argument). However, Marshall and Swift (1993; Marshall et al. 1997) have shown that individuals' class of origin has a substantial influence on whether or not they eventually achieve a 'service-class' position – regardless of the level of qualification obtained.

For example, their data show that 43 per cent of men of service-class origins but with only middling levels of qualification (above GCSE and up to A level) reached service-class occupational positions.[8] However, only 15 per cent of men of working-class origins, with the *same* level of qualifications, reached service-class positions (Marshall and Swift 1993). There has been a general increase in the numbers of people gaining qualifications, but class differences in access to education have been maintained. However, there does seem to have been some weakening of the 'class effect' over the last twenty years, in that, 'Given the same level of educational attainment, the odds of a man reaching the salariat from a class I or class II background have been approximately halved, relative to those for a man from an unskilled manual background' (Marshall et al. 1997: 129).

In contrast, Saunders has argued that ability and effort, rather than class background, are the most important features leading to occupational success (1996, 1997). Saunders uses evidence from the National Child Development Survey, a longitudinal survey based upon an initial panel of over 17,000 children born during one week in 1958. This survey carried out an intelligence test when the children were 11; Saunders's analysis uses a further survey carried out when the same subjects were aged 33. His results (using the technique of logistic regression) show that measured intelligence (at 11), together with other individual attributes such as motivation and work attitudes, were the most important factors predicting whether or not people achieved higher-level occupational positions. Thus he concludes that Britain is indeed a meritocracy, rather than a class-ridden society.

We have here, therefore, two positions which are apparently in complete contrast with each other. Marshall and Swift argue that class origins override educational levels, Saunders that ability and effort are more important than class background. However, it may be suggested that both of these apparently conflicting sets of arguments have some validity. Class inequalities will continue to give many an 'unfair' advantage, but in a society such as Britain, able and hard-working people (of whatever class origin) are more likely to be occupationally successful than those who possess neither of these characteristics.[9] Indeed, both 'sides' of this particular argument produce evidence that might be used to support the other's case. We have seen that Marshall et al. have suggested that the 'class effect' on occupational attainment has declined somewhat over the years, suggesting a move in the direction of greater meritocracy. Saunders's evidence shows that private schooling is important for class I/II children in avoiding downward mobility, 'suggesting that the private schools may offer middle-class parents some means of insuring their less able offspring against downward mobility' (1997: 273). In respect of this particular debate, therefore, there are good grounds for taking a 'both/and' rather than an 'either/or' position.

In this section, therefore, we have used the topic of social mobility in the manner of a 'worked example' in order to illustrate a number of themes we have been developing in this book. We have demonstrated the continuities with a series of important debates in the social sciences concerning the explanation and origins of inequality, including conflict versus consensus approaches, and functionalist (liberal) versus radical (class) accounts of social inequality. We have seen that, although the level of social mobility has increased, relative rates of mobility have remained remarkably stable. However, an important point to emphasize is that the overwhelming emphasis on constant social fluidity (i.e. the stability of *relative* chances of social mobility depending on class of origin) to be found within the 'Nuffield' approach has had the effect of suggesting that nothing has 'really' changed; for example, 'British society is no more open now than it was at the time of the First World War' (Marshall 1997: 1). Nevertheless, the enormous increase in *absolute* mobility rates (or structural mobility) means that the opportunities of upward mobility for children of working-class parents have in fact expanded dramatically. As far as people's lived experiences are concerned, this absolute increase will have had more impact than the stability of relative rates.

A similar argument may be developed in respect of women and class analysis. The energies of those associated with the Nuffield programme have been largely devoted to demonstrating that *relative* mobility rates for women are similar to those of men, that a woman's partner's occupational class gives a better account of her political attitudes than her own, and so on.[10] That is, all of the emphasis has been upon the *lack* of change in gender, and gender relations, in relation to 'class' as defined within the programme. However, the entry of women into paid employment has had a considerable impact on both individuals and families, particularly within the middle classes. The experiences of children growing up with two working parents will be very different from those of children who grew up in a 'male breadwinner' family. The entry of women into higher-level occupations appears to be leading to new cleavages within the middle classes, in that women tend to be disproportionately concentrating in professional, and particular managerial, occupations (chapter 6). This restructuring is projected back into the family itself, as women in managerial occupations are less likely to have childcare responsibilities (and have fewer children) than professional women (Crompton and Harris 1998). Even more important, perhaps, is the increase in social and economic polarization brought about by the widening gulf between two-wage and no-wage households.

Thus there are significant shifts in the morphology of inequality in Britain (and other similar countries). In the next section, therefore, we will examine the *processes* of social and economic polarization. As we shall see, class remains very important to the understanding of these processes, but other changes – in gender relations, technology, the organization of production and the political reshaping of institutions – need to be considered as well.

Social polarization

The recent and rapid increase in the extent of social polarization in many of the advanced service economies has served to re-emphasize the point that 'reflexive', 'late modern' and/or 'postmodern' societies remain *capitalist* societies, whatever kinds of labels social scientists might decide to apply to them. (Indeed, many of the trends which have been described as 'postmodern' might be seen as the consequence of the spread and intensification of capitalism. For example, we may point to the commodification of lifestyle, feelings and emotions, through the services which have been developed to accompany the biographical (self-) construction of the reflexive individual.) Capitalist societies have always been unequal societies. However, as we have seen in preceding chapters, social reforms associated with the development of citizenship (both the elaboration of citizenship via social citizenship and its extension to categories such as women), together with the development of social security protections, the expansion of the welfare state, and (in some periods) progressive taxation regimes, have served to reduce the scale of inequalities during the mid-twentieth century. As well as declining inequalities, absolute rates of social mobility were also increasing, and living standards rose for the majority of people.

From the end of the 1970s, however, inequalities in Britain widened considerably. Growing income inequality during this period has not been a universal trend cross-nationally. An eighteen-country comparison showed that the rate of the increase of inequality in the UK (between 1979 and 1990) was greater than that of any other country besides New Zealand. Longitudinal data suggest a decline in income inequality in the UK from the 1960s, but a sharp reversal from 1976–7. This gathered pace during the 1980s, increasing by 10 percentage points by 1990, and since 1977 the proportion of the population with less than half the average income has more than trebled (Rowntree 1995). In chapter 7, we have already discussed the debate relating to the supposed expansion of the 'underclass'. It was emphasized that this problem is to a considerable extent *spatial*, in that poverty is often concentrated in particular, relatively isolated, areas or regions of declining industry. Social polarization and widening inequalities, however, might be indicative of a more profound change in the nature of society.

There can be no single explanation for the widening gap between the rich and poor. Changes in the occupational structure have meant that the expansion of professional and managerial jobs has been accompanied by a proportional decline in manual jobs particularly unskilled manual occupations. Technological innovation has meant that fewer people are required in order to achieve a rising level of manufacturing output. The service sector has expanded. Esping-Andersen (1993) distinguishes between consumer services, social services and business services. The rates of expansion of these different sectors will vary between different countries – for example, the Scandinavian social democratic welfare states have had a very rapid rate of expansion of social services, and the jobs created have been relatively 'good' jobs. However, in Britain, the low-level service jobs which have been a major source of occupational expansion over the last two decades are on the whole low-paid and are frequently 'non-standard' – that is, they are not permanent, full-time jobs but are part-time, short-contract, and temporary. One question which might be raised, therefore, is whether a new 'service proletariat' is in the process of emerging. On the other hand, the rapid expansion of education, health and financial services has also created higher-level professional and managerial service occupations.

These changes in the occupational structure have run in parallel with significant changes in gender relations, and (rather more gradual) changes in the gender division of labour and the articulation of the household with the market economy. Women's employment has become increasingly important in maintaining household living standards. However, the increasing number of women moving into higher-level and well-paid jobs (discussed in chapter 6) means that the positive impact of women's employment is much greater in some households than others. Thus there has been a widening gulf between households in which there are two earners, and households in which there are none (and the latter group of households has increased owing to both rising unemployment and an increase in early retirement). Indeed, the gap between households in which at least one person has a full-time job, and those without an earner, has widened dramatically. Average incomes have risen in earner households (and as we shall see, some have risen very dramatically indeed), whereas households without a full-time earner have lower average incomes, in real terms, than in 1979. Inequalities are also widening amongst earners. In respect of male, full-time wages, the Rowntree Report has shown that: 'Between 1966 and 1977 all wages grew at much the same rate. After 1978, the experiences of the three parts of the distribution diverged: wages for the lowest paid hardly changed, and by 1992 were lower in real terms than in 1975; median wages grew by 35 per cent; but high wages grew by 50 per cent' (Joseph Rowntree Foundation 1995: 20).

Over the last fifteen years, therefore, the material impact of occupational success or failure has, relatively speaking, become increasingly important, as the gap between the lowest- and highest-paid has widened. One consequence has been that educational credentials have become ever more important in the labour market. The Rowntree Report (1995: 20) argues that the 'stakes have become higher for young people entering the labour market, with greater differences between those who do well (linked to high educational levels) and those who do not than there were twenty, or even ten, years ago.' Similarly, Esping-Anderson concludes that: 'Access to educational credentials (and social skills) is clearly a potential catalyst of a new class axis' (1993: 236).

The increasing importance of education for occupational attainment and thus 'life chances', as noted above, is an important part of the argument that societies are becoming more open, that is, moves toward a meritocracy mean that there is increasing equality of opportunity, if not absolute equality. However, sociologists have argued that class (i.e. social origins) distorts this relationship because levels of educational achievement vary by social class. This is because the middle classes are more efficient at ensuring that their children acquire educational credentials through a number of strategies, including the use of the private ('public') school system, moving to areas (usually of high house prices) with good (i.e. selective) state schools, and so on. Thus, as Halsey argues, 'ascriptive forces find ways of expressing themselves as "achievement" ' (1977: 184). As Halsey's work has demonstrated (see also Heath and Clifford 1996, Marshall et al. 1997), the expansion of educational opportunities during the twentieth century may have resulted in improved opportunities for working-class children, but, relatively speaking, middle-class children have retained their advantages. Thus, if education is becoming *more* important to occupational success, then class differences are becoming more significant, not less, as some postmodernists have argued.

It has been argued that the British educational system is particularly elitist, in that the role of the private schools is very important. (In France and Germany, for example, the top schools are certainly elitist and highly selective, but they are nevertheless state schools. Adonis and Pollard 1997.) Of the top 200 schools in Britain in 1996 (in terms of A level performance), all but twenty-two were in the private sector. The private sector accounts for only 7 per cent of the school population, but for over half of the entrants to Oxford and Cambridge universities. Private schools have more resources, smaller classes and much better academic results than state schools. At private schools 80 per cent of pupils achieve five or more A–C passes at GCSE, as compared to a national average of 43 per cent; this difference is carried over into A level grades, and almost 90 per cent go on to some form of higher education. Private schools, therefore, are extremely effective at producing good academic results. However, this has not always been their *major* objective. Private schools have always been elite establishments, but in the nineteenth and early twentieth centuries the production and maintenance of 'gentlemanly' cultures was seen as being more important than examination successes. As the demands for educational qualifications have been ratcheted up in the occupational race, however, so have the private schools expanded and improved their credential-producing capacities (Adonis and Pollard 1997). Even Saunders, who, as we have seen, is foremost amongst those arguing that it is individual ability, rather than class background, which accounts for occupational success, has conceded that private schools play a major part in securing class advantages for middle-class children.

Over the last twenty years, as we have seen, there has been a marked shift to service employment together with a continuing increase in women's employment. These trends might be seen as contributing to social and economic polarization. Many service-sector jobs have always been low-paid, and the increase in service jobs has been accompanied by a decline in the demand for unskilled labour in manufacturing industry. An increase in two-income households, particularly if the two people are both well-paid, will increase the difference between two-, single-, and no-income households. Thus it might be argued that the recent increase in social inequality is no more than some kind of 'natural' development, and that as the 'industrial' proletariat has declined, so an even more disadvantaged 'service proletariat' has emerged. This important topic has been systematically investigated, through cross-national comparisons, by Esping-Andersen and his colleagues (1993). They argue that (national) institutional variations are of crucial significance in shaping stratification systems. Thus welfare states, education systems, collective bargaining systems and the modern corporation are decisive 'institutional filters' through which class (i.e. occupational) structures emerge. These also affect the nature of service jobs. Perhaps the best-known example here is that of the Scandinavian social democracies, in which the state-managed expansion of welfare services has led to a massive expansion of relatively low-level, but nevertheless reasonably paid and protected, service jobs.[11]

In fact, Esping-Andersen concludes that unskilled service jobs do not constitute an emerging new service proletariat in the sense of 'a class imprisoned in a collectively shared, underprivileged, dead-end career' (1993: 231). This is partly because of the national institutional variations we have already mentioned, but also because the fluidity and mobility patterns around such jobs are simply too extensive for any significant social closure to occur (for example, many such jobs are held by young people, often students, who move on to better jobs). However, in the case of Britain Esping-Andersen concludes:

> The British unskilled workers are, as in North America, a sizeable stratum and mainly concentrated in private sector services. They are, however, clearly less mobile and when they do move it is much less likely to be in an upward direction. Indeed, for males the most likely

move is to manual work . . . Hence, unskilled service workers in Britain seem to combine the worst features of the American and German model: large but relatively immobile – a potential proletariat. (1993: 233)

It may be argued that politically-led changes in British institutions over the last two decades have had the (intentional) effect of increasing social and economic polarization. Social polarization was not a primary aim of the Conservative government elected in 1979 (although the intention to increase the extent of rewards to the better-off was deliberate), rather, the marketization of society was seen as necessary to regenerate the economy. Whether or not these policies were successful is an important topic that we cannot discuss here (see Johnson 1991 for an accessible discussion). However, there can be absolutely no doubt that government policies in Britain from 1979 onwards have served to increase the level of inequality.

Indeed, it may be suggested that one major reason for the persistence of the perpetually criticized structure → consciousness → action (Pahl and Wallace 1988) links in the sociological class analysis chain is that the capitalist class *does* manifest all the signs of being both conscious of its material interests and capable of protecting them. Offe and Weisenthal (1985) have argued that the stability of the dominant or capitalist class is not only a question of its superior resources, but also of the distinctive organizational capacities of the dominant, in contrast to the subordinate, classes. Capitalist interests are not difficult to identify, and the legitimacy of this interest (enterprise success and profitability) is widely accepted in society, and supported by the state. As a consequence, capitalist organizational forms are 'monological', that is, interest transmission is direct via the leadership. Not all capitalists need to be organized in order to represent the interests of the whole, and short-term conflicts of interest may be accommodated. In contrast, oppositional forms of organization are 'dialogical'; they do not possess the same 'taken-for-granted' legitimacy. Workers have to be persuaded that their interests have to be articulated (and are distinct from those of the capitalists), and organization is rarely successful unless all workers are involved. In short, the capitalist upper class is at an advantage not only in terms of its resources, but also in that its organizational strategies are simpler to generate and sustain than oppositional forms.[12]

The 1979 Conservative government claimed that unemployment was caused by workers 'pricing themselves out of jobs'. Thus legislation was introduced which facilitated the payment of lower wages to workers who were often poorly paid in the first place. These policies included the removal of rights granted by the Employment Protection Act of the mid-1970s;[13] the privatization of public-sector services, as a consequence of which those workers who did not lose their jobs were often re-hired at lower rates of pay; subsidies to encourage low wage rates for young workers; and the removal of wages council protection in low-paid industries. At the same time, the abandonment of wage and salary controls allowed the incomes of the very highest earners to spiral up to previously unheard-of levels. As a consequence of these changes, as we have seen, the wages of the best-paid increased by more than 50 per cent, whilst those of the lowest-paid actually fell in relative terms. Sustained high levels of unemployment, together with legislation against trade union strategies such as picketing and the closed shop, have further eroded the basis of collective action and thus the capacity to protect wage levels. By 1988 trade union membership in the United Kingdom had declined by fully 24 per cent from its peak level of 13.3 million members in 1979 to just over 10 million (Bird et al. 1991).

During the same period, direct tax cuts disproportionately benefited the better-off. Between 1979 and 1986, it has been calculated that out of the £8.1 billion in tax cuts, nearly half went to the richest 10 per cent and almost two-thirds went to the richest 20 per cent. As a result of rising unemployment, declining wage levels, and demographic changes such as the increase in households headed by single parents, the proportion of households dependent on social security benefits has risen – social security payments accounted for a fifth of all income in 1992 and 1993 (Goodman et al. 1997). Since 1980, social security benefits have been indexed to prices, rather than wages. As wages (except those of the lowest-paid) have risen faster than prices, the value of benefits in relative terms has been declining.

It is clear, therefore, that the material impact of Conservative government policies, ostensibly designed to improve economic performance, disproportionately affected different groups – or classes – within the population. This might be taken as an illustration of the force of Offe and Wiesenthal's argument – that policies clearly in the interests of a particular class (capitalists) are seen as being in the 'national' interest. The Conservatives sought – and achieved – changes in the 'institutional filters' of class, particularly in respect of collective bargaining and the welfare state, and as a consequence inequality has increased. The government's restructuring of other institutions has increased inequality by opening up opportunities to 'earn' very high incomes. Amongst the most important examples here are deregulation of the financial sector in 1986, together with the selling-off of state-owned utilities over the government's whole period in office. Financial deregulation (which was accompanied by 'sweeteners' such as encouraging individuals to cash in their occupational pensions and transfer to the private sector) resulted in an explosion of finance-related jobs, some of them very highly paid indeed. The 1996 annual report of KPMG, one of the 'Big Six' accountancy firms, revealed that the earnings of their 586 partners ranged from £123,000 to £740,000 a year (Adonis and Pollard 1997: 87). For the very highest of flyers in the financial sector, yearly bonuses can run into millions of pounds. The directors of privatized industries found they were able to award themselves huge salaries. A high-profile example was that of Cedric Brown, Director of British Gas, whose 75 per cent pay rise in 1994 brought his annual salary up to £475,000.

Increasing social polarization over the last two decades, therefore, has a number of different sources. In part, the morphology of inequality has changed – women's earnings, for example, have become much more important than they once were. The shift to the service sector has meant that *how* people earn a living through employment has changed. Class processes remain crucial to the maintenance of educational advantage and, given that educational qualifications have become more important in getting a good (i.e. secure and well-paid) job, this aspect of class inequality has become more important. In addition, the institutional filters of class in Britain have been adjusted so as to increase levels of inequality and benefit the better-off, that is, in the interests of capital, rather than labour. All of these trends suggest, as Westergaard (1995) has argued, a hardening of class inequalities rather than the 'death of class'.

Conclusions

Our brief review of the evidence relating to social polarization suggests that the material consequencies of class inequalities continue to be highly significant. Indeed, it may be suggested that in Britain, where politically driven marketization has had a substantial impact, they have become even more so. Thus as Wright (1997) has recently argued: 'To say that class counts, then, is to claim that the distribution of rights and powers over the basic productive resources of . . .

society [has] significant, systematic consequences.' To take a crude but telling example: the directors of privatized utilities in Britain only achieved their massive salary increases *after* these utilities had been released from governmental control (and thus controls over their salary levels).

There have been shifts in the morphology of inequality. At the level of the household, women's market work has become more important. Another feature of note is the decline in the kinds of unskilled jobs in manufacturing which once provided a relatively low but still 'family' (male) wage. However, as a recent review has demonstrated, skill shifts alone cannot account for the increase in wage inequality, as there has been increasing inequality *within* groups of people with the same skills. Thus institutional changes – particularly the removal of protections for the lowest-paid as well as restrictions on higher level salaries – have increased inequality (Goodman et al. 1997: 166–7). The increasing importance of formal qualifications has meant that the struggle to preserve class advantages has become even more intense. It is true that the most intelligent and able offspring of working-class parents are likely to succeed occupationally (Johnson and Reed 1996), but at the same time it is becoming ever more difficult for those of average abilities to overcome the disadvantages of location amongst the (relatively) declining material circumstances of the poorest 20–30 per cent of the British population.

We have demonstrated, therefore, that it is *not* consumption patterns, or 'status communities', or whatever, that determine life chances and levels of social and material reward but, rather, a combination of market position and rights and powers over productive resources. Classes may have changed, but they still count. There remain, however, the vexed questions of identity and action. If 'class', in the sense of membership of a cohesive occupational group (such as miners and steelworkers once were), or of living in a stable community where one 'knew one's place', no longer has the power to engender any sense of collectivity, then can it be argued to be meaningful in political terms? In chapters 4 and 5, we saw that one of the major arguments for the 'death of class' related to these kinds of arguments, particularly in relation to 'class' (i.e. occupation-related) voting behaviour. As with all such debates, there can be no simple answer. A persisting, although not particularly stable or consistent, association can be demonstrated between occupational class and voting (Goldthorpe 1996). More generally, it may be suggested that the concrete linkages between 'class' and politics have never been straightforward in any case. Religious affiliation, ethnicity and gender have all cross-cut class politics. Neither have politics necessarily had an explicit focus on class issues – both historically and in the present day, nationalism and the different interests of competing elites have often been more important.

What, therefore, of the postmodernist critique which has been so influential in denying the relevance of 'class'? First – and this is a very important point – it should be noted that postmodernist theories, by their very nature, do not give any clear account of social structures and divisions (Bradley 1996: 43). Indeed, one of the major thrusts of this chapter has been to argue that approaches which have been developed within the broad framework of 'class analysis' can in fact do just this. We have also suggested that many of the changes associated with the 'perfectionalisation of the market' (Waters 1996) are in fact *politically* driven, rather than a reflection of some underlying 'postmodern' trend. Nevertheless, the social changes brought about by increasing individuation cannot be simply ignored. Class structures may still determine life chances, but increasingly societal fragmentation may render these facts more opaque. This is not to retreat into the arguments relating to 'false consciousness' which have been so comprehensively criticized (e.g. by Lockwood). Rather, it is simply to recognize that, at the level of lived experience, there have been in train a series of changes and developments which are likely to make an *explicitly* collective sense of belonging or circumstance less likely.[14] One need not adopt a postmodernist stance relating to the causal role of cultural consumption, the supposed collapse of the modernist separation of societal spheres, or the playful reflexivity of the postmodern individual, in order to recognize and identify these trends.

In particular, changes in the nature of employment have been very significant in increasing social fragmentation. There is the obvious point that the rise in unemployment, and insecure employment, have contributed to increasing marginalization for a substantial minority. The shift to service employment (which, besides often being low-paid is also associated with flexible and non-standard working), is a further source of fragmentation. Not only is this type of employee most unlikely to develop any form of collective identity, but the rapid turnover of personnel is a further fragmenting factor. As Esping-Andersen has argued: 'The unskilled service workers ... are not condemned to know their future. They are structurally quite undetermined, fluid particles on the way to something else, be it careers, unemployment or mothering. They are not a class, but people temporarily willing or forced to take unpleasant jobs' (1993: 239).

Organizational changes brought about by technological developments and increased competition, as well as changes in management techniques, have also contributed to increasing individuation. The stable hierarchies which were once associated with middle-class careers have been transformed by organizational 'downsizing' and 'delayering'. Rather than being presented with a series of hierarchical positions which have to be worked for and achieved, individuals are encouraged to construct their own career portfolio in order to enhance their 'employability'. The reflexive biographical construction of the self, it may be suggested, is becoming embedded in the organization and management of labour. This does not necessarily mean, as some postmodernists and post-Fordists have suggested, that conception and execution are being reintegrated in 'reflexive production systems' (Lash and Urry 1994). Rather, it may be suggested that chronic change and insecurity have become elements in the management of those members of a 'service class' relatively lacking in organizational power and/or highly marketable skills.

Besides the temporal fragmentation of lower-level employment, modern management techniques also individualize in their requirements that the workforce internalize new norms (e.g. 'total quality'), and develop social skills, conducive to the organizations' goals. The whole focus of these strategies is on the worker as an individual, rather than as a member of a (potential) collectivity. Survey evidence suggests that workers do see their skill levels as having been enhanced by these kinds of development. The consequences of these developments for increasing fragmentation are not difficult to discern.

Technological change has also played a part in increasing individuation in society at large. Kumar (1995) has argued that the growth of the 'information society' has not only reshaped (although not changed in any fundamental sense) the business enterprise, but has also fuelled the development of a 'home-centred' society. Home entertainment, tele-shopping, tele-banking and, of course, tele-working have all been facilitated by technological developments. The most recent developments, such as the Internet, enable individual linkages to be made across the globe. However, Kumar argues: 'The home becomes the preferred site of individual activities, but it generates no collective purpose or sense of shared family values. Individuals can effectively choose to live their lives independently of and in isolation from each other ... The information society, paradoxically, is the private or privatized society' (1995: 158–9).

Individuation and fragmentation, therefore, have been associated with a weakening of overtly expressed strong class identities.[15] The institutions that once articulated working-class interests at the meso-level (e.g. trade unions, the Labour Party) have themselves been weakened or transformed (into 'New Labour'). As we have seen in this chapter, the political 'marketization' of British society has played its part in increasing fragmentation and social polarization. These trends have weakened the social fabric in that a substantial minority are unable to participate in 'society' and a majority experience increasing insecurity. It is increasingly being recognized that 'the market' is *not* 'self-regulating' (and never has been; see Polanyi 1957), and in any case is insufficient for the regulation of human affairs (Joseph Rowntree Foundation 1995; Hutton 1995). Margaret Thatcher once (in)famously claimed that there was no such thing as 'society', but only individual men, women and families. However, as Stinchcombe (1997) following Banfield (1958) has argued, the public goods on which capitalist institutions depend – such as law and order, city organization, material infrastructures, etc. – will be undermined if the 'family' is the major mode of organization – whether this is the nuclear family, the Mafia, the Cosa Nostra or the Triads. The aim of such groupings is to corrupt whatever institutions get in the way of the short-run maximization of 'family' interests. Neither families nor markets can be relied upon as principles of societal organization.

In conclusion: one of the major aims of this chapter has been to demonstrate that the concept of 'class' – in all its many manifesta-tions – remains essential to the understanding of our contemporary social condition. Our closing discussion has suggested that there is much about this condition which should give some cause for con-cern. The strategies that might be developed in respect of these more negative aspects would form the subject of another, and rather different, book. However, it might be suggested that such a book would still, despite the rapid nature of change in contemporary soci-eties, need to draw upon the concepts and theories already devel-oped in the analysis of class and stratification.

Notes

1   Goldthorpe (1987: 27). Ch. 1, 'Social mobility and social interests', provides an excel-lent account of the history and background of research and theorizing in the area of social mobility.

2   Blau and Duncan were at pains to emphasize the fact that their general findings were not applicable to the black population, and were very critical of the extent of struc-tured racial inequality in the United States.

3 As we have seen in earlier chapters, it should be noted that Goldthorpe's scheme includes employment relations only and therefore not all of the structural constraints identified by Crowder.

4 Glass's original enquiry has been subject to extensive criticisms which have argued, amongst other things, that it underestimated the actual extent of mobility. See Payne (1987: ch. 6).

5 The statistical techniques used in social mobility research are extremely complex and impossible to summarize briefly. A useful description for the beginner may be found in Appendix B of Marshall et al. (1997). They have also been criticized; see Saunders 1997.

6 This group corresponds to the International Sociological Association's Research Committee 28 on Social Stratification. For a descriptive summary, see Marshall (1997).

7 One obvious example would be the case of the societies of what used to be referred to as the 'Eastern bloc'. For ideological as well as economic and organizational reasons, such societies have been more likely to designate particular occupations as belonging to the 'working class', and the size of the non-manual category is correspondingly reduced. Thus if 'occupation' is taken as an index of 'class', the 'class structure' of Eastern bloc societies is quite different from that of Western societies, although they are both 'industrial' societies (Parkin 1972; Goldthorpe 1967).

8 Marshall and Swift re-analyse the Essex survey; see Marshall et al. (1988).

9 The question as to whether this state of affairs is actually just raises another set of issues which are extensively discussed in Marshall et al. (1997).

10 In fact Wright (1989) suggests that this is not the case in Sweden.

11 The entirety of Esping-Andersen's argument is simply too complex to summarize here. Much of the debate following his work has focused on women's employment in particular, see Lewis (1959), Sainsbury (1994).

12 There is an interesting parallel between Offe and Weisenthal's discussion of 'dialogical' organization forms and Lockwood's critique of the Marxist theory of action. 'Dialogical' forms of organization, it may be argued, attempt to create the 'higher-order' rationality which Lockwood associates with Marx's account of proletarian action. However, Lockwood's critique of Marx does not affect the argument being advanced here – i.e. that the essentially utilitarian legitimacy accorded to capitalist ends makes organization in their pursuit easier to achieve.

13 The Employment Protection Act had been a major piece of legislation enacted during the period of the neo-corporatist 'social contract' of the previous Labour government.

14 The emphasis has been made in order to make the point, as Offe and Weisenthal have suggested, that the 'monological' organizations of the capitalist class do not have to be explicitly collective in any case.

15 Skeggs (1997) found that the topic of 'class' was very difficult to discuss with her working-class informants, even though they were acutely conscious of it. This was not least because the label was seen as something stigmatizing, to be avoided. It may be suggested that this response is actually a reflection of the increasingly difficult economic circumstances of this group.

References

Abercrombie, N. and Turner, B. S. 1978: The dominant ideology thesis. *British Journal of Sociology*, 29 (2), 149–70.

Abercrombie, N. and Urry, J. 1983: *Capital, Labour, and the Middle Classes*. Allen & Unwin: London.

Abrams, P. 1980: History, sociology, historical sociology. *Past and Present*, 87.

Adonis A. and Pollard, S. 1997: *A Class Act*. Hamish Hamilton: London.

Althusser, L. 1969: *For Marx*. Penguin: Harmondsworth, Middlesex.

Andrews, G. (ed.) 1991: *Citzenship*. Lawrence & Wishart: London.

Archer, M. 1982: Morphogenesis versus structuration: on combining structure and action. *British Journal of Sociology*, 33 (4), 445–83.

Archer, M. 1996: Social integration and system integration: developing the distinction. *Sociology*, 30 (4), 679–99.

Bagguley, P., Mark-Lawson, J., Shapiro, D., Urry, J., Walby, S. and Warde, A. 1989: *Restructuring Place, Class and Gender: Social and Spatial Change in a British Locality*. Sage: London.

Banfield, E. C. 1958: *The Moral Basis of a Backward Society*. Free Press: New York.

Banks, O. 1981: *Faces of Feminism*. Martin Robertson: London.

Bannock, G. and Daly, M. 1990: Size distribution of UK firms. *Employment Gazette* (May), 255–8.

Banton, M. P. 1967: *Race Relations*. Tavistock: London.

Barbalet, J. M. 1988: *Citzenship: Rights, Struggle and Class Inequality*. Open University Press: Milton Keynes.

Barrett, M. 1980: *Women's Oppression Today*. Verso: London (2nd edn 1988).

Bauman, Z. 1982: *Memories of Class*. Routledge: London.

Beatson, M. 1995: *Labour Market Flexibility*. Department of Employment: London.

Bechhofer, F. and Elliot, B. (eds) 1981: *The Petite Bourgeoisie: Comparative Studies of the Uneasy Stratum*. Macmillan: London.

Beck, U. 1992: *Risk Society*. Sage: London.

Bell, D. 1973: *The Coming of Post-industrial Society*. Basic Books: New York.

Bell, D. 1976: *The Cultural Contradictions of Capitalism*. Heinemann: London.

Bendix, R. 1964: *Nation-Building and Citizenship*. John Wiley: New York.

Bendix, R. and Lipset, S. M. (eds) 1967a: *Class, Status and Power* (2nd edn). Routledge: London.

Bendix, R. and Lipset, S. M. 1967b: Karl Marx's theory of social classes. In Bendix and Lipset 1967a.

Benton, T. 1984: *The Rise and Fall of Structural Marxism*. Macmillan: London.

Berger, P. L. 1987: *The Capitalist Revolution: Fifty Propositions about Prosperity, Equality and Liberty*. Gower: Aldershot.

Berger, P. L. and Luckmann, T. 1966: *The Social Construction of Reality*. Penguin: Harmondsworth, Middlesex.

Berle, A. A. and Means, G. C. 1968: *The Modern Corporation and Private Property*. Harcourt, Brace: New York.

Bird, D., Stevens, M. and Yates, A. 1991: Membership of trade unions in 1989. *Employment Gazette* (June), 337–43.

Blackburn, R. M. and Mann, M. 1979: *The Working Class in the Labour Market*. Macmillan: London.

Blackburn, R. M. 1967: *Union Character and Social Class*. Batsford: London.

Blau, P. and Duncan, O. D. 1967: *The American Occupational Structure*. John Wiley: New York.

Blau, P. M. and Scott, W. R. 1963: *Formal Organizations*. Routledge: London.

Borthwick, G., Ellingworth, D., Bell, C. and Mackenzie D. 1991: The social background of British MPs. *Sociology*, 25 (4), 713–17.

Bottomore, T. 1991: *Classes in Modern Society* (2nd edn). HarperCollins Academic: London.

Bottomore, T. and Brym, R. J. (eds) 1989: *The Capitalist Class: An International Study*. Harvester Wheatsheaf: London.

Bourdieu, P. 1973: Cultural reproduction and social reproduction. In R. Brown (ed.), *Knowledge, Education and Cultural Change*. Tavistock: London.

Bourdieu, P. 1986: *Distinction: A Social Critique of the Judgement of Taste*. Routledge: London/New York.

Bourdieu, P. 1987: What makes a social class? *Berkeley Journal of Sociology*, 22, 1–18.

Bowles, S. and Gintis, H. 1976: *Schooling in Capitalist America*. Routledge: London.

Bradley, H. 1996: *Fractured Identities*. Polity Press: Cambridge.

Braverman, H. 1974: *Labor and Monopoly Capital.* Monthly Review Press: New York.

Breen, R. and Rottman, D. B. 1995: *Class Stratification: A Comparative Perspective.* Harvester Wheatsheaf: London.

Brown, C. 1984: *Black and White Britain.* Heinemann: London.

Brown, R. and Brannen, P. 1970: Social relations and social perspectives amongst shipbuilding workers, I & II. *Sociology,* 4 (1), 71–84; 197–211.

Brubaker, R. 1985: Rethinking classical theory. *Theory and Society,* 14, 745–73.

Bulmer, M. 1975: *Working-class Images of Society.* Routledge: London.

Burawoy, M. 1979: *Manufacturing Consent: Changes in the Labor Process under Monopoly Capitalism.* University of Chicago Press: Chicago.

Burawoy, M. 1989: The limits of Wright's Marxism and an alternative. In Wright 1989.

Butler, T. and Savage, M. (eds) 1996: *Social Change and the Middle Classes.* UCL Press: London.

Byrne, D. 1987: Rich and poor: the growing divide. In Walker and Walker 1987.

Calvert, P. 1982: *The Concept of Class.* Hutchinson: London.

Carchedi, G. 1975: On the economic identification of the new middle class. *Economy and Society,* 4 (1).

Castells, M. 1977: *The Urban Question.* Edward Arnold: London.

Chalmers, A. F. 1982: *What is this Thing called Science?* (2nd edn). Open University Press: Milton Keynes.

Child, J. 1986: New technology and the service class. In K. Purcell, S. Wood, A. Waton and S. Allen (eds), *The Changing Experience of Employment.* Macmillan: Basingstoke.

Clark, T. N., Lipset, S. M. and Rempel, M. 1993: The declining political significance of social class. *International Sociology,* 8 (3), 293–316.

Clark, J., Modgil, C. and Modgil, S. (eds) 1990: *John H. Goldthorpe: Consensus and Controversy.* Falmer Press: Basingstoke.

Clark, T. and Lipset, S. M. 1991: Are social classes dying? *International Sociology,* 6 (4), 397–410.

Coates, D. 1989: Britain. In Bottomore and Brym 1989.

Coates, K. and Silburn, R. 1970: *Poverty: The Forgotten Englishmen.* Penguin: Harmondsworth, Middlesex.

Cockburn, C. 1991: *In the Way of Women.* Macmillan: Basingstoke.

Cohen, G. A. 1978: *Karl Marx's Theory of History: A Defence.* Oxford University Press: Oxford.

Collins, R. 1971: Functional and conflict theories of educational stratification. *American Sociological Review,* 36, 1002–19.

Connell, R. W. 1982: A critique of the Althusserian approach to class. In Giddens and Held 1982.

Cox, O. C. 1959: *Caste, Class and Race.* Review Press: New York.

Crompton, R. 1979: Trade unionism and the insurance clerk. *Sociology,* 13 (3), 403–26.

Crompton, R. 1986: Women and the 'service class'. In R. Crompton and M. Mann (eds), *Gender and Stratification*. Polity Press: Cambridge.

Crompton, R. 1987: Gender, status and professionalism. *Sociology*, 21 (3), 413–28.

Crompton, R. 1989a: Women in banking. *Work, Employment and Society*, 3 (2), 141–56.

Crompton, R. 1989b: Class theory and gender. *British Journal of Sociology*, 40 (4), 565–87.

Crompton, R. 1990a: Professions in the current context. *Work, Employment and Society* (special issue).

Crompton, R. 1990b: Goldthorpe and Marxist theories of historical development. In Clark et al. 1990.

Crompton, R. 1991: Three varieties of class analysis: comment on R. E. Pahl. *International Journal of Urban and Regional Research*, 15 (1), 108–13.

Crompton, R. 1992: Patterns of social consciousness amongst the middle classes. In R. Burrows and C. Marsh (eds), *Comsumption and Class*. Macmillan: Basingstoke.

Crompton, R. 1996a: The fragmentation of class analysis. *British Journal of Sociology*, 47.

Crompton, R. 1996b: Consumption and class analysis. In S. Edgell, K. Hetherington and A. Warde (eds), *Consumption Matters*. Blackwell: Oxford.

Crompton, R. 1996c: Gender and class analysis. In Lee and Turner 1996.

Crompton, R. and Gubbay, J. 1977: *Economy and Class Structure*. Macmillan: London.

Crompton, R. and Harris, F. 1998: Gender relations and employment: the impact of occupation. *Work, Employment and Society*.

Crompton, R. and Jones, G. 1984: *White-collar Proletariat: Deskilling and Gender in the Clerical Labour Process*. Macmillan: London.

Crompton, R. and Le Feuvre, N. 1996: Paid employment and the changing system of gender relations: a cross-national comparison. *Sociology* 30 (3), 427–45.

Crompton, R. and Sanderson, K. 1990: *Gendered Jobs and Social Change*. Unwin Hyman: London.

Crompton, R., Hantrais, L. and Walters, P. 1990: Gender relations and employment. *British Journal of Sociology*, 41 (3), 329–49.

Crossick, G. 1978: *An Artisan Elite in Victorian Society*. Croom Helm: London.

Crowder, N. D. 1974: A critique of Duncan's stratification research. *Sociology*, 8.

Dahrendorf, R. 1959: *Class and Class Conflict in an Industrial Society*. Routledge: London.

Dahrendorf, R. 1969: On the origin of inequality among men. In A. Beteille (ed.), *Social Inequality*. Penguin: Harmondsworth, Middlesex.

Dahrendorf, R. 1988: *The Modern Social Conflict*. University of California Press: Berkeley/Los Angeles.

Dale, A. and Joshi, H. 1992: The economic and social status of British women. *Social Statistics Research Unit, City University: London.*

Dale, A., Gilbert, G. N. and Arber, S. 1985: Integrating women into class theory. *Sociology,* 19 (3), 384–409.

Davidoff, L. and Hall, C. 1987: *Family Fortunes.* Hutchinson: London.

Davis, J. 1985: Rules not laws: outline of an ethnographic approach to economics. In B. Roberts, D. Gallie and R. Finnegan (eds), *New Approaches to Economic Life.* Manchester University Press: Manchester.

Davis, K. and Moore, W. E. 1945; 1964: Some principles of stratification. Reprinted in L. A. Coser and B. Rosenberg (eds), *Sociological Theory.* Collier-Macmillan: London.

Dawley, A. 1979: E. P. Thompson and the peculiarities of the Americans. *Radical History Review,* 19 (Winter), 33–60.

Dean, H. 1991: In search of the underclass. In P. Brown and R. Scase (eds), *Poor Work: Disadvantage and the Division of Labour.* Open University Press: Milton Keynes.

Department of Employment 1988: *Employment for the 1990s.* HMSO: London (White Paper).

DeVault, I. A. 1990: *Sons and Daughters of Labor.* Cornell University Press: Ithaca, New York.

Devine, F. 1992: Gender segregation in the engineering and science professions. *Work, Employment and Society,* 6, 557–75.

Devine, F. 1997: *Social Class in America and Britain.* Edinburgh University Press: Edinburgh.

Dollard, J. 1957: *Caste and Class in a Southern Town.* Doubleday: New York.

Douglas, J. W. B. 1964: *The Home and the School.* Panther: London.

Douglas, M. and Isherwood, B. 1980: *The World of Goods.* Penguin: Harmondsworth, Middlesex.

Du Gay, P. 1993: Numbers and souls: retailing and the de-differentiation of economy and culture. *British Journal of Sociology,* 44.

Dubin, R. 1956: Industrial workers' worlds: a study of the central life interests of industrial workers. *Social Problems,* 3.

Duke, V. and Edgell, S. 1987: The operationalisation of class in British sociology: theoretical and empirical considerations. *British Journal of Sociology,* 38 (4).

Dunleavy, P. 1980: *Urban Political Analysis: The Politics of Collective Consumption.* Macmillan: London/Basingstoke.

Durkheim, E. 1957: *Professional Ethics and Civic Morals.* Routledge: London.

Durkheim, E. 1968: *The Division of Labour in Society.* Free Press: New York.

Edgell, S. and Duke, V. 1991: *A Measure of Thatcherism.* HarperCollins Academic: London.

Eisenstein, Z. 1981: *The Radical Future of Liberal Feminism.* Longman: New York.

Emmison, M. 1991: Wright and Goldthorpe: constructing the agenda of class analysis. In J. Baxter, M. Emmison and J. Western, *Class Analysis and Contemporary Australia*. Macmillan: Melbourne.

Engels, F. 1940: *The Origin of the Family, Private Property and the State*. Lawrence & Wishart: London.

Equal Opportunities Commission 1990: *Annual Report*. HMSO: London.

Erikson, R. and Goldthorpe, J. H. 1988: Women at class crossroads: a critical note. *Sociology*, 22, 545–53.

Erikson, R. and Goldthorpe, J. H. 1993: *The Constant Flux*. Clarendon Press, Oxford.

Erikson, R., Goldthorpe, J. H. and Portacarero, L. 1982: Social fluidity in industrial nations. *British Journal of Sociology*, 33 (1), 1–34.

Esping-Andersen, G. 1990: *The Three Worlds of Welfare Capitalism*. Polity Press: Cambridge.

Esping-Andersen G (ed.) 1993: *Changing Classes: Stratification and Mobility in Post-Industrial Societies*. Sage: London.

Evans, R. J. 1987: *Comrades and Sisters: Feminism, Socialism and Pacifism in Europe 1870–1945*. Wheatsheaf: Brighton.

Evetts, J. 1994: Women and career in engineering. *Work, Employment and Society*, 8, 101–12.

Featherman, D. L., Jones, L. and Hauser, R. M. 1975: Assumptions of mobility research in the U.S.: the case of occupational status. *Social Science Research*, 4, 329–60.

Featherstone, M. 1987: Lifestyle and consumer culture. *Theory, Culture and Society*, 4 (1), 55–70.

Featherstone, M. 1991: *Consumer Culture and Postmodernism*. Sage: London.

Field, F. 1989: *Losing Out: The Emergence of Britain's Underclass*. Basil Blackwell: Oxford.

Finch, J. and Groves, D. 1983: *A Labour of Love*. Routledge: London.

Foucault, M. 1977: *Madness and Civilization*. Tavistock: London.

Francis, A. 1980: Families, firms and finance capital. *Sociology*, 14 (1), 1–27.

Frenkel, S., Korczynski, M., Donoghue, L. and Shire, K. 1995: Re-constituting work: trends towards knowledge, work and info-normative control. *Work, Employment and Society*, 9 (4), 773–96.

Friedson, E. 1986: *Professional Powers*. University of Chicago Press: Chicago and London.

Gallie, D. 1978: *In Search of the New Working Class: Automation and Social Integration in the Capitalist Enterprise*. Cambridge University Press: Cambridge.

Gallie, D. 1988: Employment, unemployment and social stratification. In D. Gallie (ed.), *Employment in Britain*. Basil Blackwell: Oxford.

Gallie, D. 1994: Are the unemployed an underclass? *Sociology*, 26, 737–57.

Gallie, D. 1996: Skill, gender and the quality of employment. In R. Crompton, D. Gallie and K. Purcell (eds), *Changing Forms of Employment*. Routledge: London.

Gallie, D. and Vogler, C. 1993: Unemployment and attitudes to work. In D. Gallie et al. (eds), *Social Change and the Experience of Unemployment*. Oxford University Press: Oxford.

Gallie, D. and White, M. 1993: *Employee Commitment and the Skills Revolution*. Policy Studies Institute: London.

Geras, N. 1987: Post-Marxism? *New Left Review*, 163 (May/June).

Gershuny, J. and Jones, S. 1987: The changing work/leisure balance in Britain: 1961–1984. In J. Horne, D. Jary and A. Tomlinson (eds), *Sport, Leisure and Social Relations*. Routledge: London.

Gerth, H. and Mills, C. W. (eds) 1948: *From Max Weber*. Routledge: London.

Giddens, A. 1973: *The Class Structure of the Advanced Societies*. Hutchinson: London (2nd edn 1981).

Giddens, A. 1982a: Hermeneutics and social theory. In *Profiles and Critiques in Social Theory*. Macmillan: London/Basingstoke.

Giddens, A. 1982b: Class division, class conflict and citizenship rights. In *Profiles and Critiques in Social Theory*. Macmillan, London/ Basingstoke.

Giddens, A. 1984: *The Constitution of Society*. Polity Press: Cambridge.

Giddens, A. 1986: *Social Theory and Modern Sociology*. Polity Press: Cambridge.

Giddens, A. 1987: *Social Theory and Modern Sociology*. Polity Press: Cambridge.

Giddens, A. 1990: Structuration theory and sociological analysis. In J. Clark, C. Mogdil and S. Mogdil (eds), *Anthony Giddens: Consensus and Controversy*. Falmer Press: Basingstoke.

Giddens, A. 1991: *Modernity and Self Identity*. Polity Press: Cambridge.

Giddens, A. and Held, D. (eds) 1982: *Classes, Power and Confict*. Macmillan: London/Basingstoke.

Giddens, A. and Mackenzie, G. (eds) 1982: *Social Class and the Division of Labour*. Cambridge University Press: Cambridge.

Glass, D. V. (ed.) 1954: *Social Mobility in Britain*. Routledge: London.

Glucksmann, M. 1995: Why 'work'? Gender and the 'Total Social Organization of Labour'. *Gender, Work and Organization*, 2 (2), 63–75.

Goldthorpe, J. H. 1967: Social stratification in industrial society. In Bendix and Lipset 1967a.

Goldthorpe, J. H. 1973: A revolution in sociology? *Sociology*, 7.

Goldthorpe, J. H. 1978: The current inflation: towards a sociological account. In F. Hirsch and J. H. Goldthorpe (eds), *The Political Economy of Inflation*. Martin Robertson: London.

Goldthorpe, J. H. (with C. Llewellyn and C. Payne) 1980: *Social Mobility and Class Structure in Modern Britain*. Clarendon Press: Oxford (2nd edn 1987).

Goldthorpe, J. H. 1982: On the service class, its formation and future. In Giddens and Mackenzie 1982.

Goldthorpe, J. H. 1983: Women and class analysis: in defence of the conventional view. *Sociology*, 17 (4).

Goldthorpe, J. H. 1984a: The end of convergence: corporatist and dualist tendencies in modern Western societies. In J. H. Goldthorpe (ed.), *Order and Conflict in Contemporary Capitalism*. Clarendon Press: Oxford.

Goldthorpe, J. H. 1984b: Women and class analysis: a reply to the replies. *Sociology*, 18 (4).

Goldthorpe, J. H. 1996: Class and politics in advanced industrial societies. In D. J. Lee and B. S. Turner (eds), *Conflicts about Class*. Longman: London.

Goldthorpe, J. H. and Hope, K. 1974: *The Social Grading of Occupations: A New Approach and Scale*. Clarendon Press: Oxford.

Goldthorpe, J. H. and Marshall, G. 1992: The promising future of class analysis: a response to recent critiques. *Sociology*, 26 (3), 381–400.

Goldthorpe, J. H., Lockwood, D., Bechhofer, F. and Platt, J. 1969: *The Affluent Worker in the Class Structure*. Cambridge University Press: Cambridge.

Goodman, A., Johnson, P. and Webb, S. 1997: *Inequality in the UK*. Oxford University Press: Oxford.

Gorz, A. 1982: *Farewell to the Working Class*. Pluto: London.

Gouldner, A. 1979: *The Future of Intellectuals*. Macmillan: London.

Granovetter, M. S. 1985: Economic action and social structure: the problem of embeddedness. *American Journal of Sociology*, 91 (3), 481–510.

Gray, R. Q. 1976: *The Labour Aristocracy in Victorian Edinburgh*. Clarendon Press: Oxford.

Gregg, P. and Wadsworth, J. 1995: A short history of labour turnover, job security and job tenure: 1975–93. *Oxford Review of Economic Policy*, 2 (1), 73–90.

Gregory, D. 1982: *Regional Transformation and Industrial Revolution*. Macmillan: London.

Gregory, D. and Urry, J. (eds) 1985: *Social Relations and Spatial Structures*. Macmillan: London/Basingstoke.

Gubbay, J. 1997: A Marxist critique of Weberian class analysis. *Sociology* 31 (1), 143–52.

Habermas, J. 1983: Modernity – an incomplete project. In H. Foster (ed.) *The Anti-Aesthetic*. Bay Press: Port Townsend, Washington.

Hakim, C. 1980: Census reports as documentary evidence: the Census commentaries 1801–1951. *Sociological Review*, 28 (3).

Halford, S. and Savage, M. 1995: Restructuring organizations, changing people. *Work, Employment and Society*, 9 (1), 97–122.

Hall, S. 1981: Cultural studies: two paradigms. In T. Bennett, G. Martin, C. Mercer and J. Woollacott (eds), *Culture, Ideology and Social Process*. Batsford Academic and Educational: London.

Hall, S. and Jaques, M. (eds) 1989: *New Times: The Changing Face of Politics in the 1990s*. Lawrence & Wishart: London.

Halmos, P. 1970: *The Personal Service Society*. Constable: London.

Halsey, A. H. 1977: Towards meritocracy? the case of Britain. In J. Karabel and A. H. Halsey (eds), *Power and Ideology in Education*. Oxford University Press: New York.

Halsey, A. H. (ed.) 1988: *British Social Trends since 1900*. Macmillan: Basingstoke/London .

Halsey, A. H. et al. 1980: *Origins and Destinations*. Clarendon Press: Oxford.

Hamnett, C. 1989: Consumption and class in contemporary Britain. In Hamnett et al. 1989.

Hamnett, C., McDowell, L. and Sarre, P. (eds) 1989: *Restructuring Britain: The Changing Social Structure*. Sage: London.

Harloe, M., Pickvance, C. and Urry, J. 1990: *Place, Policy and Politics: Do Localities Matter?* Unwin Hyman: London.

Hartmann, H. 1981: The unhappy marriage of Marxism and feminism: towards a more progressive union. In L. Sargent (ed.), *Women and Revolution*. South End Press: Boston.

Harvey, D. 1990: *The Condition of Postmodernity*. Basil Blackwell: Oxford.

Heath, A. 1981: *Social Mobility*. Fontana: London.

Heath, A. and Britten, N. 1984: Women's jobs do make a difference. Sociology, 18 (4), 475–90.

Heath, A. and Clifford, P. 1996: Class inequalities and educational reform in twentieth-century Britain. In Lee and Turner 1996.

Heath, A., Curtice, J., Jowell, R., Evans, G., Field, J. and Witherspoon, S. 1991: *Understanding Political Change: The British Voter 1964–1987*. Pergamon: Oxford.

Heath, A., Jowell, R. and Curtice, J. (eds) 1994: *Labour's Last Chance? The 1992 Election and Beyond*. Dartmouth: Aldershot.

Hernes, H. 1987: *Welfare State and Woman Power*. Norwegian University Press: Oslo.

Herrnstein, R. J. and Murray, C. 1994: *The Bell Curve*. Free Press: New York.

Hindess, B. 1973: *The Use of Official Statistics in Sociology*. Macmillan: London.

Hindess, B. 1987: *Politics and Class Analysis*. Basil Blackwell: Oxford.

Hirsch, F. 1977: *Social Limits to Growth*. Routledge: London.

HMSO 1966: *Census 1961*: Occupation Tables. London.

Hodge, R. W., Siegel, P. M. and Rossi, P. H. 1964: Occupational prestige in the United States: 1925–1963. *American Journal of Sociology*, 70, 286–302.

Hodge, R. W., Treiman, D. J. and Rossi, P. H. 1967: A comparative study of occupational prestige. In Bendix and Lipset 1967a.

Holmwood, J. and Stewart, A. 1983: The role of contradictions in modern theories of social stratification. *Sociology*, 17 (2).

Holton, R. 1996: Has class analysis a future? In Lee and Turner 1996.

Holton, R. J. and Turner, B. 1989: *Max Weber on Economy and Society*. Routledge: London.

Hout, M., Brooks, C. and Manza, J. 1993: The persistence of classes in post-industrial societies. *International Sociology*, 8 (3), 259–77.

Humphries, J. 1982: Class struggle and the persistence of the working-class family. In Giddens and Held 1982.

Hutton, W. 1995: *The State We're In*. Jonathan Cape: London.

Ingham, G. K. 1970: Social stratification: individual attributes and social relationships. *Sociology*, 4 (1), 105–13.

Ingham, G. K. 1974: *Strikes and Industrial Conflict*. Macmillan: London.

Inglehart, R. 1981: Post-materialism in an age of insecurity. *American Political Science Review*, 75 (4), 880–900.

Jenkins, R. 1988: Discrimination and equal opportunity in employment: ethnicity and 'race' in the United Kingdom. In D. Gallie (ed.), *Employment in Britain*. Basil Blackwell: Oxford.

Jensen, J. 1986: Gender and reproduction: or babies and the state. *Studies in Political Economy*, 20.

Jensen, J., Hagen, E. and Reddy, C. (eds) 1988: *Feminization of the Labour Force: Paradoxes and Promises*. Oxford University Press: New York.

Johnson, C. 1991: *The Economy under Mrs Thatcher*. Penguin: Harmondsworth, Middlesex.

Johnson, P. and Reed, H. 1996: *Two Nations? The Inheritance of Poverty and Affluence*. IFS: London.

Johnson, R. 1979: Culture and the historians. In J. Clarke, C. Critcher and R. Johnson (eds), *Working-class Culture: Studies in History and Theory*. Hutchinson: London.

Johnson, T. 1990: Ideology and action in the work of John Goldthorpe. In Clark et al. 1990.

Jones, F. L. 1988: Stratification approaches to class measurement. *Australian and New Zealand Journal of Sociology*, 24 (2), 279–84.

Joseph Rowntree Foundation 1995: *Inquiry into Income and Wealth*. York.

Joyce, P. (ed) 1995: *Class*. Oxford University Press: Oxford.

Kaye, H. J. 1984: *The British Marxist Historians*. Polity Press: Cambridge.

Keat, R. and Urry, J. 1975: *Social Theory as Science*. Routledge: London (2nd edn 1981).

Kelley, J. 1990: The failure of a paradigm: log-linear models of social mobility. In Clark et al. 1990.

Kelly, G., Kelly, D. and Gamble, A. (eds) 1997: *Stakeholder Capitalism*. Macmillan: Basingstoke.

Kerr, C., Dunlop, J. T., Harbison, F. and Myers, C. A. 1973: *Industrialism and Industrial Man*. Penguin: Harmondsworth, Middlesex (1st edn 1963).

Klein, J. 1965: *Samples from English Cultures*. Routledge: London.

Klingender, F. D. 1935: *The Condition of Clerical Labour in Britain*. Martin Lawrence: London.

Korpi, W. 1978: *The Working Class in Welfare Capitalism*. Routledge: London.

Kumar, K. 1995: *From Post-Industrial to Postmodern Society*. Blackwell Publishers: Oxford.

Kurz, K. and Muller, W. 1987: Class mobility in the industrial world. *Annual Review of Sociology*, 13, 417–42.

Laclau, E. and Mouffe, C. 1985: *Hegemony and Socialist Strategy*. Verso: London.

Laclau, E. and Mouffe, C. 1987: Post Marxism without apologies. *New Left Review*, 166 (Nov./Dec.), 79–106.

Lakatos, I. 1978: *The Methodology of Scientific Research Programmes.* Cambridge University Press: Cambridge.

Lash, S. 1994: Reflexivity and its doubles. In U. Beck, A. Giddens and S. Lash (eds), *Reflexive Modernization, Politics, Tradition and Aesthetics in the Modern Social Order.* Polity Press: Cambridge.

Lash, S. and Urry, J. 1987: *The End of Organized Capitalism.* Polity Press: Cambridge.

Lash, S. and Urry, J. 1994: *Economies of Signs and Space.* Sage: London.

Layder, D. 1990: *The Realist Image in Social Science.* Macmillan: Basingstoke.

Layder, D. 1994: *Understanding Social Theory.* Sage: London.

Lee, D. and Turner, B. 1996: *Conflicts about Class.* Longman: London.

Leidner, R. 1993: *Fast Food Fast Talk.* University of California Press: Berkeley/Los Angeles.

Leiulfsrud, H. and Woodward, A. 1987: Women at class crossroads: repudiating conventional theories of family class. *Sociology*, 21 (3), 393–412.

Lenski, G. 1988: Rethinking macrosociological theory. *American Sociological Review*, 53, 163–71.

Lewis, O. 1959: *Five Families: Mexican Case Studies in the Culture of Poverty.* Basic Books: New York.

Lipset, S. M. and Bendix, R. (eds) 1959: *Social Mobility in Industrial Society.* Heinemann: London.

Lipset, S. M. and Rokkan, S. (eds) 1967: *Party Systems and Voter Alignments.* Free Press: New York.

Lipset, S. M. and Zetterberg, H. L. 1959: Social mobility in industrial societies. In Lipset and Bendix 1959.

Lockwood, D. 1956: Some remarks on 'The Social System'. *British Journal of Sociology*, 7, 2.

Lockwood, D. 1958: *The Blackcoated Worker.* Allen & Unwin: London (2nd edn 1989).

Lockwood, D. 1964: Social integration and system integration. In G. K. Zollschan and W. Hirsch (eds), *Explorations in Social Change.* Houghton Mifflin: Boston.

Lockwood, D. 1966: Sources of variation in working class images of society. *Sociological Review*, 14 (3), 244–67.

Lockwood, D. 1974: For T. H. Marshall. *Sociology*, 8 (3), 363–7.

Lockwood, D. 1981: The weakest link in the chain? In S. Simpson, and I. Simpson (eds), *Research in the Sociology of Work: 1.* JAI Press: Greenwich, Conn.; reprinted (1988) in D. Rose (ed.), *Social Stratification and Economic Change.* Unwin Hyman: London.

Lockwood, D. 1986: Class, status and gender. In R. Crompton and M. Mann (eds), *Gender and Stratification.* Polity Press: Cambridge.

McNall, S. G., Levine, R. F. and Fantasia, R. 1991: *Bringing Class Back In.* Westview Press/Praeger: New York.

McPherson, K. and Coleman, D. 1988: Health. In Halsey 1988.

McRae, S. 1991: Occupational change over childbirth: evidence from a national survey. *Sociology*, 25 (4), 589–605.

Mann, M. 1973: *Consciousness and Action among the Western Working Class*. Macmillan: London.

Mann, M. 1986: A crisis in stratification theory. In R. Crompton and M. Mann (eds), *Gender and Stratification*. Polity Press: Cambridge.

Mann, M. 1987: Ruling class strategies and citizenship. *Sociology*, 21 (3), 339–54.

Marsh, C. 1986: Social class and occupation. In R. Burgess (ed.), *Key Variables in Social Investigation*. Routledge: London.

Marsh, C. and Blackburn, R. M. 1992: Class differences in access to higher education. In R. Burrows and C. Marsh (eds), *Consumption and Class: Divisions and Change*. Macmillan: Basingstoke.

Marshall, B. 1994: *Engendering Modernity*. Polity Press: Cambridge.

Marshall, G. 1982: *In Search of the Spirit of Capitalism*. Hutchinson: London.

Marshall, G. 1983: Some remarks on the study of working class consciousness. *Politics and Society*, 12 (3), 263–302.

Marshall, G. 1988: The politics of the new middle class: history and predictions. Paper presented at the annual conference of the British Sociological Association.

Marshall, G. 1991: In defence of class analysis: a comment on R. E. Pahl. *International Journal of Urban and Regional Research*, 15 (1), 114–18.

Marshall, G. 1997: *Repositioning Class*. Sage: London.

Marshall, G. and Rose, D. 1990: Out-classed by our critics. *Sociology*, 24 (2), 255–67.

Marshall, G. and Swift, A. 1993: Social class and social justice. *British Journal of Sociology*, 44 (2), 187–211.

Marshall, G., Newby, H., Rose, D. and Vogler, C. 1988: *Social Class in Modern Britain*. Hutchinson: London.

Marshall, G., Roberts, R. and Burgoyne, C. 1996: Social class and underclass in Britain and the United States. *British Journal of Sociology*, 47.

Marshall, G., Swift, A. and Roberts, S. 1997: *Against the Odds?* Clarendon Press: Oxford.

Marshall, T. H. 1963: Citizenship and social class. In *Sociology at the Crossroads*. Heinemann: London.

Martin, J. and Roberts, C. 1984: *Women and Employment: A Lifetime Perspective*. HMSO: London.

Marx, K. 1843: On the Jewish Question. In L. Colletti (ed.) 1975: *K. Marx: Early Writings*. Penguin: Harmondsworth, Middlesex.

Marx, K. 1955: *The Poverty of Philosophy*. Progress Publishing: Moscow.

Marx, K. 1962a: The Eighteenth Brumaire of Louis Bonaparte. In K. Marx and F. Engels, *Selected Works*, vol. 1. Foreign Languages Publishing House: Moscow.

Marx, K. 1962b: Preface to *A Contribution to the Critique of Political Eco-*

nomy. In K. Marx and F. Engels, *Selected Works*, vol. 1. Foreign Languages Publishing House: Moscow.

Marx, K. 1974: *Capital*, vol. 3. Lawrence & Wishart: London.

Marx, K. and Engels, F. 1962: *Manifesto of the Communist Party*. In K. Marx and F. Engels, *Selected Works*, vol. 1. Foreign Languages Publishing House: Moscow.

Marx, K. and Engels, F. 1970: *The German Ideology*. Lawrence & Wishart: London.

Massey, D. 1984: *Spatial Divisions of Labour*. Macmillan: London/ Basingstoke.

Maurice, M., Sellier, F. and Silvestre, J. J. 1986: *The Social Foundations of Industrial Power*, trans. A. Goldhammer. MIT Press: Cambridge, Mass.

Mayer, K. 1959: Diminishing class differentials in the United States. *Kyklos*, 12, 605–28.

Mayer, K. 1963: The changing shape of the American class structure. *Social Research*, 30, 458–68.

Mayo, E. 1975: *The Social Problems of an Industrial Civilization*. Routledge: London.

Meillassoux, C. 1973: Are there castes in India? *Economy and Society*, 2 (1).

Merton, R. K. 1959: Notes on problem-finding in sociology. In R. K. Merton, L. Broom and L. S. Cottrell (eds), *Sociology Today*. Harper & Row: New York.

Merton, R. K. 1965: Social structure and anomie. In R. K. Merton, *Social Theory and Social Structure*. Free Press: New York.

Merton, R. K. 1982: Institutionalized altruism: the case of the professions. In R. K. Merton, *Social Research and the Practicing Professions*. Abt Books: Cambridge, Mass.

Miliband, R. 1989: *Divided Societies*. Oxford University Press: Oxford.

Millar, R. 1966: *The New Classes*. Longmans Green: London.

Millward, N. et al. 1992: *Workplace Industrial Relations in Transition*. Dartmouth: Aldershot.

Mitchell, J. 1975: *Psychoanalysis and Feminism*. Penguin: Harmondsworth, Middlesex.

Mitchell, J. C. 1983: Case and situation analysis. *Sociological Review*, 31.

Molyneux, M. 1979: Beyond the domestic labour debate. *New Left Review*, 116.

Morishima, M. 1982: *Why Has Japan Succeeded?* Cambridge University Press: Cambridge.

Morris, L. 1994: *Dangerous Classes*. Routledge: London.

Morris, L. 1995: *Social Divisions*. UCL Press: London.

Morris, L. 1996: Classes, underclasses and the labour market. In Lee and Turner 1996.

Morris, L. and Scott, J. 1996: The attentuation of class analysis. *British Journal of Sociology*, 47 (1), 45–55.

Mouffe, C. 1981: Hegemony and ideology in Gramsci. In T. Bennett, G.

Martin, C. Mercer and J. Woollacott (eds), *Culture, Ideology and Social Process*. Batsford Academic and Educational: London.

Muller, W. 1990: Social mobility in industrial nations. In Clark et al. 1990.

Mullins, P. 1991: The identification of social forces in development as a general problem in sociology: a comment on Pahl's remarks on class and consumption relations as forces in urban and regional development. *International Journal of Urban and Regional Research*, 15 (1), 119–26.

Murphy, R. 1984: The structure of closure: a critique and development of the theories of Weber, Collins and Parkin. *British Journal of Sociology*, 35, 547–67.

Murphy, R. 1986: The concept of class in closure theory. *Sociology*, 20, 2.

Murray, C. A. 1984: *Losing Ground*. Basic Books: New York.

Murray, C. A. 1990: *The Emerging British Underclass*. IEA Health and Welfare Unit: London.

Murray, C. A. 1994: *Underclass: The Crisis Deepens*. IEA: London.

Murray, R. 1989: Fordism and post-Fordism. In Hall and Jaques 1989.

Myrdal, G. 1962: *An American Dilemma*. Harper & Row: New York.

Neale, R. S. (ed). 1983: *History and Class*. Basil Blackwell: Oxford.

Newby, H. 1977: *The Deferential Worker*. Allen Lane: London.

Nichols, T. 1979: Social class: official, sociological and Marxist. In J. Irvine, I. Miles and J. Evans (eds), *Demystifying Social Statistics*. Pluto: London.

O'Connor, J. 1973: *The Fiscal Crisis of the State*. St James Press: London.

Offe, C. 1985a: 'Work' – a central sociological category? In *Disorganized Capitalism*. Polity Press: Cambridge.

Offe, C. 1985b: New social movements: challenging the boundaries of institutional politics. *Social Research*, 52 (4).

Offe, C. and Weisenthal, M. 1985: Two logics of collective action. In C. Offe, *Disorganized Capitalism*, Polity Press: Cambridge.

Pahl, R. E. 1984: *Divisions of Labour*. Basil Blackwell: Oxford.

Pahl, R. E. 1988: Some remarks on informal work, social polarization and social structure. *International Journal of Urban and Regional Research*, 12, 247–67.

Pahl, R. E. 1989: Is the emperor naked? Some questions on the adequacy of sociological theory in urban and regional research. *International Journal of Urban and Regional Research*, 13 (4), 709–20.

Pahl, R. E. 1996: A reply to Goldthorpe and Marshall. In Lee and Turner 1996.

Pahl, R. E. and Wallace, C. D. 1988: Neither angels in marble nor rebels in red: privatisation and working-class consciousness. In D. Rose (ed.), *Social Stratification and Economic Change*. Hutchinson: London.

Pakulski, J. 1993: The dying of class or of Marxist class theory? *International Sociology*, 8 (3), 279–92.

Pakulski, J. and Waters, M. 1996a: The reshaping and dissolution of social class in advanced society. *Theory and Society*, 25, 667–91.

Pakulski, J. and Waters, M. 1996b: *The Death of Class*. Sage: London.

Parkin, F. 1972: *Class Inequality and Political Order*. Paladin: London.

Parkin, F. (ed.) 1974: *The Social Analysis of Class Structure.* Tavistock: London.

Parsons, T. 1965: Full citizenship for the Negro American? A sociological problem. *Daedalus*, 94, 1009–54.

Parsons, T. and Clark, K. B. 1967: *The Negro American.* Beacon Press: Boston.

Pateman, C. 1988: *The Sexual Contract.* Polity Press: Cambridge.

Pateman, C. 1989: *The Disorder of Women.* Polity Press: Cambridge.

Paukert, L. 1984: *The Employment and Unemployment of Women in OECD Countries.* OECD: Paris.

Pawson, R. 1989: A *Measure for Measures.* Routledge: London.

Pawson, R. 1990: Half-truths about bias. *Sociology*, 24 (2), 229–40.

Payne, G. 1987: *Mobility and Change in Modern Society.* Macmillan: Basingstoke/London .

Peacock, A. 1991: Welfare philosophies and welfare finance. In T. Wilson and D. Wilson (eds), *The State and Social Welfare.* Longman: London/New York.

Perkin, H. J. 1989: *The Rise of Professional Society.* Routledge: London.

Peters, T. J. and Waterman, R. H. 1982: *In Search of Excellence.* Harper & Row: New York.

Pfau-Effinger, B. 1993: Modernisation, culture and part-time employment. *Work, Employment and Society*, 7 (3), 383–410.

Phillips, A. 1990: Citizenship and feminist theory. In G. Andrews (ed.), *Citizenship.* Lawrence & Wishart: London.

Piachaud, D. 1991: Revitalising social policy. *Political Quarterly*, 62 (2), 204–25.

Pickvance, C. G. 1977: From 'social base' to 'social force': some analytical issues in the study of urban protest. In M. Harloe (ed.), *Captive Cities: Studies in the Political Economy of Cities and Regions.* Wiley: London/New York.

Pickvance, C. G. 1992: Comparative analysis, causality and case studies. In A. Rogers and S. Vertovec (eds), *The Urban Context: Ethnicity, Social Networks and Situational Analysis.* Berg: London.

Pirenne, H. 1936: *Economic and Social History of Medieval Europe*, trans. I. E. Clegg. Routledge: London.

Plant, R. 1991: Welfare and the enterprise society. In T. Wilson and D. Wilson (eds), *The State and Social Welfare.* Longman: London/New York.

Plant, R. and Barry, N. 1990: *Citizenship and Rights in Thatcher's Britain: Two Views.* IEA Health and Welfare Unit: London.

Polanyi, K. 1957: *The Great Transformation.* Beacon Press: Boston.

Pollard, S. 1983: *The Development of the British Economy: 1914–1980.* Edward Arnold: London.

Pollert, A. 1988: The flexible firm: fixation or fact? *Work, Employment and Society*, 2 (3), 281–316.

Posner, C. (ed.) 1970: *Reflections on the Revolution in France: 1968.* Penguin: Harmondsworth, Middlesex.

Poulantzas, N. 1975: *Classes in Contemporary Capitalism*. New Left Books: London.

Prandy, K. 1991: The revised Cambridge scale of occupations. *Sociology*, 24 (4), 629–56.

Prandy, K. and Blackburn, R. M. 1997: Putting men and women into classes. *Sociology* 31 (1), 143–52.

Price, R. and Bain, G. S. 1988: The labour force. In Halsey 1988.

Pringle, R. 1988; *Secretaries Talk: Sexuality, Power and Work*. Verso: London.

Przeworski, A. 1985: *Capitalism and Social Democracy*. Cambridge University Press: Cambridge.

Rattansi, A. 1985: End of an orthodoxy? The critique of sociology's view of Marx on class. *Sociological Review*, 641–69

Reid, I. 1981: *Social Class Differences in Britain*. Grant McIntyre: London.

Reid, I. 1998: *Class in Britain*. Polity Press: Cambridge.

Reiss, A. J. 1961: *Occupations and Social Status*. Free Press: New York.

Rex, J. 1961: *Key Problems of Sociological Theory*. Routledge: London.

Rex, J. 1986: *Race and Ethnicity*. Open University Press: Milton Keynes.

Rex, J. 1987: Ethnicity and race. In P. Worsley (ed.), *The New Introducing Sociology*. Penguin: Harmondsworth, Middlesex.

Rex, J. and Tomlinson, S. 1979: *Colonial Immigrants in a British City*. Routledge: London.

Ritzer, G. 1996: *The McDonaldization of Society*. Pine Forge Press: Thousand Oaks, Calif.

Rose, D. 1988: Introduction. In D. Rose (ed.), *Social Stratification and Economic Change*. Hutchinson: London.

Rose, D. and Elias, P. 1995: The revision of OPCS social classifications. *Work, Employment and Society*, 9 (3), 583–92.

Rose, D. and Marshall, G. 1986: Constructing the (W)right classes. *Sociology*, 20 (3), 440–55.

Rose, D. and O'Reilly, K. 1997: *Constructing Classes: Towards a New Social Classification for the UK*. ESRC/ONS: Swindon and London.

Rose, D., Marshall, G., Newby, H. and Vogler, C. 1987: Goodbye to supervisors? *Work, Employment and Society*, 1 (1), 7–24.

Rosenthal, P., Hill, S. and Pecci, R. 1997: Checking out service. *Work, Employment and Society*, 11 (3), 481–503.

Rubery, J. and Fagan, C. 1994: Occupational segregation: plus ça change? In R. Lindley (ed.), *Labour Market Structures and Prospects for Women*. EOC: Manchester.

Runciman, W. G. 1990: How many classes are there in contemporary British society? *Sociology*, 24 (3), 377–96.

Rutter, M. and Madge, N. 1976: *Cycles of Disadvantage*. Heinemann: London.

Sabel, C. F. 1982: *Work and Politics*. Cambridge University Press: Cambridge.

Sainsbury, D. (ed.) 1994: *Gendering Welfare States*. Sage: London.

Sarlvik, B. and Crewe. I. 1983: *Decade of Dealignment: The Conservative Victory of 1979 and Electoral Trends in the 1970s*. Cambridge University

Press: Cambridge.

Sarre, P. 1989: Recomposition of the class structure. In Hamnett et al. 1989.

Saunders, P. 1987: *Social Theory and the Urban Question*. Unwin Hyman: London.

Saunders, P. 1990a: *Social Class and Stratification*. Routledge: London.

Saunders, P. 1990b: *A Nation of Home Owners*. Unwin Hyman: London.

Saunders, P. 1996: *Unequal but Fair? A Study of Class Barriers in Britain*. Institute of Economic Affairs: London.

Saunders, P. 1997: Social mobility in Britain. *Sociology*, 31 (2), 261–88.

Savage, M. 1991: Making sense of middle-class politics: a secondary analysis of the 1987 British general election survey. *Sociological Review*, 39 (1), 26–54.

Savage, M. and Warde, A. 1993: *Urban Sociology, Capitalism and Modernity*. Macmillan: London.

Savage, M., Dickens, P. and Fielding, T. 1988: Some social and political implications of the contemporary fragmentation of 'service class' in Britain. *International Journal of Urban and Regional Research*, 12 (3).

Savage, M., Barlow, J., Dickens, A. and Fielding, T. 1992: *Property, Bureaucracy and Culture: Middle Class Formation in Contemporary Britain*. Routledge: London.

Sayer, A. 1984: *Method in Social Science: A Realist Approach*. Hutchinson: London.

Sayer, A. 1989: Post-Fordism in question. *International Journal of Urban and Regional Research*, 13 (4), 666–95.

Sayer, A. and Walker, R. 1992: *The New Social Economy*. Basil Blackwell: Oxford.

Scase, R. 1992: *Class*. Open University Press: Milton Keynes.

Scott, J. 1982: *The Upper Classes*. Macmillan: London.

Scott, J. 1991: *Who Rules Britain?* Polity Press: Cambridge.

Scott, J. 1996: *Stratification and Power*. Polity Press: Cambridge

Seccombe, W. 1974: The housewife and her labour under capitalism. *New Left Review*, 83. 3–24.

Sewell, G. and Wilkinson, B. 1992: Empowerment or emasculation. In R. Blyton and P. Turnbull (eds), *Reassessing Human Resource Management*. Sage: London.

Skeggs, B. 1997: *Formations of Class and Gender*. Sage: London.

Smelser, N. J. 1959: *Social Change in the Industrial Revolution: An Application of Theory to the Lancashire Cotton Industry 1770–1840*. Routledge: London.

Smelser, N. J. (ed.) 1988: *Handbook of Sociology*. Sage: Beverly Hills, Calif.

Smiles, S. 1859: *Self-Help: With Illustrations of Conduct and Perseverance* (4th edn). Murray: London.

Smith, C. 1987: *Technical Workers, Class, Labour and Trade Unionism*. Macmillan: London.

Sombart, W. 1906: *Why Is There no Socialism in the United States?* Repr. 1976: International Arts and Sciences Press: White Plains, NY.

Stacey, M. 1960: *Tradition and Change: A Study of Banbury*. Oxford University Press: London.

Stacey, M. 1981: The division of labour revisited or overcoming the two Adams. In P. Abrams, R. Deem, J. Finch and P. Rock (eds), *Practice and Progress: British Sociology 1950–1980*. Allen & Unwin: London.

Stanworth, M. 1984: Women and class analysis: a reply to Goldthorpe. *Sociology*, 18 (2), 159–70.

Stark, David 1980: Class struggle and the labour process. *Theory and Society*, 9 (1).

Stedman Jones, G. 1976: From historical sociology to theoretical history. *British Journal of Sociology*, 27 (3), 295–305.

Stedman Jones, G. 1983: *Languages of Class: Studies in English Working-class History*. Cambridge University Press: Cambridge.

Stewart, A., Prandy, K. and Blackburn, R. M. 1980: *Social Stratification and Occupations*. Macmillan: London/Basingstoke.

Stinchcombe, A. 1997: On the virtues of the old institutionalism. In *Annual Review of Sociology*, vol. 23. Annual Reviews: Palo Alto, Calif.

Stoecker, R. 1991: Evaluating and rethinking the case study. *Sociological Review*, 39 (1), 88–112.

Szelenyi, S. and Olvera, J. 1996: The declining significance of class: does gender complicate the story? *Theory and Society*, 25, 725–30.

Szreter, S. R. S. 1984: The genesis of the Registrar-General's social classification of occupations. *British Journal of Sociology*, 35, 522–46.

Therborn, G. 1983: Why some classes are more successful than others. *New Left Review*, 138 (March–April).

Thomas, R. and Elias, P. 1989: Development of the standard occupational classification. *Population Trends*, 55, 16–21.

Thompson, E. P. 1968: *The Making of the English Working Class*. Penguin: Harmondsworth, Middlesex.

Thrift, N. 1989: Images of social change. In C. Hamnett et al. 1989.

Thrift, N. and Williams, P. (eds) 1987: *Class and Space*. Routledge: London.

Touraine, A. 1977: *The Self-Production of Society*. University of Chicago Press: Chicago.

Tumin, M. 1964: Some principles of stratification: a critical analysis. In L. A. Coser and B. Rosenberg (eds), *Sociological Theory*. Collier–Macmillan: London.

Turner, B. S. 1986: *Citizenship and Capitalism: The Debate over Reformism*. Allen & Unwin: London.

Turner, B. S. 1988: *Status*. Open University Press: Milton Keynes.

Turner, B. S. 1990: Outline of a theory of citizenship. *Sociology*, 24 (2), 189–217.

Urry, J. 1981: *The Anatomy of Capitalist Societies*. Macmillan: London/Basingstoke .

Veblen, T. 1934: *The Theory of the Leisure Class*. Modern Library: London.

Wacquant, L. J. D. 1989: Social ontology, epistemology, and class. *Berkeley Journal of Sociology*, 34, 165–86.

Wacquant, L. J. D. 1991: Making class: the middle class(es) in social theory and social structure. In McNall et al. 1991.

Walby, S. 1986: *Patriarchy at Work*. Polity Press: Cambridge.

Walby, S. 1988: Gender politics and social theory. *Sociology*, 22 (2), 215–32.

Walby, S. 1990: *Theorizing Patriarchy*. Basil Blackwell: Oxford.

Walker, A. 1990: Blaming the victims. In Murray 1990.

Walker, A. and Walker, C. (eds) 1987: *The Growing Divide: A Social Audit 1979–1987*. Child Poverty Action Group: London.

Walker, P. 1979: *Between Capital and Labor*. Monthly Review Press: New York.

Warde, A. 1990: Introduction to the sociology of consumption. *Sociology*, 24 (1), 1–4.

Warner, L. 1963: *Yankee City*. Yale University Press, New Haven, Conn.

Waters, M. 1991: Collapse and convergence in class theory: the return of the social and the analysis of stratification arrangements. *Theory and Society*, 20 (2), 141–72.

Waters, M. 1996: Succession in the stratification system. In Lee and Turner 1996.

Weber, M. 1948: Class, status, party. In Gerth and Mills 1948.

Weber, M. 1976: *The Protestant Ethic and the Spirit of Capitalism*, trans. Talcott Parsons. Allen & Unwin: London.

Westergaard, J. 1995: *Who Gets What?* Polity Press: Cambridge.

Westergaard, J. and Resler, H. 1975: *Class in a Capitalist Society*. Heinemann: London.

Willener, A. 1970: *The Action-image of Society*. Tavistock: London.

Willis, P. 1977: *Learning to Labour: How Working Class Kids Get Working Class Jobs*. Saxon House: London.

Willmott, H. 1993: Strength is ignorance, slavery is freedom: managing culture in modern organizations. *Journal of Management Studies*, 30 (4), 515–52.

Wilson, E. 1977: *Women and the Welfare State*. Tavistock: London.

Wilson, W. J. 1987: *The Truly Disadvantaged: Inner City Woes and Public Policy*. University of Chicago Press: Chicago.

Wilson, W. J. 1991: Studying inner-city social dislocation: the challenge of public agenda research. *American Sociological Review*, 56, 1–14.

Wilson, W. J. (ed.) 1993: *The Ghetto Underclass*. Sage: London.

Womack, J. P., Jones, D. T. and Roos, D. 1990: *The Machine that Changed the World*. Macmillan: New York.

Wood, E. M. 1986: *The Retreat from Class*. Verso: London.

Wootton, B. 1955: *The Social Foundations of Wage Policy*. Allen & Unwin: London.

Wright, E. O. 1976: Class boundaries in advanced capitalist societies. *New Left Review*, 98.

Wright, E. O. 1979: *Class Structure and Income Determination*. Academic Press: New York.

Wright, E. O. 1980: Class and occupation. *Theory and Society*, 9.

Wright, E. O. 1985: *Classes*. Verso: London.

Wright, E. O. 1997: *Class Counts*. Cambridge University Press: Cambridge.

Wright, E. O. (ed.) 1989: *The Debate on Classes*. Verso: London.

Wright, E. O. and Martin, B. 1987: The transformation of the American class structure, 1960–1980. *American Journal of Sociology*, 93 (1).

Wright, E. O. and Singlemann, J. 1982: Proletarianization in the changing American class structure. *American Journal of Sociology*, 88 (Supplement), 176–209.

Wrong, D. 1966: The oversocialized conception of man in modern sociology. Reprinted in L. A. Coser and B. Rosenberg (eds), *Sociological Theory*, Collier-Macmillan: London.

Wynne, D. 1990: Leisure, lifestyle and the construction of social position. *Leisure Studies*, 9, 21–34.

Zeitlin, M. 1982: Corporate ownership and control: the large corporation and the capitalist class. In Giddens and Held 1982.

Zukin, S. 1988: *Loft Living: Culture and Capital in Urban Change*. Radines/Century Hutchinson: London.

Zweig, F. 1961: *The Worker in an Affluent Society*. Heinemann: London.

Index

Abercrombie   31, 57, 151
Adonis and Pollard   221, 225
Alford index   87, 105, 132, 206
Althusser   30
analytical dualism   168 n9

Banks   183
Beck   18, 83, 128, 157
Bell   152–3
Bendix and Lipset   13, 36, 37, 117
Beveridge Report   181
Blau and Duncan   58, 60, 209–11,
   213
Bourdieu   22, 51, 148–50
bourgeoisie   26–7, 29, 71
Bradley   207, 227
Braverman   17, 39, 55, 70–1, 74
Breen and Rottman   107, 114
Brubaker   148
bureaucratic career   83, 156, 157, 228
Butler   107, 151

capitalism   4, 170, 218, 223;
   development of   93, 129;
   organized   129
case studies   80, 119, 122–3, 190
CASMIN   64, 66, 75, 98, 102, 108,
   214

caste   1–2
citizenship   3, 8, 21, 121, 171–9,
   200; and women   180–5; and race
   186–90
Clark and Lipset   98–9
class   4–5; action   29, 33, 89–92;
   American tradition of   117; conflict
   29, 200; consciousness (identities)
   xiv, 14, 28, 31, 34, 37, 38–9, 41, 46,
   226, 229; cultures   205–6; decline
   of   9, 91–2, 98–100, 226, 227;
   definitions of   4, 5, 9–12, 26;
   employment aggregate approach
   55, 80, 99, 104–6, 108–10,
   113–16, 118–19, 145–6, 164, 190,
   197, 198, 204; formation   48, 55,
   69, 77, 80, 114, 134–5; and history
   40–3; and occupation   11, 14,
   56–64, 70, 95–6, 143, 144; and
   politics   86–9; processes   56, 77,
   80, 114, 115, 119, 148, 150, 166,
   190, 197, 198, 203–4; schemes
   14–16, 55, 56–61, 63–76, 95,
   100–1; and status   10; structure
   30, 33, 37–40, 42, 47, 79; and
   voting   105–6, 143, 144
'class analysis'   207; critiques of
   16–22, 136–7

clerical work 38, 65, 95–6
Cockburn 182
Collins 35
conflict approach 8–9, 12, 13, 25,
    42, 63, 77, 79, 112, 217
Conservative government 223, 224
consumption 19–20, 22, 115,
    120–1, 126, 127, 129, 131, 133,
    141, 151, 167, 226; sector cleavages
    142–6
corporatism 19, 75, 82, 130, 142
Crowder 210–11
culture 19, 22, 40–2, 49, 129, 142,
    146–8, 151–2, 155–6, 166
culture of poverty 21, 196, 197

Dahrendorf 38–9, 42, 175–6
Davis and Moore 6, 58
Devine xiii, 160, 191
domestic labour debate 93
Du Gay 161–2
Durkheim 7, 133, 175

education 104, 105, 216–17, 220–2
employment 16–17, 131, 141–2; in
    banking 157–8; changes in
    81–4, 227–8; relationships in
    161–4; of women 84–6, 158–60,
    206
'employment aggregate' class analysis
    see class, employment aggregate
    approach
'employment relations' 39, 65, 66, 67
Engels 93
Enlightenment 123
equality 3, 5–6; of opportunity 7
Erikson and Goldthorpe 14, 66, 69,
    97, 214
Esping-Andersen 21, 160, 219, 220,
    222–3, 227–8
exploitation 72–4

Featherstone 125, 126, 154
feminism ix, 19, 92, 94, 177, 180,
    182–5; feminist criticisms of 'class
    analysis' 65, 92–4

feudalism 2, 28–9, 37
Fordism 18, 84, 85, 87, 129, 131
Foucault 124
Frenkel 162–3
functionalism(ist) 25, 79; theory of
    stratification 6–7, 8, 58, 62–3, 68,
    91, 215–16, 217

Gallie 163, 197
gender 19, 220; and class 65,
    92–8, 158–60; and 'employment
    aggregate' approach 94–8; see
    also feminism
Giddens 12, 44–6, 96, 125,
    129–30,165, 176–7
Glass 62, 211–12
globalization 19, 113, 134
Goldthorpe 4, 39, 57, 62, 75, 99,
    105, 113–16, 211–15; class scheme
    64–9; gender and class 96–7; see
    also Erikson and Goldthorpe
Goodman et al. 224, 226
Gorz 17
Gramsci 30, 43
Granovetter 134
Gubbay 102–3

Habermas 123
Halsey 105, 204, 221
Hamnett 144
Hartmann 93
Harvey 126–7
Hayek 6
Heath 105–6, 107
Hirsch 5, 8
historical materialism 28–9, 35
Holton 135
housing 143–4, 146
Hout 98–9, 101

income 191, 219, 220, 224, 225
individualization (individuation) 18,
    83, 127–8, 167, 169, 205, 227, 228
'industry society' thesis 12, 63, 69,
    74, 86–7, 112–13, 213; and
    citizenship 173

inequality 1–6, 11, 20, 191, 198;
  conflict theory of 8–9; functional
  theory of 6–8; growth of 218–25
Ingham 104

Jones, F. 101
Jones, G. 157
Joyce 125

Keat and Urry 49
Kerr 112
Kumar 126, 129, 228

Labour government 82; see also 'New
  Labour'
Laclau and Mouffe 124–5, 174
Lash and Urry 84, 129–34, 141, 153,
  161, 162, 228; see also Urry
Layder xiii, 48
Lee 135–7
Leidner 163
life chances 33, 35, 121, 138, 151, 167
lifestyle see consumption
Lipset and Bendix 210
Lipset-Rokkan thesis 87
Lockwood 13, 37, 38–9, 46, 64–5,
  89–90, 94, 95, 171, 175

'male breadwinner' 65, 84–5, 96
Malthus 199
management 17; see also new
  management techniques; Total
  Quality Management
Mann 175, 177
market situation 33, 38–9, 64–5
markets (market forces, marketization)
  83, 133–4, 156, 170, 176, 227, 229
Marshall, G. 34, 99, 103, 119, 197,
  198, 207–8, 216–17
Marshal, T. H. 8, 121, 171–9, 187
Marx 4, 13, 24, 26–32, 37, 50–1,
  63, 89–90, 136–7, 172–3, 209
Merton 21, 196
middle classes 13, 17, 22, 49, 70, 95,
  107, 109–10, 121, 150–8, 213, 217,
  221, 222, 228; and gender 158–60

Mitchell 122
modernity 3, 4, 55, 123
Morris 109, 196–7, 198, 207–8
Mullins 91
Murray 192, 193–4, 198–9

national statistics 14, 107–8
'New Labour' 88–9, 185, 229
new management techniques 84,
  161–3, 228
new social movements see social
  movements
Nichols 57

occupational segregation 19, 93, 158,
  160
occupational structure 12, 14, 47, 54,
  56–8, 77–8; see also class and
  employment aggregate approach;
  class and occupation
Offe 84, 87–8, 106, 177, 223, 224
'orthodox consensus' (in sociology)
  12, 15, 46, 86, 112

Pahl 9, 89, 90–1, 103
Pakulski 99, 130–6, 141, 161,
  169–70
Parkin 56, 63, 209
Parsons 36, 42, 187–8
Pateman 180–1
patriarchy 92–3, 180, 181, 184–5,
  200
petty bourgeoisie 71
Pickvance 90
Pirenne 2
Plant 191
Polanyi 134
political economy 47
positivism 12, 13, 25, 45, 49
post-Fordism 18, 84, 160, 228
post-Marxism 124–5
postmodernism 55, 80, 113, 125–7,
  131, 133, 151, 155, 160, 166, 205, 227
post-structuralism 80, 123–5, 205
poverty 14, 193; see also culture of
  poverty; underclass

Poulantzas 30
Prandy and Blackburn 66, 101
prestige *see* status
production 4, 18, 28, 33, 35, 39, 93,
130, 131, 132–3, 142, 228
proletariat *see* working class
pseudo-debate xiii, 21, 80, 115–16,
206

race 94, 186–90; and 'underclass'
debate 194–6
realism 48–50, 52 n8, 119, 122
reflexive (reflexivity) 128, 129, 130,
131, 132, 161, 163, 228
Registrar-General 11, 58–61
Reid 56, 59
relational class schemes 44, 57,
64–76, 80, 211; development of
37–40; *see also* class, employment
aggregate approach
Rex 186–90
Roemer 72
Rosenthal 162
Rowntree Report 191, 219, 220
Rutler and Madge 196

Saunders 8, 20, 142–6, 192,
214–16, 221
Savage 49, 107, 147, 151, 154–5,
156
Sayer and Walker 57, 132–3
Scott 101–2, 109, 120, 170
service class *see* middle classes
services (service employment)
132–3, 160–1, 219–20, 222, 227
Skeggs 205
Smelser 42
social mobility 57, 68, 69, 102, 151,
208–18
social movements 18–19, 87–8,
124, 177–8, 179
socialism 31–2; 'state' 18, 31, 86
'societal shift' debates 18, 20, 80–1,
99, 110, 127–34, 135, 137–8, 190
sociology: development of viii–ix,
xii, 36–7

'stakeholding' 174, 190
Stark 44
status (prestige) 10, 21, 35, 36, 56,
116–23, 165–7, 169–71, 179;
scales 15, 61–4
Stinchcombe 229
stratification: defined 1; *see also*
functionalist theory of stratification
structuration 13, 44–6, 49, 51
structure-action model xiii, 13, 39, 46,
51, 68, 89–90, 136, 142, 148, 223
Swift 216

Therborn 51–2
Thompson 41–3, 48, 90, 91
Thrift and Williams 46–7
Total Quality Management 84
trade unions 82, 176, 178, 224; and
race 188–9
Turner 31, 120, 135–7, 175, 177–8

underclass 21–2, 130, 143, 189–90,
190–9; defined 192
unit of analysis 111 n7
urban sociology 47–50
Urry 29; *see also* Keat and Urry;
Lash and Urry

Veblen 140

Walby 182, 185
Warde 141, 146
Warner 36, 117, 119–20
Waters 130–6, 141, 151–2, 161,
169–70, 227
Weber 24, 32–5, 50–1, 63, 101–2,
119–20, 136–7, 169–70
Weisenthal 223, 224
welfare state 172, 180–5; deal 83,
188–9; and 'underclass' 191
Westergaard 54, 57, 225
Willis 43
Wilson 194–6
women: and class 19, 217–18; and
citizenship 180–5; employment
84–6; entry into management and

professions 158–60; *see also* feminism; gender
Wood 124–5
work *see* employment
work situation 38–9, 46, 64–5, 111 n15
working class (proletariat) 4, 17, 18, 27, 28, 29, 46, 71, 83, 86, 89–90, 95, 118, 200, 223, 226
Wright 14, 32, 39, 63, 99–101, 108, 113–16, 204, 225–6; class scheme 69–76; gender and class 97–8
Wynne 154–5